Fiction Writer's Brainstormer

FICTION WRITER'S
BRAINSTORMER

JAMES V. SMITH JR.

WRITER'S DIGEST BOOKS

CINCINNATI, OHIO
www.writersdigest.com

Fiction Writer's Brainstormer. Copyright © 2000 by James V. Smith Jr. Manufactured in the United States of America. All rights reserved. No part of this book may be reproduced in any form or by any electronic or mechanical means including information storage and retrieval systems without permission in writing from the publisher, except by a reviewer, who may quote brief passages in a review. Published by Writer's Digest Books, an imprint of F + W Publications, Inc., 4700 East Galbraith Road, Cincinnati, Ohio 45236. (800) 289-0963. First edition.

Visit our Web site at www.writersdigest.com for information on more resources for writers.

To receive a free weekly e-mail newsletter delivering tips and updates about writing and about Writer's Digest products, send an e-mail with "Subscribe Newsletter" in the body of the message to newsletter-request@writersdigest.com, or register directly at our Web site at www.writersdigest.com.

10   09   08   07   06   6   5   4   3   2

Library of Congress Cataloging-in-Publication Data

Smith, James V.
    Fiction writer's brainstormer / by James V. Smith Jr.
      p.   cm.
    Includes index.
    ISBN 13: 978-0-89879-943-9 (alk. paper)
    ISBN 10: 0-89879-943-0 (alk. paper)
    1. Fiction—Authorship. I. Title.
PN3365.S63   2000
808.3—dc21   00-043725
                                                CIP

Designed by Sandy Kent
Cover designed by Sandy Weinstein, Tin Box Studio Inc.
Cover illustration by John Pack © SIS
Production coordinated by Mark Griffin

DEDICATION

For Sue
What I do,
I do for you.

Acknowledgments

Dave Borcherding, thanks for your extraordinary patience and thoughtful editing. Every writer should have such an editor with the good instincts and the professional touch.

Lori Perkins and Peter Rubie, thanks for landing this contract. What a provocative, pleasurable assignment it has been.

About the Author

James V. Smith Jr., is published both in fiction and nonfiction, including seven novels.

His novels include three published action-adventure novels and a psychological thriller from Dell. *Beastmaker*, *Beaststalker* and *Almost Human* chronicle the horrifying results of genetic experimentation gone wrong. *The Lurker* is a psychothriller. His fifth novel, from Penguin USA, is *Cradle of Fire*, a techno-thriller set in the Persian Gulf. His latest novels are called *Force Recon*, a military action-adventure series for Berkley.

In nonfiction, Smith collaborated with Harry S. Dent Jr. on *The Great Boom Ahead*, a futuristic economic forecast in hardcover from Hyperion in 1993, and a 1995 release from St. Martin's Press, *Job Shock,* a forecast for America's work revolution. Smith also wrote *Word-of-Mouth Marketing* with Jerry R. Wilson (Wiley, 1991). His *You Can Write A Novel,* a "how-to with attitude" from Writer's Digest Books, was published in 1998.

Smith is a former news and feature writer for the *Dallas Morning News* and the *Indianapolis News*. He has published articles in *Writers Digest*, *American Legion* magazine, and *Family Circle*. As a freelance technical writer, he has published numerous articles in trade magazines.

A Montana native, Smith is retired as an Army lieutenant colonel and is the managing editor of a weekly community newspaper, the *Shelby Promoter*. He lives in Montana with his wife, Susan, daughter, Kathryn, and two golden retrievers, Gus and Kelly.

TABLE OF CONTENTS

Part I
10 BRAINSTORMER STRATEGIES

CHAPTER 1

How to Get Your Mind Right for Brainstorming...3
10 strategies for accessing your right-brain resources

Part II
THE FICTION WRITER'S
BRAINSTORMER IN ACTION

Part III
ADVANCED WRITING—THE SEVEN HABITS OF HIGHLY EFFECTIVE WRITERS

"If a writer has to rob his mother, he will not hesitate: The 'Ode on a Grecian Urn' is worth any number of old ladies."

—WILLIAM FAULKNER

Part I

TEN BRAINSTORMER STRATEGIES

Brainstormer Warm-Up ✳

Feeling creative?

Let's see what you've got. Solve this puzzler, a remark by a famous American. It'll warm up your brain before you dig into the first chapter.

Genius is . . .

spir1/¢ation n 9t9/¢/spiration

Did you solve it? Good. Was it because . . .

uryy4me?

Or

miee e uuuu?

If you didn't get it, look at the quote at the top of page 3. Then check out the Solutions on page 274.

Now that you know what you're in for, let's brainstorm, shall we?

> "Genius is 1 percent inspiration and 99 percent perspiration."
> —THOMAS EDISON

How to Get Your Mind Right for Brainstorming

Ten strategies for accessing your right-brain resources

> "More brain, O Lord, more brain!"
> —GEORGE MEREDITH

 Before you get going on brainstorming strategies, I have a question: What's a brainstormer, anyhow?

Thanks for asking. Start with the word ***brainstorming:*** *a process in which two or more heads spin out creativity with more zap than any one mind.*

Leading to ***brainstormer:*** *a book of tools to help you access the little-used areas of your mind.* Think of this brainstormer as a box of flints. Strike one of its tools against the steel of your gray matter to create sparks of genius.

I wrote the book for fiction writers, amateurs and pros, including screenwriters and playwrights. But writers of every stripe can also benefit from it—ad writers, authors, PR staffers, editors, reporters, columnists, writing coaches, speechmakers, teachers—anybody who writes as a hobby or career. If you want to solve a writing problem, this book can help you put the "creative" in creative writing.

Researchers tell us we use only 15 percent of our right brain. With some of us, it's closer to 1 percent. Either way, tap into the genius you never use. Find a brainstormer tool to help shake down a little of that dazzle from the sky and use it in your work.

Now, let's get going, shall we?

Brainstormer Strategy 1—THEBEGIN ✳

"All this will not be finished in the first one hundred days . . . nor even perhaps in our lifetime on this planet. But let us begin."
—JOHN F. KENNEDY

To identify this strategy, you'll have to solve this simple puzzler:

THEBEGIN

If it gives you trouble, stay tuned. It'll come to you. In fact, you'll find the correct response right before your eyes.

Meanwhile, solve the maze in Figure 1 on page 5. Time yourself.

Ready, set, *GO*!

Even if you solve the puzzle instantly, check out the solution beginning on page 274.

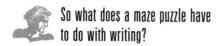 **So what does a maze puzzle have to do with writing?**

Plenty. Figure 1 teaches many lessons. Let's look at a few.

One, try to see the maze as a story plot with all of its twists, turns and dead ends. Using Strategy 1, a writer knows the end before she writes the tale. Now she can see the path from start to end (or from end to start, if you like). She can also texture a story by leading a reader into dead ends—without losing her own way.

Two, if a writer knows the end of his story before writing it, he can judge scenes before he creates them. He'll know whether the action moves his tale toward the climax or peters out before reaching the climax. He might choose not to write a scene and fill in gaps with narration. This saves him hours of time and energy. Think of how much time he'd waste if he wrote the novel first and then saw he had to cut fifty pages of action that he should have seen as surplus from the start.

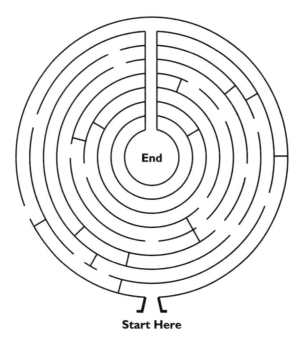

End

Start Here

FIGURE 1. Puzzler for Strategy 1—Begin at the End

Three, foreshadowing is so much easier when you know where the story's going. You know foreshadowing, right? That's when you plant a detail early in the story, and that detail comes into play much later.

THEBEGIN helps a writer foresee, so he can foreshadow.

And it leads us right to Strategy 2.

Brainstormer Strategy 2— Reject the Conventional Wisdom

"Only the gamefish swims upstream."

—JOHN MOORE

Here's another puzzler for you to solve. Don't think about this exercise too long. Just fill in the blanks. Give the answers writing teachers always teach.

Five Conventional Rules for Conventional Writers

1. _____ stereotypes.
2. Write about things you _____ .
3. _____ SASE.
4. _____ multiple submissions.
5. _____ clichés.

Did you fill in words like *avoid, know, enclose, do not send* and *don't use*?

Of course you did. Those rules show up in every writer's manual since Moses set down his own *Ten Commandments for Scribes*.

The trouble with conventional wisdom is that it is *soooooooooo* conventional. And so automatic. We accept it at its face value. We don't give it a single critical thought. We don't dare go against the grain or swim against the current.

 Wait a sec. If it says so in *all* the writing manuals, it *must* be so. I mean, isn't it suicidal to go against publishing protocol?

You'd think. But when we buy into these sacred rules of writing like sheep in a flash flood, we close our eyes to hundreds of creative prospects.

 Sheep in a flash flood?
What does that mean?

I have this on good authority—a local who's tended sheep all his life. In a torrential rain, sheep tend to move downhill. More than one flock has dropped into a gully full of raging water and drowned. No matter how hard the shepherd tries to steer them away from certain death, the sheep keep going into the roiling muck, one after another, until they're all swept away.

Don't let the conventional wisdom do that to you. Don't be ruled by habit. "Habit," Wordsworth writes, "rules the unreflecting herd." And flock.

How will you ever develop an original, creative writing style if you slavishly follow every rule set down by those who write writing manuals? Creative writing, by definition, means breaking a convention every so often. If you don't believe me, look it up. You'll find the definition includes *originality*. If you want to sell something original—that is, different from that of every other writer—you'll have to write outside the lines.

Instead of baaa-ing, *Yes, sir, yes, sir, three bags full,* take some risks. When the conventions close in on you, push back. Stretch your creative muscles. Say no to the rules.

As far as I know, the only unbreakable rule of writing is from Richard Walter's *Screenwriting:*

Never be boring.

To me, every other writing rule—even mine—is carved in wax.

Here's a war story. I used to teach creative writing seminars. To prod my audience, by the end of the session I would offer every student a surefire tool for writing a best-selling novel. *Guaranteed.*

I told my students I felt so sure of my technique that I would bet any one of them a quarter that I could back up my claim. Nobody among the hundreds of so-called creative writers ever took my bet. I still sadly reflect on that, and not only because I might have made hundreds of quarters. Had I been sitting in the audience when somebody made such a goofy proposition, it would've been worth risking the twenty-five cents just to see how the idiot at the front of the class would talk himself out of the corner.

But not for provocation's sake alone do I suggest you find a fresh approach to the conventional situations posed in my puzzler. I have committed a sin against each of those conventions—and avoided going to writer's prison besides. You can, too. Just do it.

I'm curious. Can you guarantee *I* can write a best-seller?

Yep. I guarantee it. Let's see your quarter. (I invite you to jump ahead and check out page 182.)

Brainstormer Strategy 3— Act a Little Crazy ✴

"There is a correlation between the creative and the screwball. So we must suffer the screwball gladly."
—KINGMAN BREWSTER

Puzzler I

Name the amazing products that sprang from the following dubious origins:

1. Cocklebur _____
2. Failed shock absorber _____
3. Twisted loop _____
4. Pie plate _____
5. Failed synthetic rubber _____

Many ideas we now consider pure genius didn't explode onto the scene in their time. (See the answers on page 275.)

Why the resistance to inventions and ideas that now seem so obvious? Simple. Either the sweeping notion of change inherent in a new idea creates fear, or people who might adopt it don't have the vision to do so. Velcro didn't exactly sweep the garment industry off its feet, but can you imagine a world without Velcro? Now *that's* the absurdity.

That's why I urge you to do more than consider outrageous extremes as an exercise in mind-bending. Step out front and exploit the limits of absurdity. You don't have to make a fool of yourself to act a little crazy. But to explore the limits of practicality, which border on the absurd, it *helps* to act a little crazy. Above all, don't fence in your creativity with artificial limitations.

With that frame of mind, try the next puzzler.

Puzzler II (in a more writerly vein)

Name something outrageous you might do with the following either in your fiction writing or your writing career. Don't worry about being safe, reasonable or practical. Just name something outrageous.

1. Clichés _____
2. A rejection letter _____
3. A stereotypical character _____
4. A dated directory of agents _____
5. An incomplete novel idea _____

There's no way I could dream up "right" answers to such an open-ended exercise, so you won't find anything in the Solutions section. Instead, I give you some possibilities I have used:

ABSURD ANTICONVENTIONS

1. **Embrace clichés.** Buy a book on clichés and employ them in all your writing. String them together like raisins and wear them as proudly as pearls.

2. **Use rejections to sell your work.** Photocopy them and send them out to editors and agents.

3. **Exploit stereotypes for all their worth.** Study them. Steal them. Use them with a clear conscience.

4. **Call agents who no longer appear in current editions of directories.**

5. **Write a pitch letter based on your incomplete idea.** Don't let on that the novel isn't finished. Give a word count in your contact letter. Offer sample chapters. Go for it.

 Naming an outrageous act isn't the same as doing it. Have you done these things you're trying to goad me into doing?

As they all say in *Fargo*, you betcha. So let's discuss how each of my suggestions might be more practical than you thought.

Clichés. Two thoughts. First, you can invent characters who think and speak in clichés. That they do so tells us something about them. In my Force Recon novel series, one main character develops a distinctive voice because of the way he mangles clichés. He utters such Yogi Berra–isms as, "Let barking dogs sleep."

Second, if you worry too much about clichés while writing first drafts, you can distract yourself. Embracing them allows you to get your story down. Do so. Then work the kinks out later. In fact, I spend much of chapter 6 telling you how to creatively work with even the most worn clichés. The exercise begins by embracing them. Feel free to jump ahead and check it out. If you avoid absurd extremes, you miss dozens of possibilities.

Rejections. One publishing convention says you should never let an editor know your material has been shown around, let alone rejected at other houses. Those of you who read my how-to *You Can Write a Novel* know that I once photocopied a rejection letter with an encouraging word from one editor and sent it to three others.

An act outrageous enough to land a contract for my first novel.

Rejections that reveal even a glimmer of criticism can help you market your fiction. Collect them. Extract the nuggets of advice from each and create a poster of do's and don'ts. Keep it in sight as you write and market your work.

One sure way to avoid getting rejected is to never send out query letters.

Stereotypes. Contrary to advice you've heard elsewhere, editors sometimes insist on stereotypes. Category books rely on types as conventions of the genre. When editors prescribe how they want a series written, they describe stereotypes they want prospective writers to use in their books. I have a handful of series proposals, called "bibles," to prove this.

Imagine how you can stun such an editor when you create a character that meets all his expectations and transcends such stereotypes besides.

Check out chapter 10. It tells how to brainstorm and create a package to sell to editors and agents who specialize in category fiction. The real-life sample includes an actual editor's list of politically correct stereotypes. You'd find the same cast of characters in almost any sitcom, cop drama and comic book you could name.

Stereotypes: Don't reject them out of hand.

Calling agents in outdated directories. Try to find an agent who's in the outdated directory but not listed in the most current one. A rep might drop out of market listings for any number of reasons. He might have quit the business, hired on at another agency, hit it big with only a few select clients or died. As I said, anything may have happened. One thing you can assume: He isn't bugged as often by amateurs asking stupid questions like: "I've got this great idea. Wanna make a million dollars?"

If you stay away from such nonsense yourself, this trick can lead to some of the more interesting conversations you'll ever have with an agent. Prepare a list of discussion points before you call. Write down a series of headlines as answers to the following:

Questions an Agent Might Ask
- What have you published (when and where)?
- What's your story about (category and brief story outline)?
- Is the piece finished? (Yes is the only acceptable answer.)
- What are your special qualifications for writing such a work?
- What's the word count?

- Does anybody else have the work under consideration? (Danger! Every agent wants to believe she's getting an exclusive look. If this question comes up, offer an answer. In return, ask for a quick response. If the query is already out, say so, but do mention if nobody has asked for chapters yet. It might earn you a request to send chapters.)

To get you started, here's a composite of exchanges I have had.

WRITER: Hello, I'm (*state your name*). Just checking to see if I have the current address of your agency before I sent out a contact letter. Are you still at (*state the address*)?

AGENT: (*Brusquely.*) How did you get my number?

WRITER: Out of the (*name the outdated directory*). Is this address still current?

AGENT: (*Confused silence, which is not a bad thing for you.*)

WRITER: I have (*state the address from the outdated directory*). If that address is still good, would you mind giving me a name I can send my letter to?

AGENT: I don't usually look at anything unless it's a referral from an editor or another agent. (*Observe the word choice,* usually. *Notice that it is not a no. The door might still be open to you. Without wasting words, find out.*) (*Oh, by the way, since the agent mentioned it, how credible is the notion that one agent would refer a sure-fire money machine of a writer to another agent? In fact, one agent told me confidentially that he never makes referrals, except for clients he doesn't like, which he sends to agents he doesn't like. And laughs about it. You have to admit—it is funny.*)

WRITER: So, are you telling me not to send my query letter unless I can get a referral? I'm pretty sure I could get another agent to refer me to you. I'll get back to you by the end of the day.

AGENT: (*Recognizing the absurdity of his own suggestion.*) Wait. What kind of project are you pitching?

WRITER: A novel. (*And here's where being prepared pays off.*) An ecological thriller about a wildlife biologist who discovers that somebody is killing off grizzly bears in Montana and selling body parts that are used in Asia as aphrodisiacs. (*Resist the urge to go into the story. Shut up. Now.*)

AGENT: (*Noncommittal grunt.*) Are you from Montana?

WRITER: No, but I (*tell how you are an expert from your research about Montana and bears. Be brief. Asking about Montana tips off that he's going to ask you to send the letter—only if you don't scare him off*).

AGENT: I'll look at your letter. Two conditions. One, keep it to one page and be sure to include an SASE. Two, I want to have an exclusive look.

WRITER: (*Never mind that he just asked for three things. Accept his conditions. Get his name and address.*) Tell me a little bit about what has gone on in your agency since this directory went out of date.

From here on, you're on your own. Remember, *listen* more than you talk. He will be curious about your background and publishing experience. Answer questions, but don't go off on tangents. Only tell him the headlines of your answer. Then shut up. Of every one hundred people an agent talks to, ninety-nine blab too much. You can distinguish yourself as being more than a half-wit merely by letting the agent fill the awkward silences.

Pitching an unfinished novel. I warn you—this is risky business. But it's also a technique powerful enough to move mountains of resistance to writing. Namely, the resistance in your own mind that prevents you from finishing your novel. Here's how it works.

You get fired up over a brilliant idea and sketch out a plan for a no-fail bestseller. You try to go through all the steps of prewriting: structuring your novel with an outline you'll never refer to, sharpening pencils you'll never use, gathering research material you don't intend to read. But an utterly seductive first line comes to you in the shower. You write it on the bathroom mirror using an eyeliner pencil. Then you stand naked and dripping before your keyboard, pounding out the opening scene. Chapters 1, 2 and 3 write themselves. However, you run face-first into that invisible brick wall—the emptiness in creativity that comes from not preparing well enough in the first place.

Instead of tossing your sample chapters into the closet with a dozen other false starts, try motivating yourself. Put your mouth where your manuscript ought to be.

Write a contact letter to an agent or editor. Pitch your novel. Don't let on that you haven't finished it. Offer to send a more detailed synopsis and chapters. Include this sentence: "Word count: 71,424 words." (Or other specific intended word count.) Send your one-page letter to a few agents and editors.

Depending on the brilliance of your idea and the expression of it in your contact letter, you now have anywhere from two to eight weeks to come up with that detailed synopsis and to polish the sample chapters you promised. You might also feel an urgency to continue writing now that you have worked out the structure somewhat, perhaps finishing another half-dozen chapters. In fact, for this technique to have any value, you *must* feel a sense of urgency to write your way around that invisible brick wall. Otherwise, you risk that prickle of shame that comes when an editor or agent asks to see the first one hundred pages and you only have fifty.

Miracles can happen. With the reputation of the publishing industry being what it is, it led me to believe I might never be invited to send a manuscript in the first year or two of trying. Instead, my very first contact letter resulted in an invitation to send chapters—chapters I had not written. You can imagine the flurry of activity that invitation generated. I ultimately sold the novel, but not before being rejected by the first publisher who had asked to see it. And not before fifty-five intervening rejections as well.

But after that first scare, I started writing furiously and didn't stop until I finished the story. I was as ready as any Boy Scout to send the manuscript by the time the editor responded to my chapters. But, alas, he did not.

CAUTION: This is a self-motivation brainstormer trick you play on yourself. Do not think of it as a trick you play on agents and editors.

If your creativity thrives under pressure, try submitting this way. If you can be motivated to work by imposing such a deadline on yourself, by all means, do it. It's a great brainstormer tactic that relies on the principles of Strategy 9.

If you know that you will not or cannot finish the chapters and manuscript in time to send them in, if asked, then beware. You're playing with napalm.

Those are some outrageous ways you can turn the conventional wisdom to your own advantage.

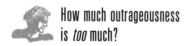

How much outrageousness is *too* much?

Depends. Which of the outrageous techniques you've seen so far do you consider *too* outrageous? One of those last five anticonventions, say, marketing an incomplete novel? The notion of inviting you to jump around rather than reading every segment of this book in order? The author speaking to you as if he were in the room? (Say, is that a hole in your sock?) The maze? The bit about the guaranteed best-seller?

Like it or not, outrageousness has ensconced itself in our popular culture. Shock radio. Assisted suicide as news video. Animal attacks and car wrecks as entertainment. Dennis Rodman's autobiography. Dennis Rodman.

For me, the chance to exploit the outrageous in writing a book like this was reason enough to take on the project. By definition, you cannot push the envelope of creativity very far if you eliminate the opportunities for stepping into the realm of the absurd. It's not always enough to reject the conventional wisdom. Sometimes you have to step out there—*really far* out there—to find a creative solution to your writing problem.

Does that mean you should write outrageous stuff or try ridiculous stunts just to get noticed? Nah. No matter how ridiculous the extents to which you let your mind wander, never use outrageousness for its own sake, but always to make a point.

And remember this: There is no point to being outrageous if you don't have a smart piece of writing you can use as the knockout punch in the fight to sell your work.

Brainstormer Strategy 4— Imagine Impossible Standards ✳

"All excellent things are as difficult as they are rare."

—SPINOZA

A quick productivity quiz: When you begin writing the first draft of your next fictional piece, what would you consider to be just out of your reach in:

1. Maximum words a minute? _____
2. Average words a minute, sustained for an hour? _____
3. Words an hour of sustained work? _____
4. Words a day of sustained work? _____
5. Total production in a given month? _____
6. Length of time between typing your first word of fiction and submitting a completed, polished novel or script? _____

First the discussion, and then my answers.

This strategy demands that you do more than think about writing or daydream about becoming a writer. You don't merely visualize your way to success. You work at success, and you start by setting standards for yourself. And not just high standards, but impossible ones.

When you set standards out of your reach and then extend your grasp to actually achieve those standards, you'll be surprised at how often you underestimate your capabilities.

For instance, check your answers to the productivity quiz above against my answers, which might sound impossible.

Standards That Are Not So Impossible, After All

- **200 maximum words a minute.** The best I've ever done is 220 words a minute. No, that's not a typo. I meant to write 220. You can do the same.
- **50 average words a minute.** I have sustained this rate for an hour at a time and have done this too many times to count.
- **3,000 words an hour of sustained work.** Yes, more than once. I even have a personal best of 3,100 words in an hour.
- **10,000 words a day of sustained work.** The most I have accomplished is 11,300 words, but 10,000 words is commonplace for me.

 You must work twenty-two hours a day. Wouldn't your rather have a life away from the computer?

I don't and I do. Here's the nifty part:

I achieved those counts working no more than four hours a day at the computer.

- **Total production in a given month: 60,000 to 80,000 words.** In the example I'm using here, I stopped production at 73,400 words. I completed the first draft of my first Force Recon novel after ten days of dictation. I used the rest of the month to revise and edit, sending off a final manuscript of 65,000 words. I usually spend another two weeks in revision once it comes back from my editor.
- **That's one month between typing my first word of fiction and submitting a completed, polished novel.** As I said, I spent one month on that last novel, a figure I intend to improve upon in future works.

By the way, did I mention that I am writing and editing this brainstormer by talking to my computer? At this very moment, I am staring out the front window of my house, both hands in my pockets, watching a late-winter snowstorm blow through. To input copy, I simply speak into a microphone strapped to my head, and my words appear as text on the screen. It's a technology called *continuous speech recognition* (CSR). Because I have trained myself and my computer to be proficient using CSR, I have been able to achieve the results I just shared. Consistently. With only the slightest exaggeration. (I produced the 220 words a minute in a speed test, reading copy as fast as I could just to push the software to its limit. When I talk that fast, I begin to sound like Alvin the chipmunk. There's no way can I create prose at that rate.)

I only mention CSR here to boggle your mind; to get your attention by hitting you between the eyes with my microphone, so to speak; to prove that a standard you might have thought impossible may very well be within your grasp. If you want to explore CSR in greater detail, check out chapter 9.

For now, let's examine a tool that's not so much a creativity tool as it is an organizer that helps you set creativity goals and objectives.

The Brainstormer's WRITE System of Setting Creativity Goals

This system helps writers plan. First, let's get to WRITE, which tells you how to put your dreams of writing success into terms you can measure, terms that lead to action. WRITE stands for:

> **W**riting-related
> **R**adical
> **I**nspirational
> **T**imed
> **E**xplicit

- **Writing-related.** Set writing goals and objectives to get you on track and keep you focused.
- **Radical.** Push yourself in setting goals and objectives. Set impossible standards.
- **Inspirational.** State your goals and objectives in a way that fires you up.
- **Timed.** Does the word "deadline" mean anything to you? Set limits for

yourself on the clock and calendar.
- **Explicit.** Be specific about your writing standards.

Look at this example of WRITE in action:

*To write and submit a completed science-fiction movie script of 110
pages to six film agents by February 14, 2004.*

 Now that looks workable. But . . . is that statement a goal or an objective?
What's the difference between goals and objectives, anyhow?

Good questions. To my mind, that statement is a goal. It's a big-picture kind of
thing, like, "To earn my MBA at the Harvard School of Write-In MBAs by February 14, 2006, graduating with a 3.5 grade average."

That's a big-picture task. The intermediate tasks, like, "Completing the Business
Ethics 501 course by February 13, 2004, earning an A," help to form your objec-
tives. And within the objective, you might have any number of tasks, for example,
"Write the first draft, three thousand words minimum, of my ethics term paper by
December 31, 2003, including a complete bibliography and draft tables."

With those distinctions in mind, try on this tool for size.

The WRITE Task List

Look at Figure 2 on page 18 for an example of a task list you can construct and
print for yourself, say for tackling Force Recon novel #3, due to the publisher on
January 1, 2001.

As you can see, I've filled in a rough list of objectives or tasks (with deadlines)
that must be completed before I can claim to have met the goal stated at the top
of the task list. Once this big-picture task list is done, I do several things with it.

I rewrite the larger goal on a 3″ × 5″ card and continually carry it around with
me in the same pocket with the rest of my personal goals. Writing your goals down
is a major first step toward accomplishing them. But like everything else in your
life, from relationships to career climbing, you have to work at it.

Check out the appendix for a view of the full-size blank form.

WRITE Task List   Date_____

Goal:

Writing-related	To submit *Force Recon* novel no. 3 of 65,000 words in final
Radical	draft form to Penguin Putnam by Jan. 1, 2001.
Inspirational	
Timed	
Explicit	

PRIORITY	TASK	NOTES
☐	Submit idea in writing to ed. by Aug.1, 2000, for approval.	Kosovo setting, Title: *Butcher of Belgrade*
☐	Sketch new char., setting, high-tech wpns by Sept. 1, 2000	New team member msn, villain
☐	Use 10-Scene Tool to sketch novel plan by Aug. 15, 2000	
☐	Write opening scene by Sept. 15, 2000	

FIGURE 2. The WRITE Task List for setting brainstormer goals and objectives.

Brainstormer Strategy 5—Never Settle

"Genius . . . is the capacity to see ten things where the ordinary man sees one."

—EZRA POUND

Puzzler time. You're faced with a writing dilemma. You've just written a scene that puts your heroine into an impossible situation, namely:

> *Villainous forces have sabotaged her plane on a flight over the Bering Sea. Radar proves the plane went down in waters so cold, nobody could survive more than four hours. Yet she must live because your novel is only half told. How?*

And your answer is?

 I'd never let a heroine of mine fly over water unless I first equipped the plane with pontoons. She'd land safe and dry.

Good, good. Is that your only answer? Did you look any further than the first idea that occurred to you? No? I thought as much. You see, we're conditioned to believe that the firstest, fastest answer is the best one. But to the brainstormer you want to become in your writing, the quick response is usually the most obvious and most boring one. And you already know that, to a fiction writer, boring is bad.

Quick now—think of the most creative person you know. What makes her seem so special? Is it because she always looks at the ordinary in extraordinary ways? And because she can express the mundane in brilliant terms?

Probably, right?

And do you think she's so creative because of an accident (or intention) of the heavens at birth? Or because she thinks differently?

Yes on all counts, right?

And do you think you can become as creative as she?

You *don't*? That's where you're wrong. You may not be able to effect change in the fates, but you can certainly approach problems in creative ways. And you can express yourself in terms every bit as startling as the person you most admire. All you have to do is quit stopping at the first solution to a problem or the obvious observation of the ordinary. All you have to remember is: Never settle. Never, never, never settle.

To help you get started, I'll restate the puzzler

> *Villainous forces have sabotaged her plane on a flight over the Bering Sea. Radar proves the plane went down in waters so cold, nobody could survive more than four hours. Yet she must live because your novel is only half told.* **Give me no less than a dozen explanations of how this is possible.**

Did you feel the earth move as you read the twelvefold increase in the demand I first made on you? I don't wonder. The first puzzler statement didn't limit you to a single answer, but now you know *I won't accept* just a single answer. Your mind shifted into overdrive to think:

> *Aha! He assumes I can find at least twelve solutions to this problem, some of them bad, some of them good. Possibly even more than one of them creative. He has set an impossible standard. I must imagine the impossibilities as possible.*

That's the attitude. Nurture it in your own creativity. Tell yourself:

From now on, no one answer, especially a first answer, will do. I will no longer be satisfied with the first thing that pokes me in my mind's eye. I will not spit out the first word that I lay my tongue on. I will not trundle out the first cliché that pops into my keyboard. I will not accept a one-dimensional character in my fiction because I'm too lazy to dig deeper into his personality and find his unique quirks. I will not let my hero out of a jam in my script by taking the foot-worn path a thousand television sitcom heroes have traveled before him. I will never again settle. Never, never, never.

I am writer. Hear me roar.

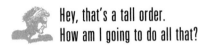 **Hey, that's a tall order.**
How am I going to do all that?

Relax. Here's a brainstormer tool that forces you to consider the extremes of a situation and every impossibility that falls in between. Once you bracket a problem using this tool, you can feel sure you've at least scanned the terrain from horizon to horizon, which is far better than staring at a spot beneath your nose until a single solution of dubious value wriggles its way into your head.

Let's bracket our puzzler problem using the following scale to find twelve possible responses along this continuum:

[**Automatic → Obvious → Commonplace → Literal → Labored →**
Interesting → Unusual → Obscure → Odd → Opposite → Inventive →
Creative → Magical → Amusing → Outrageous → Ridiculous →
Obscene → Preposterous → Over-the-top]

FIGURE 3. The brainstormer tool for bracketing possibilities between extremes.

To use this tool, put your problem alongside each category of possible solutions. If you don't hit upon an answer right away, move on to the next category. If a solution strikes you, look for a second, then a third within the same category. After you've traveled from the left bracket across the spectrum to the right bracket, retrace your steps and try again to fill in the blanks. Then look for a fourth, fifth and then a twelfth response in a category that might not have been vacuumed dry. After you reach a dozen, go for a baker's dozen. Then two dozen. Keep going until you're exhausted. Then get some rest and attack the possibilities again.

Naturally, if your creativity grabs you by the nape of the neck and drags you outside the brackets to examine whole new worlds of possibilities, strap it on and go. Anywhere you go is likely to be better than buying into the first solution and quitting the search.

Using the puzzler I stated earlier, fill in the blanks below. I've already done the first and last responses—the extremes—for you.

THE BRACKETING TOOL

Automatic	*Impossible* (Not an option for a true brainstormer).
Obvious	_____
Commonplace	_____
Literal	_____
Labored	_____
Interesting	_____
Unusual	_____
Obscure	_____
Odd	_____
Opposite	_____
Inventive	_____
Creative	_____
Magical	_____
Amusing	_____
Outrageous	_____
Ridiculous	_____
Obscene	_____
Preposterous	_____
Over-the-top	Willy, the freed Orca (killer whale), swims by and offers the heroine his dorsal fin as a convenient handle, then transports her to shore.

The simplest application of this strategy involves purging your mind of the two extremes indicated in Figure 3. I entered *impossible* to cover the automatic answer, putting it out of your mind so you could work on the possibilities. As an over-the-top response, I suggested Willy, which is too hokey for words.

But that's not my point, anyhow. When you're stumped in any writing situation, open your mind to all of the possibilities that lie between the extremes—but not just any quantity of possibilities. I invented the tool to help you generate high-quality responses by changing your mind-set many times over.

Here's my solution with the inevitable commentary. How did I do? Feel free to critique my responses. Naturally, there are no right answers to this puzzler. The idea is to generate a variety of answers. Creative answers, if you don't mind.

Automatic	*Impossible* (Not an option for a true brainstormer).
Obvious	The heroine breaks out the over-water survival kit, which includes a raft, and saves herself.
Commonplace	A passing fishing boat rescues her.
Literal	She hoists herself from the sea onto a floating cushion or other debris. Then she paddle-kicks to safety, the exertion providing warmth enough to save her.
Labored	She disarms the sabotaging device in flight, fakes the crash at sea, then flies under radar to safety to make the villains think she died.
Interesting	She ditches the plane and in the minute the plane stays afloat, fashions a raft by lashing together her baggage.
Unusual	She sets an explosive charge of her own so the plane will explode and burn on impact, the flames acting as a rescue beacon. Then she parachutes to safety.
Obscure	She helped design the plane and knows it will float if it doesn't break apart on landing. She sets it down gently and waits for rescue.
Odd	She discovers the sabotage device, flies over the nearest land and aims the plane out to sea on autopilot. Then she parachutes to safety as the plane disintegrates over the ocean.
Opposite	She discovers and disarms the sabotage device and arranges for air traffic controllers to issue a false crash report. No crash after all.
Inventive	She unpacks her luggage and dresses in multiple layers of wool clothing, which will reduce loss of heat.

Creative	Before the crash, she tears insulation from the plane's interior and straps it to her body to help her float and retain heat.
Magical	She suspects sabotage and forces the villain to accompany her in flight, leaving the villain to reveal and disarm the sabotage device.
Amusing	She discovers the sabotage early enough to return to the villain's hideout and crash-land there to resume action.
Outrageous	She ditches at sea, swims to a convenient, uncharted island in the Aleutian chain, and survives on raw shellfish.
Ridiculous	She ditches the plane and goes to the bottom, surviving on trapped air until she hears a ship's screws passing by, then swims to the surface.
Obscene	She decides to commit suicide, riding the plane to her death, ending the novel prematurely, letting her twin take over the fight for justice, truth, and the American way.
Preposterous	She crash-lands on a passing aircraft carrier.
Over-the-top	The *Free Willy* thing.

You may not find these ideas as spectacular as your own. Heck, I didn't even get into your idea of the plane having pontoon landing gear. No matter. What's important is getting down more than one answer, which is something we writers don't do often enough. After you've finished blitzing my responses, go back to work and finish filling in any blanks you've left. When you're finished, you'll have at least seventeen ideas besides those at the extremes of the brackets. Surely one of them is better than the first automatic response that dribbled out of your brain.

That's the bracketing tool.

TIP: You can set up a scale of your own, replacing my adjectives with useful gradations that fit more into your genre or line of work. You might choose terms like: business, spiritual, biblical, journalistic, poetic, musical, math-related, academic, scientific, gibberish. Whatever moves your creativity quotient.

Most important, keep in mind that the tool can have dozens of uses in your writing beyond this simple application. We'll be exploring some of those applications later, especially in dealing with clichés in chapter 6.

Brainstormer Strategy 6—Simplify ✳

"Speak plain and to the purpose."
—SHAKESPEARE

A simplicity puzzler: Tally the number of times the letter *f* occurs in the following selection:

> *Funding for scientific research is a matter of increasing influence for lobbyists of the academic and federal communities.*

What could be simpler than that puzzler and my instructions for solving it? Consult the answer on page 276 to compare your response to the correct one. And brace yourself for another dissertation.

In researching this book, I consulted agents, editors and other writers to discuss problems that a brainstormer might fix. The most common problem contained the word *over*. So I give you this litany:

The *Over* Problem

- Overemoting by characters
- Overwriting, including overdescribing by authors
- Overresearching
- Overmusing of both characters and authors
- Overmotivating of characters
- Repetition (over and over again)

I fall victim to the *over* sins myself, especially in early drafts. I tend toward the massive brain dump, getting all the junk down no matter how messy it looks at first. Then I compound the problem by exploring every detail and nuance of it. Because part of my training is in journalism, I try to be accurate, which leads me to excessive research. Finally, once I have created a semibrilliant passage (no matter that it's irrelevant) I resist every instinct to edit or eliminate the "little darling," as William Faulkner called such passages.

The *over* problem comes at you from every point of the compass, creeping into every writing job. But you can fight it off.

Three Defenses Against the *Over* Problem

1. **Plan to simplify.** That is, you can't leave simplicity to the mercy of a good intention. Or to a cute saying like the KISS formula: *Keep it simple, stupid.* Write a work plan before you write your story. Set down your writing goals and objectives for the project. Use the WRITE system. Lay out a straight path for your novel's central structure from beginning to end. No detours, subplots, complex complications. See the ten-scene tool and screenplay format in chapter 5, the nugget in chapter 2 and the character cards in chapter 4.

2. **Simplify as you go.** Write simply at every level. Write simple scenes, simple paragraphs, simple sentences. Use simple words. Think simple thoughts. You can impress editors and agents more with elegant simplicity than with a ten-dollar vocabulary and fifty-word sentences.

3. **Edit for simplicity.** Your tool of last defense against the briar patch of complexity is the editing pencil. Wield it like a hatchet. Before you write another word in your fiction career, check into the study of the results I made on ten best-selling authors in chapter 8. It includes the best lesson I've ever learned about editing for simplicity—a lesson that would have served me better (and earned better reviews for my books) if I'd mastered it much earlier in my writing career. But I have learned it at last and I'm sharing it with you.

We'll address creative solutions to specific *over* problems as we encounter them in the coming chapters, including chapter 16, in which we discuss writing in the white space. (That is, how to communicate ideas and images without writing them at all.) Until then, remember Henry David Thoreau's advice:

Simplify, simplify.

By the way, shouldn't that simply be *Simplify,*
in keeping with Thoreau's own advice?

You think? Me, too.

Brainstormer Strategy 7—
Tap Into Genius

"I hate quotations."

—RALPH WALDO EMERSON

Emerson hated quotations? Not me. I love 'em.

What is a quotation but a priceless gem mined from the total genius of a writer, speaker, leader, thinker, poet or prince? You sift through the life's work of history's most brilliant minds. Then, by using a quote from that work, you shine a light on one of its most lustrous fragments. You honor the speaker's most creative words just by reframing and reusing them. And, when you rub up against genius, a bit of it sticks to you like pollen to a bee's drumstick.

Why, just by using Emerson's quote here and disputing it, I feel as if I've brainstormed with him. (And the great thing is, he can't come back to trounce me verbally, as he might if he were alive.)

So study the works of others as a way of tapping into genius. You can use quotes as brainstorming tools in every aspect of your writing. You can find themes in them to explore in your stories. You can find titles for your works. You can put exact quotes into the mouths of your characters, and you can bend famous words into creative new phrases.

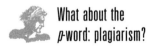 What about the
p-word: plagiarism?

Short of transcribing somebody else's work, it'd be nigh impossible for a fiction writer to plagiarize. I'd like to have a dollar for every time an author blended a fragment of W.B. Yeats's poem, "The Second Coming," into her work. You might remember the poem best for its famous last lines:

And what rough beast, its hour come round at last,
Slouches towards Bethlehem to be born?

I took key words from five unique phrases in the poem's twenty-one lines and ran them through the search engine of Amazon.com to see how many book titles would turn up. Here's the result:

Ceremony of innocence—sixteen hits

Rough beast—six hits

Slouch Bethlehem—five hits

Blood-dimmed tide—four hits

Spiritus Mundi—two hits

Of course, the search did turn up duplicate titles, one each for the hardcover and paperback versions of the same book. Even so, that's quite a hit list—thirty-three book titles from one poem of only 168 words. You can only imagine the countless times writers have borrowed a line to fit their own fiction need.

Puzzler Time

A two-parter. Identify the phrase from a literary source in each quote below. Answers are on page 276.

The bricklayer says, "I wanna talk to a guy name Tug Grey."
"Doug Gray?" Marty shakes his head. "I don't know a Doug Gray."
It's so Clintonesque. How can the guy be both lame and funny in the
face of disaster? "You guys know a Doug Gray?"
Marty is a liar of the worst magnitude, and I am going to have to
work with him.

PHRASE: _____ SOURCE: _____

The bricklayer is flanked by a pair of smaller, younger clones of himself and one slouching greasy gangster who hasn't shaved in days. An altogether stiff-necked people.

PHRASE: _____ SOURCE: _____

I have faith. The solid wall of my staunchest friends will stiffen up so he cannot get at me.
    But, no they are better strangers than friends.

PHRASE: _____ SOURCE: _____

The bricklayer says, "Which one of you is Tug?"
    Sturgis does the right thing. He fingers me with a toss of his head, his smile as stupid as the Mona Lisa's.
    "I'm Tug." I thrust out my hand as if there is safety in stupidity.

PHRASE: _____ SOURCE: _____

The selections come from a single page of my own experimental novel, *Love Busters, Inc.* You can read the novel's summary in chapter 2, if you like.

I wrote the novel using Strategy 7 to the extreme. I borrowed more than five hundred quotations from Anonymous to Zola, with Byron, Confucius, Hitler, Homer, Keats, Milton, Nietzsche, Plath, Pound, Twain and Woody (Allen) between.

Including one from "The Second Coming." Yeats wrote:

> *The best lack all conviction, while the worst*
> *Are full of passionate intensity.*

And Tug Grey observes of his sometimes friend Jack Sturgis:

> *He's run out of steam. His best arguments lack all conviction, and his delivery lacks passionate intensity besides.*

 How can I borrow from these giants without adding footnotes and other bizarre devices to my fiction?

Several ways. Here's how to . . .

Brainstorm With Genius

Read. Take notes. Lots and lots of notes. Except for books that I borrow from the library, I usually read with a pen in hand. I write in the margins, underlining, circling and highlighting passages that I find particularly ingenious. I look for wordplay, puns, irony, wit, beauty and creative technique. When one of these passages strikes a creative chord with me, I turn to a blank page at the back of the book and write a note to myself. It might be a title or an idea for a novel, or something I might adapt to a character or situation in an existing novel (or work of nonfiction, for that matter). If the book doesn't belong to me, I write a note on a 3″ × 5″ card, or photocopy a page and write in the margin of the copy.

I must mention the *p*-word again. Never borrow a lengthy passage word for word without giving complete credit. You can do that in a piece of fiction by allowing a character to give credit. For example:

> *"I'm the white Aunt Jemima of the women's movement," she said.*
>
> *"Don't give me that tripe—" He remembered the thick book with the blue cover lying open. "Aunt Jemima? You didn't think that up. You ain't that smart. You stole it out of that book on your nightstand by that Moonie guy."*
>
> *"It's Moon," she said, sniffing at him. "William Least Heat-Moon. He's an Indian."*
>
> *He laughed harshly, more like a dog snarling. "Indian? I read the back cover. Guy's name is Trogdon, William Trogdon."*

Naturally, you're not going to be able to use such a labored device more than once in any piece of fiction. Even if you do something like,

> *"To be or not to be, that is the question, isn't it?" she asked.*
> *He snorted at her. "Don't quote Shakespeare at me."*

It would sound strained if you tried it twice. Of course, Shakespeare is in the public domain, so you wouldn't have to credit him at all. I only did so for illustration's sake (and to set you up for what is to come).

Take this excerpt from *Mr. Perfect,* a novel I'm now marketing:

> *She held her silence for mere seconds less than five minutes, a long time by Bender's standards. Finally, nearing the bottom of her martini*

funnel, she came at him. "There he sits cruel, but composed and bland,
dumb, inscrutable, and grand as a cat."

Was that rehearsed or not? He doubted it. She was quoting. He
didn't know who and didn't want to show off his ignorance by asking.

Or, from the same chapter, this exchange:

"I'm not making eyes at you," he said.

"You're telling me I don't know what I see? You think a woman has
to be a truth detective to tell when a man is making eyes?"

"It's not that kind of a look."

"So it's making eyes in only a professional sense."

He thought about it and nodded. "An appraisal, if you like. I'm
calibrating my awareness, trying to establish a baseline reading on
your honesty." She looked crestfallen. "Don't get me wrong," he blur-
ted. "I'm not saying I don't like you."

She tossed her short hair and gave him a civil leer. "I hate dragging
a compliment out of a man only to discover faint praise."

You might recognize "It's not that kind of a look" as a twist on a line from
Schindler's List: "It's not that kind of a kiss." "Faint praise" and "a civil leer"
come from Alexander Pope. These passages do not require attribution but do add
flavor to the narrative by sounding a familiar note in the ear of an alert reader.

In most cases, I recommend bending a brief quote (and not long passages,
remember) to freshen it up, twisting it to serve your dramatic purpose (with no
particular concern about giving credit), as in:

She pursed her lips. "He didn't have to tell me about your famous trial.
I followed everything on television."

"So." The sum of modern mankind: They fornicated and watched
Geraldo.

Which is adapted from Albert Camus's *The Fall*:

A single sentence will suffice for modern man: he fornicated and read
the papers.

Or:

To see or not to see, that is the question.

Which comes from—well, you know where it comes from. I might use any one of half a dozen verbs that rhyme with *be*, depending on the context of what I'm writing. From *To me or not to me* to *To tea or not to tea*. And anything in between.

Finally, remember that there may be no such thing as an original idea. Theologian William R. Inge might have stolen:

What is originality? Undetected plagiarism.

From Abraham Lincoln's remark:

Books serve to show a man that those original thoughts of his aren't very new after all.

Which might have come from Goethe, who wrote in *Faust*:

What wise or stupid thing can man conceive
That was not thought of in ages long ago?

Perhaps bending and borrowing from René Descartes, who came before and wrote in *The Discourse on Method*:

One cannot conceive anything so strange and so implausible that it has not already been said by one philosopher or another.

Who might well have relied on Cicero, who wrote in the first century B.C.:

There is nothing so ridiculous but some philosopher has said it.

Who knows where Cicero stole his stuff? Maybe Terence, who put it down in the second century B.C. that:

Nothing is ever said that has not been said before.

Don't get hung up on it. Live and write by Chateaubriand's observation:

An original writer is not one who imitates nobody, but one whom nobody can imitate.

A final word on this strategy: Don't get into the habit of borrowing quotations as a way of advancing your writing life. The idea is to make creative associations.

Use the brilliance of others to stimulate your genius. Don't tap into somebody else's genius to pad your word count. Or worse, to sell somebody else's words as your own.

Brainstormer Strategy 8—UROPIIII ✳

"There is only one trait that marks the writer. He is always watching."
—MORLEY CALLAGHAN

Here's a puzzler to help you identify the name of this strategy.

The Granddaddy of All Brainstormer Strategies

Hidden in the following string of letters is the best advice you'll ever get in your writing career. For the message to make sense, just cross out five vowels.

O F P I E V N E V Y O O W U R E E L Y E S S

You know where to find the solution if this puzzler gives you fits—Appendix 1.

When you're finished, let's examine some techniques that will help you unlock the gift of eureka!

CHANGE YOUR POINT OF VIEW

Brainstormer Shuffle
- **Hold the problem at arm's length to look at it**. If you'll recall, that was the quickest way to solve the maze puzzler.
- **Use a splatter vision technique to escape the problem of tunnel vision**. The term *splatter vision* comes from the author Tom Brown, whose books on survival and tracking in the outdoors are masterpieces in the field. Brown talks about viewing a scene by gazing ahead, looking at nothing in particular, yet taking in everything within your field of view. You can take such a view of your own writing in a variety of ways. Speed-read your manuscript. Speed-read it aloud. Listen to somebody else speed-read your words. These

are several ways of stepping back from the words on the screen or on a page and getting a wider view.

- **Approach the situation by working backward.** Remember THEBEGIN? Use it here to get a fresh look at an old problem. For instance, one of the best proofreading tricks of all time is to read copy backward, word by word, aloud. Misspellings, stylebook faults and punctuation errors pop off the page.
- **Turn the situation upside down.** This happened to me as I looked for solutions using the bracketing tool mentioned earlier. Remember the heroine's plane crash at sea? Turning the problem upside down led me to put the villain into the plane so he risked falling victim to his own villainy.
- **Restate the question or problem.** I direct your attention to the puzzler at the beginning of this strategy discussion.
- **Challenge every assumption.** Here you apply two earlier strategies: reject the conventional wisdom and exploit the outrageous by acting a little crazy.
- **Get a second opinion.** Sometimes the best solution to brainstorming requires you to seek the assistance of another brain. I can't tell you the number of times a brief brainstorming session with my best friend and wife produced a solution seven times better than anything I developed on my own.
- **Ask questions.** Go to the experts, either through researching or by asking them outright.

 Those sound like good ideas. Give me another puzzler so I can try out what I've just learned.

Happy to. Here are two. Don't go on to the Solutions section until you've tried to solve both. I wouldn't want you to peek at the second answer while checking out the first puzzler.

> *I live in Montana in the house my father built. I weigh in on the wrong side of two hundred pounds, stand six feet tall and wear size twelve boots. My dogs, both golden retrievers, are named Gus and Kelly, and my son's name is Chris. How many hard-boiled eggs can Chris eat on an empty stomach?*

Did you do okay on that one? Then try something even easier:

Without contacting the Montana Bureau of Vital Statistics, what's my father's full name?

STAY ALERT

No problem vexes me more than losing a fleeting creative gem because I was unaware of its potential when it popped into my consciousness. You're asking yourself, "How can you lose a thought if you're aware of losing it?" Simple. I do it all the time because I'm too often a blockhead. Somebody will make a tiny speech blunder like *mute point*. The first thought that comes to my arrogant, oversized head is, "It's *moot* point, moron, not *mute*." Later I might remember that the speaker had handed me an expression with wonderful ironical potential, something that could be used to great effect in a story I'm doing. As in,

> *She glared at me in the long silence that followed, making her mute point all too loudly.*

But I neglected to have paper and pencil handy to write down the gem and subsequently forgot it. Now who's the moron?

All of which could have been avoided if I had been prepared, both mentally and logistically at the moment of eureka! Don't be caught unprepared. Remember this quote from Laurence J. Peter:

> *Of all the sad words of a writer's pen,*
> *saddest are these, "I didn't jot it when!"*

I carry $3'' \times 5''$ cards for this reason. I find them easy to sort and resequence. Plus, I find plenty of occasions to use them to leave notes or memos for others. And when anybody asks, "Do you have a sheet of paper?" out comes a card.

You may find it an extravagance, but I also use the same $3'' \times 5''$ cards as calling cards, with my name, number and e-mail address on one side.

The entry on this eureka! card is "Pontiff Kate," a gem that came to me quite literally out of nowhere. Earlier in this chapter, I dictated the word *pontificate*. Because I didn't enunciate clearly, my CSR program interpreted it as *Pontiff Kate*. Fortunately, something prompted me to capture the misunderstanding. It most likely struck me because I have a daughter, Kathryn, variously nicknamed Katy, Kate, Kates, Kit-Kat and half a dozen others. I see two possibilities for the acciden-

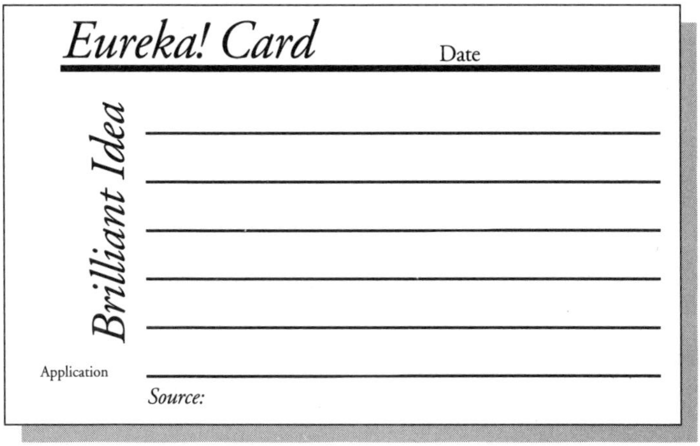

Eureka! Card   Date _____

Brilliant Idea _____
    _____
    _____
    _____
    _____
    _____

Application _____
    Source:

FIGURE 4. The Brainstormer's Eureka! Card.

tally invented expression. One, it sounds like a good title. Two, it could be an epithet for a character named Kate, the way *Saint Maybe* was used in the title of the Anne Tyler novel and television movie of the same name. You can find a reproduction of the eureka! card suitable for photocopying on page 281.

ELEVATE YOUR AWARENESS

Tricky stuff, this. Most of the time we are so lacking in self-awareness that we are not aware of moving around in a fog. We let the noise of daily life overwhelm us. We sink into trivial things like gossip and news items that have spawned countless talk shows without adding much enlightenment to our lives. Or we drift along in the raging torrent of racket created by our popular culture.

Remember this commercial advertising image, both in print and on television? A man sits before a television in an easy chair caught in a blast of noise and light pouring out of the tube. The image represents any one of us sitting in the daily wind tunnel of mindless minutiae. Our jackets are blown open, and our hair ribbons and neckties fly back in the assault of the slipstream. When we accept everyday distractions by sitting still for them, creativity and personal awareness have little chance of escaping death by drowning in our cluttered consciousness.

Here are several thoughts about how to elevate your own awareness and a brief exercise to help you put those thoughts into practice.

Wake Up to Your Personal Brainstormer Potential
Start with the acronym ELEVATE:

Eyeball
Listen
Embellish
Visualize
Absorb
Take notes
Explore possibilities

Eyeball. Another way of saying, "Open your eyes." Every situation, no matter how common or usual, is replete with discovery if only you'll take time to see the possibilities in it. Look around you. No matter how many times you've found yourself in this precise setting, try to find three things you haven't noticed before. Don't just smell the roses—see them up close. Touch their satin petals and thorny spikes. Taste them. Listen to them (but be careful of bees).

Once you've satisfied yourself, don't stay that way. For the next three weeks, wherever you go and whatever you do, look at your surroundings and coinhabitants with a fresh eye. You tone your awareness muscles by exercising them.

Listen. Is the room quiet? Are you sure? Try to distinguish and identify every tiny sound. Do you hear that computer fan running? The refrigerator compressor? A clock? The air conditioner? The traffic outside? It's not so quiet after all, is it? At the opposite end of the spectrum, is the roar of noise around you making it impossible to distinguish specific sounds? Are you sure? Put yourself to a test. Play some music. Try to identify every instrument and voice on that sound track. Make it a habit to listen to what's going on around you. Exercise powers of awareness that might have been dormant in you for years.

Finally, when somebody talks to you, don't spend valuable listening time formulating a reply. Just listen to what the person is saying.

Embellish. No matter how mundane your surroundings or circumstances are, energize them for dramatic effect. Embellish pure coincidence by exaggeration, by creating stories to explain the circumstances. As humans, we tend to accept that most of what happens around us is random and unmotivated. As a writer, coincidence and accident are unacceptable as standard fare. You must create stories, motivations, contentious objectives.

Here's a tip that might help you. As I blunder about in my daily life, I often encounter noises and occurrences that cannot be easily explained. If no explanation immediately occurs to me, my first tendency is to dismiss the incident. But if I happen to be operating on an elevated awareness that day, I apply this dramatic rule of thumb.

Nothing happens for nothing.

Then I set about finding an explanation. If I come up empty in the reality department, I invent an explanation. The idea for my third novel, *The Lurker*, occurred to me as I sat alone in the house listening to odd sounds. The explanation I invented? *Somebody is living in this house without our knowledge. It's not a burglar who breaks in, steals and leaves. It's a lurker who stays and eats our food and lounges around when we're asleep. If he gets bored, he could turn deadly.*

Visualize. I love the concept of shutting your eyes to see things better. Do so now, reevaluating your surroundings. What impressions can your senses detect when you focus on them? For instance, how cold or warm is the air? Is a breeze moving? Is the ground hard? Inventory your body, counting the number of places where your skin is irritated or feels itchy. This exercise alone gives you an appreciation for how your body can suppress trivial discomforts. But when you concentrate, trying to locate aches and itches, I have no doubt you will be able to find at least half a dozen. Now all you have to do is get those discomforts out of your head and exercise the larger powers of your awareness.

Absorb. Take in everything. What geometric patterns do you see? How many parallel lines exist right in front of you? Right angles? Regular circles? What is distinctive and unique in your field of view—those things that will not be duplicated anywhere else on the planet? When was the last time you looked straight up and examined the sky, especially at night? What would be different if you deviated from your usual routine within the next five minutes? Change cabs. Have the carpool drop you off. If you're outside, go inside. And vice versa.

You can't read a book outside in the rain? Oh, yeah? Where does it say that in the rules for living? I can think of a dozen ways to do it.

Take notes. As I've said, ideas and observations are fleeting. Write them down.

Explore possibilities. What applications do you find for all your new discoveries in this exercise of flexing your awareness muscles?

That's how you ELEVATE your awareness. Trouble is, can you sustain new heights of awareness? The answer is yes. Marketing wizard Jerry Wilson, author of *Word-of-Mouth Marketing*, is fond of saying, "If you want to cultivate a good habit, do it for twenty-one days." After that, the theory goes, the activity will become automatic. Give it a try and see. What can it hurt?

Brainstormer's Awareness Exercises

1. **When watching television, practice looking at parts of the screen other than where the director wants you to look.** Check out the furniture in the background, the writing on the chalkboard, the titles of the books on the shelves behind the actors. I practiced this exercise recently and found that Dodge truck commercials often have no backgrounds and no more than one actor, making it difficult for you to look at anything but the product. Chevrolet commercials tend to have a great deal of scenery and many pretty people competing with the automobiles. Victoria's Secret commercials use quite another strategy for keeping your eyes from wandering away from the television.

2. **Keep an awareness journal for a week.** No need to be elaborate about this. Just keep track of the times of day when you generate the most fresh ideas and when you are most effective as a writer. Keep track of when you are tired or bored, the time of day that you crash physically, when you are the most thoughtful or conversational, and when you want to be alone.

   Then use this journal to help you decide when you should set aside time for writing, brainstorming and napping.

3. **Practice looking.** You'll find what you're looking for. Don't believe me? How many Volkswagen Bugs have you seen today? Likely none, if you weren't looking for them. Try looking for the rest of the day and see what happens.

   Even if you don't seek the Bugs, you know how this principle works. You buy a unique article of clothing in a fashionable store. You're sure you'll be fashionably out front at school or work. Then you notice that every other person is wearing what you thought was so distinctive. Why? Because now that you have it, you're constantly on the lookout to see if anyone else is wearing it.

   Likewise, when you start looking for solutions to daily writing problems, you find them. Need a plot device to solve your hero's dilemma? Don't just walk away from the keyboard hoping that something will randomly occur to you. Set down the problem. Use the bracketing tool on it. Intentionally think about it as you're riding to work.

Seek genius and you shall find it.

Finally, let me end the discussion of this strategy with a piece of advice:

4. **Never say no to creativity.** How many times have you heard people say things like:

"I guess I'm just a left-brain person."

"I just don't know where creative people get all their ideas."

"I can't write (tell a story, tell a joke)."

"After a day at work, I don't have the time or energy to write a letter, let alone a novel."

Erase such statements from your speech banks and eliminate them from your attitude vault.

You must be ready to fling open the doors to creativity at any moment. These moments will become frequent and full of energy if you elevate your awareness. But you must first say yes to creativity—every day, all day long.

Brainstormer Strategy 9— Reverse Polarity ✴

"The gift of fantasy has meant more to me than my talent for absorbing positive knowledge."

—ALBERT EINSTEIN

By this I mean your creative polarity. Capitalize on brainstormer bipolarity by moving from the extreme of active creativity to passive polarity. It's a powerful way to give yourself the gift of fantasy.

 Whoa, whoa! What's bipolarity, and what does it have to do with creative writing?

First another brainstormer exercise.

Identifying Your Creativity Zone

Under what circumstances are you creative? When do brilliant gems occur to you? Check one or more of the following from this list:

☐ **Sensory deprivation.** Being in total quiet, pitch darkness, an empty setting, with no distractions to the ordered march of your creativity. This most passive state might include being drowsy or even in a deep sleep.

☐ **Bucolic inspiration.** Being outdoors or lakeside, sitting or walking in the forest, being at sea, watching glorious sunsets, listening to birds sing, finding poetry and music in the air and inspiration for your writing.

☐ **Motion detachment.** Traveling as a passenger. Riding on any form of transportation and being lulled by the movement. New ideas occur to you as gradually and regularly as a cloud changing shape.

☐ **Activity.** Watching a film or television show. Listening to music. Driving. Showering. Reading. Working out. Absorbed in anything but creative thinking so that ideas can fly at you from anywhere.

☐ **Sensory overload.** Walking in a crowded mall. Sitting in the audience of a spectator event, including concerts. Walking a busy city street. New ideas fall like hail from the thunderstorm of stimuli.

☐ **Other situations.**

SCORING YOUR CREATIVITY ZONE INVENTORY

How many circumstances did you check? If you selected:

Five or more, congratulations! Your mind is open to creative inspiration at any time, including circumstances beyond the five I offered you. You are very creative, indeed. It's likely that you often awaken in the dead of night and reach for that pen and pad beside your bed. While driving in rush-hour traffic, you capture an idea on your voice recorder. You have opened your eyes—and all of your other senses—to creative possibilities. You have built the field, so to speak. The creative sparks will come.

Four or fewer circumstances? Sorry, you have failed the test. You should never reject a situation as not having creative potential. Go back to the inventory. Circle the circumstances you did not check. Get involved in as many of the listed activities as soon as possible. Force yourself to generate as many gems of genius as possible under as many circumstances as possible.

Even if you check my five circumstances, I recommend that you periodically create each of the brainstormer environments. This will let you exercise your creative muscles under a variety of situations. When you find one area in which you are particularly creative, by all means, capitalize on it. I often go to a fast-food restaurant, tune out the racket and constant comings and goings of the clientele, and scribble on a legal pad. Any time we travel, I ask my wife to drive. That frees me to do more scribbling. I love the crush of airport terminals and flying coach. I don't know what it is, but some of my best ideas have come out of that chaos.

Bipolarity

In general, we are subject to mood swings. In the extreme, this condition is known as manic depression. Some sufferers of bipolarity fall victim to certifiable psychosis. Some of the true geniuses in music, art, mathematics and, yes, authorship were subject either to mania or depression. To name some: William Blake, Emily Dickinson, T.S. Eliot, Walt Whitman; as well as writers Hans Christian Andersen, Charles Dickens, F. Scott Fitzgerald, Ernest Hemingway, Mary Shelley, Mark Twain and Émile Zola. In fact, the list is much longer. See *Touched With Fire* by Kay Redfield Jamison.

Some of these geniuses cultivated their illnesses, pushing themselves to the brink of madness to touch the most seductive side of their genius. Others fell victim to it and killed themselves.

Those of us who function between the extremes of bipolarity recognize that, at a minimum, some days we're more enthusiastic than others. On any given day, we're likely to experience mood swings to some degree. Older people are more productive in the morning. Youngsters are more creative in the afternoon, according to some experts.

What about you? As a writer, you may be inclined to find excuses for not working except when your mood is perfect. This common writer's dodge is a variation on one I'll be introducing under the next strategy.

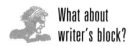 What about
writer's block?

Doesn't exist. Skip ahead to chapter 12 and get it out of your system. Then come back here and get creative.

As in the exercise at the beginning of this segment, I do not recommend eliminating any of the possibilities for tapping into your own genius. I recommend writing at all times of the day, no matter what your mood or level of alertness. Simply insist that you will write when you are tired, bored, excited, sad, glad and any other emotional adjective you can name, including angry and desperate.

I recommend doing this because I find that during high-energy times, my mind erupts with creative possibilities and ideas by the dozen. When I'm feeling down, I am able to connect with a darker side of my nature. I tend to be cynical, but that cynicism often helps me develop aspects of my characters, settings and scenes that usually go unnoticed when I'm feeling bright and bubbly.

Obviously, you'll not always be able to match your mood with a narrative need of the moment. You may be in an effervescent frame of mind while the character you're writing about is in a deep depression. At the risk of being accused of inciting mood abuse, I have some suggestions that might help you create the frame of mind you need for a particular writing situation.

Manage Your Creative Mood

First, this no-kidding disclaimer:

CAUTION: Never, under any circumstances, use drugs or alcohol to manage your mood. No matter how witty or insightful you feel under the influence of intoxicants or depressants, your prose will probably suffer rather than be improved by them. Besides, these things can kill or injure you.

ENERGIZING THE BRAINSTORMER'S BODY AND MIND

First, a list of the obvious, nonchemical stimulants to creativity.

- **Exercise.** Do anything from walking to more strenuous activities.
- **Listen to music.** High-energy or inspirational music both work. I like classical, swing and jazz-lite.
- **Take a refreshing nap.**
- **Soak in a hot bath.** I've read that soaking in hot water warms the blood to the brain and makes it more effective, but I can't say. I keep falling asleep and ruining my tape recorder.
- **Get some fresh air.**
- **Eat high-protein, high-fiber meals.**
- **Read fiction or poetry that inspires you to rise to the level of its author.**

The neat thing about this is the likelihood that you can find one book or poet who will fire you up every time you read the work. The poetry of e.e. cummings does this for me.

- **Read nonfiction that energizes you.** *The Western Canon* by Harold Bloom fills me with enthusiasm just by reading the segment on Shakespeare's unique writing qualities and contributions to our literature.
- **Visualize a nightmare.** When you get drowsy at writing time, relive a nightmare. Fill in the details with your imagination when your memory fails. If you don't have a nightmare of your own, borrow one of mine—the grizzly attack in chapter 5.

You don't need me to tell you what makes you feel good, awake or creative. Maybe it's a shopping trip. Or playing with a puppy. Or something as simple as working in a brightly lit room. Whatever works, capitalize on your knowledge of your moods by creating energy to fit an energetic fiction situation.

 ## What about coffee and caffeine?

One cup of coffee can help you concentrate, according to an article on brain power in *USA Weekend* magazine (January 1–3, 1999). "But if you're prone to anxiety," the piece stated, "you're probably better off not jazzing up your brain with a jolt of java."

Here's my take on coffee:

CREATIVE TIP: You can be more productive by cutting in half the amount of coffee you drink each day.

If you drink three or more lattes, it's very likely you spend a good deal of your creative energy traveling back and forth to the bathroom. Plus, high caffeine levels can make you jittery.

CREATING THE BRAINSTORMER'S BLUES IN YOUR FICTION

- **Create fatigue** by exercising or working long hours—or just by capitalizing on existing fatigue.

- **Experiment with odd hours.** Set your alarm clock to awaken you in the middle of the night. Get up and get to work writing.
- **Don't nap.** Work through your customary nap time, fighting off the advance of sleep.
- **Eat high-carbohydrate foods.** Pasta, bread and yellow veggies will make you sleepy. Work through it.
- **Listen to music,** particularly tunes that make you sad.
- **Read.** Try fiction, poetry or nonfiction that brings on melancholia.

As before, you know the things that can bring on feelings that tend toward depression. It may be pondering a personal grief. It may come from talking to soulful people or watching a sad video. Just remember, the point is not to incapacitate yourself, but to create a somber mood that you can connect with for a given writing situation.

And, I suppose, this being the litigious age, I should warn you:

WARNING: Don't try any technique in this book except on the advice of your personal physician.

Sheesh.

A BRAINSTORMER'S GUARANTEED PRODUCTIVITY BOOSTER

The most effective logistical measure you can take for improving your creativity and productivity is so simple, you'll wonder why you hadn't thought of it yourself.

PEAK BRAINSTORMER'S PRODUCTIVITY TIP: Work standing up.

Use a lectern that will hold your keyboard and mouse pad. Find the right level and get used to working on your feet. If necessary, find a stool that works to support you when you get tired. Eventually, you won't even need that. Stand on a foam pad to be kind to your joints.

I give credit for this tip to Tom DeCoster, a productivity expert from Indiana University–Purdue University Indianapolis. The practice will help you focus as much as anything else you do when you write at work or at home. When you work standing up, you will find yourself being more attentive. You tend not to nap or nod off when standing. Rarely do parts of your anatomy fall sleep. No matter how creative or effective you already are, this technique will help you improve on your existing performance. It's not an idea you can dismiss intellectually, either. You have to try it to experience it. Once you do, you'll be a believer.

Finally, let's turn the puzzler at the beginning of Strategy 9 into a brainstormer tool. Using the outline below, create the appropriate circumstance and record the mood you experience in each. Then duplicate that mood whenever you need to create particular sensations in yourself to match a fictional mood you hope to write about.

The Mood Tool

1. **Subject yourself to sensory deprivation.** Seek total quiet, pitch darkness, an empty setting, no distractions. Try to write.
2. **Employ bucolic inspiration.** Spend time outdoors, lakeside or walking in the forest, at sea, watching glorious sunsets, listening to birds sing, finding poetry and music in the air.
3. **Experience motion detachment.** Travel as a passenger, riding on any form of transportation, but as an intentional passenger, with paper and pen in hand.
4. **Get actively engaged.** Watch a film or television show. Listen to music. Drive. Shower. Read. Work. Get absorbed in anything but creative thinking. Be alert for creativity sneak attacks.
5. **Bring on sensory overload.** Work in a crowded mall. Sit in the audience of a spectator event, including concerts. Walk a busy city street. Again, pen and paper or audiocassette recorder in hand.
6. **Invent your own creative locale.**

Brainstormer Strategy 10— Make Words Instead of Excuses ✳

"The great end of life is not knowledge but action."
—THOMAS HUXLEY

When all else fails, stop thinking about writing and write. Plant your butt in a chair and write. If you use CSR and stand up to work, I might add: *Stand before your computer and talk into the mike.*

Thinking about writing, no matter how earnestly, won't get the novel written. To make these happy words—*check enclosed*—happen, you're going to have to write and sell your piece of fiction.

 Say, is it my imagination, or have you forgotten
to lay a puzzler on me?

Nah. Rather than a puzzler to this segment, I've decided to give you a final test to finish off the chapter. The test is based on the following.

The Brainstormer's Journal of Creativity

English teachers love to assign writing a journal to students. But that won't inspire as much creativity as a directed, focused assignment.

Use the following checklist to energize your personal creativity. If you do nothing else in this book to prompt your creativity, elevate your awareness and tap into the right-side capabilities of your brain, this exercise will bring out the best in you.

Even if you don't feel like it, complete all one hundred items in the checklist. Don't wait for tomorrow. Don't put it off until you feel particularly creative. Do it now. Complete this exercise before you move on to the final test.

ONE HUNDRED CREATIVE GEMS TO FIND IN THE WORLD AROUND YOU EVERY DAY

1. **List ten expressions people have used or misused** that demonstrate creative potential. If you must, capture these items from radio or television, preferably from unscripted shows like news interviews or unrehearsed conversations.
2. **List ten expressions you've found in written matter,** from newspapers to novels to nonfiction books.
3. **In ten words or fewer, write an image of ten characters** you have seen today with fiction potential. Select at least five from life and no more than five from photographs, film or television.

4. **List ten settings or situations** that you could put into a novel, film, screenplay, stage script or short story. Use commonplace settings but indicate how you could make them uncommon.

5. **Select ten clichés** and use any tool you like to turn them into usable, creative gems.

6. **Find ten ordinary vocabulary words or expressions** and use them to create puns or other wordplays.

7. **Write ten titles** for a piece of fiction. (Check out chapter 3 for the brainstormer's title writing tool.)

8. **Capture ten of your own emotional moments,** describing each in ten words or fewer. Write how you can use them in your work.

9. **Identify ten images,** ordinary or otherwise, and in a few words, indicate how each might be used in your fiction.

10. **Identify ten sentences from any source,** written or spoken. Edit each to improve upon them.

GRADING THE FINAL TEST ON YOUR CREATIVITY ATTITUDE

How many of the one hundred items did you generate?

101 or higher—You are a Certifiable Creative Brainstormer. If you exceeded my expectations for you, in terms of creativity, by generating all one hundred requested responses and continuing to record ideas that might have occurred to you, even if it was only one, give yourself an A+. You are truly creative. More important, you are energetic and enthusiastic. You have demonstrated the willingness to generate the 99 percent of genius that comes from perspiration. I have no doubt the inspiration will follow. Congratulations!

80 to 100—You are a Brainstormer. Now that you have seen the terms I'm using to grade this final test, I wouldn't be surprised if you went back to the drawing board and either started from scratch to create a new journal or filled in the blanks you left the first time around. I see no problem in that. You'd merely be showing an inclination to correct shortcomings, another important element of creativity. Good work.

60 to 79—You are a Brainstormer Wanna-Be. You gave the exercise the old college try. I wouldn't be surprised that many of your entries were certifiably creative. You want to be creative. You want to be a published writer. I regret to inform you that, no matter how talented you are, if you don't apply yourself, it's not likely you will be published. Sorry to be harsh about it. Publishing is a rough, unforgiving industry.

40 to 59—You're a Dabbler. Not that there's anything wrong with making a hobby of either creativity or writing. Have fun. But don't expect to make any money.

39 or lower— _____ . Fill in the blank on your own. You know what you are. You know what to say. I doubt you'll even finish reading this chapter, let alone the book, let alone actually writing anything. I hope you don't think I'm being cruel about this. Just realistic.

The Last Word

From now on, anytime you don't feel like writing, drag out the checklist and complete a new journal of creativity. By forcing your mind to work on the problems that I present to you, you will generate creative sparks. If you think you are oppressed by that disease some call writer's block, refer to chapter 12, then come back to this exercise. Complete it every day until you feel like writing again. It won't be long before you'll be back at the keyboard (or microphone) writing fiction.

You've been a good student so far. As a reward, here's the mother of all puzzlers. Does it seem familiar? It should. You'll find the solutions on page 276, but I hope you've paid close enough attention to solve all ten. And quickly.

PUZZLER FINAL QUIZ

theIN	_____
ject ject alwisconventdom	_____
act crazy	_____
impimagossible standard standard . . .	_____
never _____	_____
fy	_____
geniustapgenius	_____
uropiiii	_____
ytiralop	_____
stemakewordwordad of excuse excuse	_____

After you've unpuzzled these ten, circle the first letter of the first word in each solution to solve the puzzle within a puzzle and identify the reason we're both here. I hope you find the result a good memory aid the rest of the way through the book and in your writing life.

You now have the brainstormer tools, strategies and attitudes. Let's get on with applying them to specific writing problems in all aspects of your fiction.

> "A writer is somebody for whom writing is more difficult than it is for other people."
>
> —THOMAS MANN

Part II

THE FICTION WRITER'S BRAINSTORMER IN ACTION

"Writing is the manual labor of the mind:
a job, like laying pipe."

—JOHN GREGORY DUNNE

CHAPTER 2

Brainstorming the Critical Elements of Your Story

Twenty-something problems and fifty-plus solutions in launching a piece of fiction

ive puzzlers to start you thinking before you undertake problems dealing with:

- Ideas
- Story structure
- Plots and subplots
- The nugget

Can you find the common phrase for each of these puzzles?

1. pppod
2. cumorrowmorrow
3. bprepre
4. 8brutebrute
5. ci ii

Answers are on page 277. Now that your brain's in gear, let's introduce a few problems and solutions to help you write your way out of the box.

Ideas

"Every idea is an incitement."

—JUSTICE OLIVER WENDELL HOLMES

 I've this great idea, but how can I
know if it will sell?

Good question. Forget about the quality of your writing, structure, story, topic, theme or plot. Just answer this: Will it sell?

If the answer is no, *fahgeddaboutit.* Forever. Only if the answer is yes should you go on to worry about the little stuff like story and plot.

Writers want to know if they can sell to agents; agents want to know if they can sell to editors; editors to bosses; bosses to marketers; marketers to booksellers; and booksellers to the public. Not to mention the other big targets of the sales pitch: the critics and Tinsel Town.

 Fine idea, but worthless if I don't know how to test an idea.
How can I *know* if my idea will sell? Or not?

Depends.

The answer can be yes, your idea will sell—absolutely yes—but only in a limited number of circumstances. If your first book was a best-seller, then it is likely that your next idea will sell. If you're a celebrity, your idea will sell.

Meanwhile, we mere mortals can improve our odds of getting a yes answer by understanding ideas before going into my two-step process for evaluating them.

 What is this two-step process for
evaluating novel ideas?

Thank you for asking. The two steps are:

- analysis
- synthesis

First, let's look at what we call an idea for a novel, what I call . . .

THE HOT FLASH

We are struck by a bizarre observation, an interesting insight or even a genuine flash of brilliance. We say to ourselves, "Hey, maybe I could write a novel about that."

Here's a for-instance: I saw such a hot flash on one of the TV news shows the other night, something called alien hand syndrome. Victims of AHS lose control of one of their hands because the left brain literally does not know what the right brain is doing. A person might try to hang up the phone, for example, but the alien hand will refuse to do it. Willpower alone doesn't get results. Only after the good hand grabs the alien hand like a wayward child and forces the issue does the phone return to its cradle. In extreme cases, victims report awakening in the night to find the offending hand trying to strangle them.

Is this an idea for a salable novel? By itself, probably not. It's merely another of those one-dimensional hot flashes of brilliance we sometimes get. At best, it is a single facet of an idea that might be shaped into an otherwise salable story.

Could it be the central element of an idea for a novel? I doubt it. It has a dated *Twilight Zone* quality to it, lending itself to a twist in a piece of short fiction with a surprise ending or a subplot within a novel at best. I don't see enough substance in it to carry a book-length story.

 Are you saying that such hot-flash ideas are useless?

On the contrary. By the time this book is published, I'll bet the AHS Syndrome has already appeared in a "ripped from the headlines" segment of a television drama like *The X-Files, ER, Law and Order, The Practice,* or *Homicide.* In fact, Stanley Kubrick used this very device as a stunning, memorable, and continuing sight gag in the film classic *Dr. Strangelove* more than thirty years ago. I think I can foresee using it myself to individualize a character in an upcoming novel. Don't be surprised if several other novelists have the same idea and get it done before me.

And if a dramatic film receives an Oscar for a story about a physically challenged character (a lá *Rain Man*) with alien hand syndrome, don't write to tell me that I was wrong about a hot flash carrying a movie. Although I doubt it now, I do not doubt the ability of the creative genius to overcome any conventional wisdom, including my own.

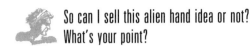

**So can I sell this alien hand idea or not?
What's your point?**

My point is that it's a mistake either to reject an idea altogether just because you don't think it can carry a piece of fiction or to build an entire novel around an insubstantial oddity.

In the first case, you might use a hot flash on a smaller scale within the novel, say, as a character trait. You ought to capture any flash, however lukewarm, by writing it down, filing it and periodically reviewing it for use in your writing.

In the second case, the most serious mistake you can make would be to invest an extraordinary effort into writing an entire novel around it—only to find out from an agent or editor that you've wasted your time. That they're titillated by the single-faceted hot flash but not seduced. That you have to start over.

Use my two-step process for evaluating salable ideas, and save yourself the grief of submitting a query that is as thin as vinegar.

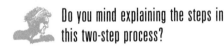

**Do you mind explaining the steps in
this two-step process?**

Not at all.

STEP ONE—ANALYZE YOUR STORY IDEA

Simply put, *analysis* means to break an element—in this case, an idea—into its individual parts.

When an idea occurs to you, wouldn't it be handy if you could throw it into a hopper, push a few buttons and have a computer crunch out its components? Wouldn't it be great if the processor would spit out a score telling you the probabilities of your story selling to a publisher? Or give you the addresses of agents who'd be the best ones to consider it? After all, some medical computers analyze blood, and crime labs analyze everything from dirt to insects to metals to shoe prints. Why not idea salability?

Why not, indeed. What do you think editors and agents do for a living? They evaluate ideas and the execution of those ideas. They study the market, previous publishing experience, sales data and popular trends. They analyze a thousand factors and compare ten thousand probabilities inside the computers they wear above and between their shoulders. And, tempered with the excitement generated in their heads, chests and guts, they make buying decisions based on their conclusions.

Or they make rejections.

You can perform the same operations to arrive at a story idea that might influence those buying decisions. Here's a simple brainstormer checklist that will help you analyze your ideas. Use it to tear your idea down into its separate components. Just put a check mark in each box where you can clearly see a connection with the elements of the idea.

Let's try it using the alien hand syndrome.

The Brainstormer Checklist of Minimum Essential Story Elements

Does your raw idea about alien hand syndrome contain the following:

- ☐ (15 points) A truly heroic character? And is that character:
  (1 point for each item checked)
  - ☐ Distinctive in voice or attitude?
  - ☐ Likable, even if quirky?
  - ☐ Interesting in career or skills?
  - ☐ Honorable, even if not saintly?
  - ☐ Flawed or vulnerable, either physically or emotionally?
  - ☐ Able to connect with readers in matters of the human condition?
  - ☐ Capable of humor or irony?
  - ☐ Capable of fear but not enduring cowardice?
  - ☐ Physically appealing but not a perfect ten?
  - ☐ Alive at the end of the story?
- ☐ (10 points) The heroic character's worthy goal? And is that goal:
  (1 point for each item checked)
  - ☐ Substantial in content?
  - ☐ Difficult to attain?
  - ☐ Generally legal and honorable?
  - ☐ Shared by potential readers?
  - ☐ Contested by any number of forces? Especially . . .
- ☐ (15 points) The heroic character's worthy adversary? And is that adversary:
  (1 point for each item checked)
  - ☐ Distinctive in voice or attitude?
  - ☐ Continually in competition with the heroic character?

- ☐ Likable or sympathetic to some extent?
- ☐ Interesting in career, crimes or skills?
- ☐ Wicked but not entirely demonic?
- ☐ Flawed or vulnerable, either physically, mentally or emotionally?
- ☐ Capable of humor or irony?
- ☐ Powerful enough to crush the heroic character?
- ☐ Physically fascinating, even if repulsive?
- ☐ Defeated at the end of the story?
☐ (10 points) Action and conflict involving the heroic character's quest? With:
(1 point for each item checked)
- ☐ Suspense or substantial tension at every turn?
- ☐ All dialogue laced with conflict?
- ☐ A varied pace?
- ☐ Action either rising to a confrontation or falling from one?
- ☐ The utter absence of boring, static scenes?
- ☐ Vivid imagery rather than lifeless description?
- ☐ Singularity of the central story line?
- ☐ Subplots that support the central story line?
- ☐ Narration carried by the characters and not the author?
- ☐ Absence of philosophizing, preaching and musing?
☐ (10 points) A perceived ending? Complete with:
(1 point for each item checked)
- ☐ A final, titanic, climactic struggle at the story's end?
- ☐ The climax being the most powerful scene in the story?
- ☐ A resolution that offers redemption to the heroic character?
- ☐ Recognition that every element in the story pointed to the end?
- ☐ Lessons learned, for both the characters and readers?

The checklist allows for 100 possible points. Tally yours according to the following scale, giving the value in parentheses after each major category you checked.

Scoring Your Idea
- ☐ A truly heroic character (15 points)   Your score: _____
- ☐ The heroic character's worthy goal?
  (10 points)   Your score: _____

☐ The heroic character's worthy adversary?
   (15 points)   Your score: _____
☐ Action and conflict involving the heroic
   character's quest? (10 points)   Your score: _____
☐ A perceived ending? (10 points)   Your score: _____

                                            Your total: _____

That takes care of 60 possible points. Unless you envision the incredible coincidence of both the heroic character and the adversary with the same syndrome (very inventive, I think, if not improbable), you probably arrive at 15 points.

Now add a single point for each of the forty remaining boxes you checked.

    Total boxes checked of the forty   Your score: _____

                                      Your new total: _____

I tallied 2 extra points: 1 for a hero who is physically flawed, and 1 for a hero who is not a perfect ten, giving a total of 17 points (or 32 if both the hero and adversary have alien hand syndrome).

Finally, use this scale:

Idea Salability Scale

POINTS	EVALUATION
0-25	This idea carry a novel? Absurd
26-50	Forget it
51-80	No way
81-95	Doubtful
96-100	Maybe

Pretty strict grading, huh? I base this rigid standard on the reports of agents to Jeff Herman's annual survey that 95 to 99 percent of all submissions, including queries, get rejected. It's a stiff-necked business.

Still, the scale makes two teaching points:

• First, raw ideas don't sell unless they come from writing superstars.

• Second, raw ideas that score high on this scale really aren't so raw after all. They're well-conceived and thoroughly developed ideas that use the second process we're going to discuss.

STEP TWO—SYNTHESIZE YOUR STORY IDEA

In synthesis, you put individual parts together to form a whole. Here's where you take a raw idea and turn it into a salable one. It's the first step of organizing to write. You should be encouraged if your idea earned 20 points or higher. Such a score indicates promise for developing the idea into a salable one. But no matter. You can generate all the points using our tool.

To synthesize that idea, you'll use the same checklist as before. This time, you'll add elements that allow you to check every box, using the brainstormer tool as a guide. Take out some paper and prepare to fill in the blank boxes with check marks supported by notes to yourself.

Let's leave alien hand syndrome behind us for the moment. Instead, we'll develop a rough idea for a novel based on a hot flash from, *Between Eternities,* a book of poetry by Grace Noll Crowell. Rather than from a physical oddity, this idea originates in a facet of common human behavior, one that affects us all. I think a broader scope offers a better chance of selling a story.

Examine these lines:

> *The hidden grief we bear we never tell.*
> *We go our several ways, dissembling well.*

How do you interpret them? Do they remind you of instances of denial in your own life, the white lies you hide behind when you can't bear to share your most hurtful emotions? Have you ever put on a brave face in the company of others when you'd rather run off and stew in your own emotions? I think that's what the poet is talking about. I like working with this theme because it shows promise for telling a story with scope and depth. Much more so than the hand thing.

 How can we turn the idea inherent in that couplet into a story worthy of a salable novel, play or film script?

UP WITH PEOPLE

Let's start with the most significant element of any story—people. You can see that the qualities of the characters dominate the scale I've given you to measure the salability of your story ideas. I believe that action and plot don't count for much if the characters are flat. No amount of special effects can rescue a film tale with boring characters.

In a previous life, I was director of the journalism department at the Department of Defense school that trains reporters, editors, photographers, broadcasters and PR staff for military base newspapers and broadcast outlets worldwide. One of the great theoretical discussions among the faculty and conventional journalists was the notion *What is news?* Oh, the debates we had. The answers ranged from the flippant (retired network television news producer: "News is what I say it is") to encyclopedia-length definitions, neither of which had much value in teaching newswriting to beginning journalists.

I studied hundreds of newspapers from military bases all over the world, checking stories that made the front pages. You'd think news would define itself by what most editors used as their top stories. Instead I identified a serious universal deficiency in most news coverage. More than half the stories in those papers dealt with technology, facilities, organizations, weapons, equipment and all too often the dicta of commanding officers. Seldom did our military journalists cover the most important asset of our armed forces: people.

So I wrote a new definition into our journalism handbook: *News is what happens to people.*

Our faculty began teaching that technology is a better story when it tells how it will help people function better. Instead of hardware, software, buildings and policies, tell us in every instance about people, people, people and people.

Brilliant, don't you think? So brilliant, in fact, I intended to adapt my definition to this book until I discovered that it had already been done. Peter Rubie, in *The Elements of Storytelling for Writers*, wrote that "The story is not about what happens, but the character to whom it happens."

Rubie, another great mind, is right on. The first important test of any flash of an idea is:

> *Does this idea lend itself to telling a story about what happens to people?*

When we ask that question about the Grace Noll Crowell excerpt, it's clear we have some work to do. So let's get to it, using the salability checklist as a guide.

Fleshing Out a Skeleton Idea

Simply keep the salability checklist on pages 55-56 at your fingertips and force yourself to answer its questions by plugging information into the right places. You try first. Then we'll compare answers.

Done? Here's what I came up with for the dissembler idea:

- **The heroic character.** A woman in her forties. She is raising three children: a girl in college, a boy in high school and a girl in elementary school. She has helped her husband establish his own business, not only by keeping house, but also by working in his office without taking a wage. She's not happy that she has grown overweight and out of fashion. Her unique quality is that strangers are drawn to her and people tend to trust her, telling her personal details in complete confidence. At the beginning of the story, many of her qualities remain hidden, even to her. She is honest, dependable, caring, pretty (although gone to seed a little). She is a survivor but is subject to dissembling, as we've defined it.

- **The heroic character's worthy goal.** At the novel's opening, she discovers evidence of her husband's affair. She struggles to keep her family together, protect the children from emotional damage and maintain the semblance of an ordinary life. Along the way she has to battle her husband, his mistress, her own emotions and tragedy in the family. And that dissembling thing.

- **The heroic character's worthy adversary.** She has several, as we've indicated: her husband; his lover; herself, as she tries to hide her grief and present a normal exterior. Together these forces combine to try crushing her spirit. One or the other of them allows us to check every box on the scale because we know the best stories are those that make life difficult for the heroic character and leave the outcome in doubt.

- **Action and conflict involving the heroic character.** There's the affair. The arguments with her husband. The effects of the affair on the children, after it is discovered. The divorce proceedings. Her attempts to begin an independent career. Her involvement with other women, characters who are also trying to hide extreme circumstances in their own lives. The ambiguous feelings she undergoes in establishing another relationship with a man who is an executive in her company. The conflict at every level from internal to out-and-out physical encounters creates an atmosphere of tension throughout.

- **Titanic struggle and heroic ending.** Denial of her problems creates dysfunctions leading to an attempted suicide in her family. She succeeds in her career path, comes to grips with her husband and family relationships and deals with her lover. She doesn't necessarily live happily ever after, but comes to terms with herself, her problems and her competence. She celebrates her independence. Most of all, she comes to the realization—both for herself and the reader—that it does little good to live a life of denial.

My new score: 99 points. More important than points is that the idea, developed in only 434 words, now gives me the basis for expanding it with enough detail, such as names and settings, to create a synopsis. From there I can build an outline of scenes that describe incidents (action) the story will include. Finally, I can condense the elements into that all-important brief statement of the idea in thirty-five to forty words. This is something I call the *nugget*. I can use that shorthand description to pitch my idea in a sales letter—the query.

More on the nugget later in this chapter.

 Your 99 is nothing. My novel was written from an idea that contained every one of these elements—that's right, 100 percent. But I haven't sold it yet. Just what are you trying to peddle?

Don't get testy. I'm not surprised that a novel wouldn't sell if it contained *only* these essential minimum requirements of fiction. Remember, the most this gets you is serious consideration. Those elements of the idea test simply help you cross your *t*'s and dot your *i*'s so you can submit a story idea and synopsis that won't get rejected because of fatal flaws such as missing teeth or bones.

Take the anatomy analogy one step further. Every supermodel hangs her beauty on the same 206 bones as you. Stripped down to her skeleton, she's no prettier than one of those Halloween suits the kids wear. Every one of us, whether a feast or a beast for the eyes, uses the basis of a skeleton just to get off the ground, so to speak. Same with stories.

Look at stories from an editor's point of view. Every professional pitch for a novel is likely to contain every one of the elements in our brainstormer checklist, whether it submitted over the phone by a frequently published author or in a formal query letter in the blind. Editors on the receiving end expect fiction ideas to conform to these minimum standards of that skeleton.

Without these elements, rejection is nigh automatic. You must understand that, although agents and editors are continually on the lookout for something above and beyond the conventions, most won't risk ridicule on anything too far out. You must go beyond the conventions to boost the odds of selling your story.

 Short of setting myself on fire, how can I get the attention of an editor or agent?

You need a grabber, a literary two-by-four applied to the forehead of agents and editors. You need a device that gets the attention of a publishing pro. The idea is not to hurt them but to make them feel good about the possibility that they might acquire a work that's new, fun and, oh, yes, in the best interest of their rising careers.

 How? What does a grabber of an idea look like?

Two quick stories will illustrate.

First, a visual example. The editor of my local newspaper asked me to help collect photographs to enter in the statewide journalism contest. Although she had a stack of excellent photographs, we rejected nearly all of them. The reason? Although they were technically excellent and visually interesting, none of the photographs displayed "stopping power." You know what I'm talking about. It's the photograph in the newspaper or magazine that grabs you by the lapels as you're thumbing past, holding you, demanding that you examine its every detail.

It's also the television commercial that brings family conversations to silence, not only the first time you watch it, but every time thereafter.

It's that quality in a movie trailer that makes you say, "I must see that film!" (And also the quality that persuades you to comment when you walk out of the theater, "The trailer for this movie was better than the #@!%$#@ film!")

Second, a nonvisual example. In a brainstorming session not long ago with an editor at Penguin Putnam, he invited me to pitch an idea for a novel series. So I did, naturally. Thinking off the top of my head, I gave him an idea in the rough, one I'd been noodling over for some time. When I finished he said, "I like it.

There's just one thing missing. I didn't hear the one thing that makes me sit up and say, *'Oh, wow!'* "

Oh, wow! As soon as he said it, I recognized how conspicuously absent it was.

I wrote the problem on a $3'' \times 5''$ card and began carrying it around with me. I'll keep this idea at the top of my consciousness until a solution occurs.

 A fat lot of help that is. Give an example of *oh, wow!* that exists in the here and now already.

Certainly.

In *Jurassic Park*, it's the startling notion of re-creating dinosaurs as theme park entertainment by recovering ancient DNA from mosquitoes trapped in amber.

In *Titanic*, it's the touching portrayal of a one-day romance that could be woven into and eternally survive an epic disaster.

In *The Truman Show*, it's the notion of growing up on a soundstage that only mirrors real life.

In *Shakespeare in Love*, it's one *oh, wow!* after another. Beginning with the Romeo and Juliet love story that evolved from writing the actual *Romeo and Juliet* love story, which speculates, often ironically, on the life and times of a genius we know little about other than the brilliance we see in his plays. And ending with a story told with all the qualities of mistaken identity, bawdiness and wit of any of Shakespeare's plays.

In Bruce Willis's film, *The Sixth Sense*, it's not Bruce as much as it is the kid who whispers in the movie trailer, "I see dead people." *Yikes!*

And, in the realm of soon-to-be-published fiction, it's an example that the editor at Penguin Putnam gave me. He said, "I just pitched a novel to my editorial board, a *Day of the Jackal* story set in the Civil War about the Confederacy commissioning the assassination of Ulysses S. Grant."

That's all I know about the book. That alone is enough to make me pick it up and peek inside with a view toward buying it.

That's *oh, wow!*

 Sometimes I have an entirely different problem. I want to write fiction, but I haven't a single idea for a story.

Really?

If you're really stumped, here are some places to seek a story idea. Use some or all of them, and write down as many as you can. Using a technique I suggest in the next segment, winnow your list down to a single idea, then run it up against the salability checklist we've already discussed. And don't forget that element of *oh, wow!*

- **Borrow from yesterday's events.** Research the news magazines from yesteryear. Many papers feature a "10, 20, 50 and 100 years ago" department. If you hit upon an idea that sounds inviting, research it. If it hasn't been novelized, use it. For instance, fifty years ago, the sheriff of my hometown was shot when ambushed. Three men were suspects. Nobody was ever arrested. That'd make a story. And the *oh, wow!* element just might be that the real killer was the sheriff's son.

- **Borrow from Smalltown, America.** Find a university library where you can examine small town newspaper stories that didn't make the national news. Literally thousands of novel ideas are lying unexploited in these places. Last year in Valier, Montana, not far from my home, a young boy was mauled by a cougar. He narrowly escaped being dragged into the forest by the cat. Later, a local lion hunter used his best dog to track down the cat. The boy's wish? To have a puppy from that dog. Tell me there's not a young adult story in that. And plenty of *oh, wow!* besides.

- **Surf the Internet.** Go anywhere online, following links, making bookmarks and writing notes to yourself. The Net is a rich resource for thousands of great ideas (and millions of bad ones). You could discover more ideas in an afternoon on the Internet than you could write into novels in a lifetime. Here's one: The chat rooms came alive with conspiracy theories about how John F. Kennedy Jr. did not die by accident but was murdered in that plane crash. You could write a celebrity thriller out of that. Or you could depart from the premise and write a novel about the kind of people who can find conspiracy everywhere but in the dictionary.

- **Write a working title for your novel.** Let the idea for a novel spring from the title. Try this one on for size: *The Pimpled Angel.* I don't know about you, but I see a tale of a sainted person who has a dark secret.

- **Write the first line of your novel.** Write a great first line, then try to puzzle out how an entire novel can grow from that seed. Use this one, if you like:

*Maybe a bad man isn't all bad, but a good man isn't good for every-
thing, either.*

Who knows? Maybe it's the first line of *The Pimpled Angel.*

- **Fictionalize your own experiences.** You may be the best source for your
  first novel idea. You have a life, experiences, interests, hobbies, careers,
  unique qualities. (Don't you?) What among them could be dramatized and
  turned into a novel? A for instance: People are always fascinated when they
  find out I flew helicopters in the army. And they're always blown away
  when I tell them that, except for the brief, stimulating moments when I
  nearly killed myself in them, it was a mostly boring job. I ought to write a
  book about that, eh?
- **Anecdotes, stories, gossip.** I talked to a farmer who hated badgers so vehe-
  mently he once nearly burnt his crop trying to rid his fields of them. I found
  it to be so hilarious, I wrote a short story about it. Whether it could be a
  novel, I'm not so sure. But he could certainly be a lively character in any
  work of any size, adding *oh, wow!*
- **Books of lists, directories, collections and references.** I went to *The New
  York Times Guide to Reference Materials* and found an entry for the *Reader's Encyclopedia of Shakespeare* by Oscar Campbell and Edward Quinn.
  It made me wonder what kind of men these were. Could they be an odd
  couple in a new setting? How would men get along as they cataloged every
  detail in the Bard's plays down to the dog, Crab, in *The Two Gentlemen of
  Verona*? It'd be a novel idea worth exploring.
- **Books of quotes.** *The Pimpled Angel* suggestion comes from a John Barth
  quote:

*Is man a savage at heart, skinned o'er with fragile Manners? Or is
savagery but a faint taint in the natural man's gentility, which erupts
now and again like pimples on an angel's arse?*

For that matter, the line, ". . . . a good man isn't good for everything"
comes from John W. Gardner. (I love quotes, remember?)

- **Local sources such as the historical society.** My county's society collects
  stories from the old-timers as a way of preserving the history of the homestead-
  ers. I'm fascinated by the tragedy of displacement of Native Americans as

both cultures struggled for survival in a harsh setting. There's a novel in that.

- **Death.** Capitalize on any or all of these:

  1. **Death of a parent.** My parents never planned to die, at least not in the estate-planning sense. Or if they did, they intended for their children to sort things out for them. The pangs I felt in combing through their personal papers and photos, the surprises, the disappointments, are the things that, if not capable of sustaining an entire novel, can enrich a story. A friend of mine wants to write a book, *When I'm Gone, Don't Fight Over My Girdle.* It stems from a true case of children contesting their mother's undergarments. Honest.

  2. **Loss of a friend or enemy.** When I came back from Vietnam after my first tour of duty there, I learned that my best friend had died in a car crash. And I found that my worst enemy had plowed his car into a bridge. I'd gone to war and back—and lived. They'd stayed home, my friend exempt from the draft because he had a baby, my enemy exempt because of his criminal record. The mix of emotions, should I ever explore them, will make a novel richer.

  3. **Death of a pet.** As a kid, I had a dog named Rusty. Meanest dog I've ever met. Bit the neighbors, chased cars, bit my sister, tore up mom's laundry, bit me. He might have survived all those things. Then he bit my dad. My dad told me the dog had to go. So me and the critter rode in the back of the truck out to a farm where a friend of the family agreed to board him for life. I cried, although that dang dog kept biting me to the end. Years later, I was struck by a telling insight. No farmer was going to abide Rusty and his needle teeth. As soon as we drove out of sight, the farmer shot my dog. There's a young adult story in that modern *Old Yeller.* Gotta be.

 You're saying that you could write a novel out of any of these ideas?

I think so. The problem is not whether you *can* write a film, play, short story or novel from a given idea. The problem is, *do you want to?* You must sell the idea to yourself, first and foremost.

If you settle on a great idea, write it.

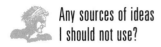

Any sources of ideas
I should not use?

No. Neither you nor I should limit your creativity. In *You Can Write a Novel*, I did advise beginners to shy away from two sources: events in the news and situations taken from television shows. That advice was fine for beginners, but you're a more advanced specimen, so here are two examples.

As for events in the news: With the strong women striking out for the top rung in politics these days, you can expect to see a film or read a novel very soon about the trials of her husband playing "First Gent." Will you be the one to write it?

And, as for sitcoms: Think how novel it'd be to write a novel about man-woman roommates, neither of which is gay. *Oh, wow!*

Story Structure and Plot

"Yes, nifty dialog helps one hell of a lot; sure, it's nice if you can bring your characters to life. But you can have terrific characters spouting just swell talk to each other, and if the structure is unsound, forget it. . . . You have to know what is absolutely crucial in the telling of your story—what is its spine?"

—WILLIAM GOLDMAN

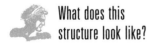

Supposing that I have isolated my salable idea,
what do I do with it?

Fit it into a story structure. In *The Elements of Storytelling for Writers*, Peter Rubie writes, "Without structure there is no real story because events and characters exist in a natural chaos on which the storyteller must impose order."

What does this
structure look like?

At its simplest, and here I borrow from teachers of creative writing, from Rubie to Aristotle, stories are comprised of beginnings, middles and endings, which seems obvious enough.

Too obvious, in fact. We need some specifics, if you don't mind. What goes into beginnings, middles and endings?

Try on this visual illustration (Figure 5) for size. It's my interpretation of the universal structure into which you can organize your story. Almost all fictional stories can be analyzed in terms of this structure.

BRAINSTORMER'S MASTER STORY STRUCTURE

I've modified this tool since first introducing it in *You Can Write a Novel.* I've decided it's a bad idea to encourage a brainstormer devotee to write falling action, so that's gone from this drawing. And a tenth master scene is included.

The profile shows two sequences of rising action. First, from a strong opening (1) to the pivotal point-of-no-return complication (3). Second, from there to the climax (9).

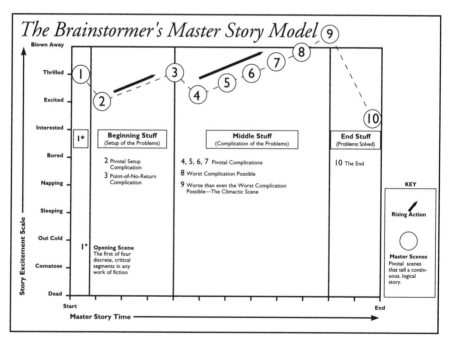

FIGURE 5. The Brainstormer's Master Story Model.

A story has four discrete, critical parts. These are:

- **The Opening Scene** (1).

- **Other Opening Stuff** (2)—Sets up the action rising to the point-of-no-return complication (3).
- **Middle Stuff**—Complications (4), (5), (6), (7) and (8), with action rising to the climactic scene (9).
- **End Stuff** (10)—Wrap-up, including the ending, epilogues and the like.

 Hey! I've always been told there are three parts to a story—beginning, middle, end. What's the deal here?

I agree with that story structure. But if you'll permit me to create a brainstormer distinction here, I think you'll see this isn't an academic or theoretical situation. Your opening, in my opinion, has to be the second most influential scene in your story, after the climax. That puts it in a class by itself.

BRAINSTORMER RULE OF THUMB: Write your opening scene with the idea that it will persuade an editor to ask to see your completed work of fiction. Write your climactic scene (and the complications along the way) with the notion that it will make the editor's buying decision.

The Opening Scene

If you like, peek ahead to chapter 3 for more remarks about first words and chapters. There you'll see why I consider the opening scene to be an entity unto itself in any piece of fiction. I've separated it from the notion of rising action that you find in most writing references.

A great opener might include any or all of the following:

- A great first line.
- Excitement. High action, high drama, high anxiety.
- An introduction to the heroic character.
- An introduction to the worthy adversary.
- Problems that stand in the way of the heroic character achieving a worthy goal.
- Your best writing style to set the tone of the story and show you can write: action, conflict, imagery, dialogue, irony.
- A feel for the story's setting and atmosphere.
- Foreshadowing of things to come.

Other Beginning Stuff

As many scenes as required to continue the momentum of the opening scene—without the necessity of achieving the relatively high level of interest. Introduce characters, commit the heroic character to her worthy goal and put the central conflict in motion, leading to the . . .

Point-of-No-Return Complication. At the end of this scene, the writer's setup for the story is done. The reader understands the problems facing all the main characters and feels with certainty that events have been set in motion toward an inevitable, climactic confrontation. An example might demonstrate better than an academic dissertation.

In the film *Fargo*, the crank scheme at the center of the story might be undone at any time, until the state trooper and two witnesses are murdered. After that point, there's no going back to the way things were for anybody in the story.

Middle Stuff—Action Rising Toward the Climactic Scene

Pivotal Complications. These are essential scenes in every kind of fiction, points at which the story changes direction because of problems introduced or solved. As the name suggests, they complicate the contest between adversaries and make it more difficult for heroic characters to achieve their quests. The number of pivotal complications in a story will vary, but as the tale proceeds, each succeeding pivotal complication ought to be more vital, more difficult and filled with more tension and action. That's how we get our concept of rising action and tension. It's what we mean by that profile that looks like a rising stock market.

The Climax

Here the central conflict of the story is settled. In many ways, the opening scene is more important than the climax because if it doesn't hook the readers, they'll never get to the climax. But the climax must be the most exciting, wondrous piece of writing and storytelling you've put into your fiction. If it doesn't deliver the goods, you'll generate bad reviews and negative word of mouth about your story. Elements of a climax:

- A titanic, epic, final struggle.
- Confrontation between your story's adversaries.
- Resolution of the story's central conflict, often in the heroic character's favor.

- Avoidance of tricks that help the heroic character win.
- A maximum of action and conflict with a minimum of explanation.

The End Stuff

- A logical conclusion. One that results from all the action that precedes the climax; one that leads to the logical ending.
- Resolution, as it is called.
- Redemption for the main characters.
- A sense of *oh, wow!*

I have a great novel, a real page-turner that heats up in the third chapter. Trouble is, I can't get an editor to read it.

It could be structure problems. Throw your first two chapters away. Start your novel at the third chapter. Apparently, all that goes before it is preliminary, as if you began your novel too early.

See chapter 3 for more on the topic of first lines, first chapters and other firsts.

Your master story model shows ten scenes. As I structure and plot my novel, how many scenes should I expect to write?

Start with ten or fewer. That's the essence of the following tool.

THE BRAINSTORMER'S TEN-SCENE TOOL

This might surprise you. Every novel I've ever written, read or heard about can be destructured into ten scenes.

That's right—ten scenes. The same goes for plays, films and teleplays.

Notice I'm not suggesting that the creators of these works of fiction used only ten scenes to tell the story. I'm just saying you should plan the central story line of your novel to go ten scenes or fewer. If you write the central story well in these ten scenes, the rest of the novel will take care of itself.

Take a look at the ten-scene tool on page 73. You can use this tool as the quintessential illustration of Strategy 6—Simplify. When you're finished, you will have the central story line intact. Adjust it as your novel progresses, adding or amending as new developments occur to you. When you get stumped in the middle of your novel, refer to these ten scenes to remind yourself where you're supposed to be going. In other words, adhere to this fundamental . . .

BRAINSTORMER TRUTH: Stick to the central story line by using the ten-scene tool and you will avoid most fatal structural mistakes made by amateur fiction writers.

You will avoid:
- Excess story complexity; overplotting
- Wandering
- Overwriting
- Being unable to explain what the story's about

And a host of other sins. All other things being equal, if you can nail down the central structure—if you have a story worth telling and the ability to write it—you can sell your fiction.

For your central plot or main story line, these ten scenes will carry the freight. Obviously, they're going to be your most exciting, most critical points in the story. Everything else having to do with the main story line involves using other devices or fiction tools to provide characterization and motivation, and to describe minor scenes that will carry a reader's interest between the ten most important scenes.

By the way, there could be fewer scenes in the middle if you like. There's nothing sacred about having ten. Only the ones marked with asterisks in Figure 6 are essential.

Subplots

"Since a story is not an exact transcript from life, it does not even mirror life, but expresses it."
—LEON SURMELIAN

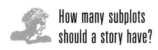 How many subplots
should a story have?

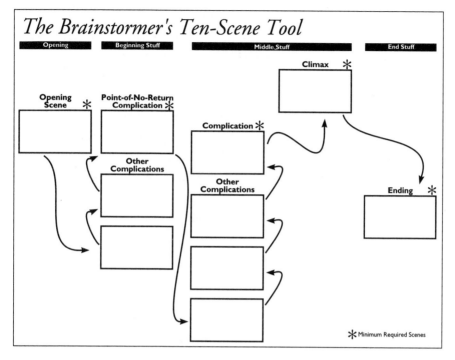

The Brainstormer's Ten-Scene Tool

FIGURE 6. The Brainstormer's Ten-Scene Tool.

So glad you framed your question in those terms. Don't let the existence of subplots trick you into creating labored contrivances. Constructing the novel is not like going to the bulk food section of your supermarket where you can dip into a variety of bins and come up with three scoops of subplots, nineteen scoops of minor characters, seven plot twists and so on.

Granted, certain subplots do seem conventional. For instance, you can expect to find a romantic interest subplot in almost every kind of fiction, from *Armageddon* to *Zorba the Greek*. Family relationships. Career ups and downs. Love affairs on the side. Rebellion against authority. Any or all of these themes might appear in your stories, as they do in many other stories.

But in the truly brilliant stories, these are not tacked onto the main story line as if stuck on with Post-it notes. You know what I'm talking about. For the last two decades or so, nearly every film you can find has the obligatory sex scene thrown in. Or else the provocative instance in which some part of the anatomy, usually but not always female, is briefly exposed. And almost every one of those films could be shown with the scene excised without damaging the central story line.

On the other hand, effective subplots woven into the fabric of the story are part of a pattern that cannot be removed without shredding the main story.

A brief example from the film *Shakespeare in Love*. The main story line concerns Shakespeare's need to write a play in order to make money. This quest lands him in the same orbit as Viola, a young woman who wants to be an actor in a Shakespearean play because she admires his writing above all others. For the moment, put aside all the action that takes place and imagine that only these two are on camera or onstage, if you will. And permit me to describe a few of the many subplots to this central story.

- Shakespeare is jealous of his contemporary, Christopher Marlowe, because of his celebrity status.
- The nobleman, Lord Wessex, arranges his own marriage to Viola.
- Queen Elizabeth, a fan of the theater, puts herself in the position to umpire a wager between Wessex and Shakespeare about whether true love can ever be represented on the stage.
- A young urchin, fond of mice, is rejected as an actor in Shakespeare's play and becomes a troublemaker.

You could name a dozen other subplots. The remarkable thing is, every one of them is so well crafted and tightly tied to the central story line that to remove it would diminish the polish of the overall tale.

Think about this. What other Hollywood production have you seen in which the lovemaking scenes are not gratuitous? Set to lines from *Romeo and Juliet*, even the sex is art in the film.

From this piece of subplot artistry, every writer can learn a valuable lesson:

> *If a subplot can be eliminated from a story without leaving a vacuum, it was likely tacked on, perhaps as a formulaic afterthought. The subplot shouldn't have been written in the first place.*

 Since you recommend writing the central story line in ten scenes first, how can subplots be included without seeming to tack them onto the main story?

Your excellent question requires a careful answer that might seem downright slippery:

A subplot reveals itself to you as a natural outgrowth of the central action, the characters and their interactions, and from the everyday experiences of life. The subplot carries the audience forward toward the outcome of the central story by posing and solving intervening problems.

If you'd like to, think of it this way: The central story line keeps you moving toward the inevitable, final conflict in the climax. You must see how the novel's main issue gets resolved. Subplots keep you moving from scene to scene and chapter to chapter to see how the smaller issues turn out.

The trick for both is to create realistic characters, fictional people with the concerns that you, your loved ones and your hated ones have to deal with day to day.

Having said that, let me illustrate with an example from my second Force Recon novel.

Sergeant Robert Night Runner is a Blackfeet Indian from Montana. He's Ivy League–educated, an excellent shot, a superb marine. In this novel, the Force Recon team must rescue the United Nations arms inspection team detained against their will in Iraq. That's the central story line. But Runner has plenty of other issues to deal with, issues that I call subplots:

1. He's a warrior in a white man's world and constantly forced to adapt to two strange cultures: modern white America and the marines.
2. He's wed to the basic skills of his ancestors but must function in the high-tech climate of today's warfare.
3. He's caught in a struggle within the overall contest, one that threatens his pride as well as his life. An Iraqi terrorist band is tracking his Force Recon team, and an Arab fighter in that band just might be even more adept at tracking than Runner.

It's a given that the good guys are going to win the struggle of the main story line: The Force Recon team will rescue the UN inspection team. Perhaps not in any way you might guess, but that's the way a category book must turn out. No editor is going to write an acceptance check if, in the end, the rescue team comes back home and says: "Welp, we tried, but we just couldn't save the good guys from Saddam."

However, on the issues of subplots, *nothing* is predetermined.

When I personalized the fight between two men, a Blackfeet warrior and a Bedouin warrior who each feel threatened by the other, the story hit an important milestone for me. It transcended its action-adventure genre, something we should all try to do.

So don't ask what you can do for your country. Ask what subplots can do for your novel.

 ## What kinds of subplots *ought* to be included in my stories?

I hesitate to make lists of such things because, as I've said, subplots are natural outgrowths of the story and of the writer's genius. They're not picked from prefabricated lists. When you see certain movies, you instantly recognize that stock plot elements were generated and plopped into the script. Things like these story lines tend to be clichés when they're dropped into films:

- The obligatory car chase, followed by . . .
- The obligatory car crash in which . . .
- The bad guy gets away, leading to the scene of . . .
- Hatred at first sight between the hero and heroine, followed by . . .
- The soft-focus sex scene between the hero and heroine after a blowup between them, followed by . . .
- The lover's spat brought about by a misunderstanding that apparently ends the romance, followed by . . .
- The lovers making up, usually with make-up sex . . .
- Then the lovers combining to defeat a legion of demons . . .
- Leading to a love scene . . .
- And so on, ad nauseum.

Nevertheless, here's a list, not exhaustive, using *Seinfeld* as an example:
- **A continuing romantic interest.** For Jerry, one an episode, with frequent references to his past relationship with Elaine.
- **Personal quirks.** For George, repeated instances of his tendency to be a tightwad, and to be obsessed with parking spaces.
- **Personal graces.** The better angels of their nature. Like . . . gee, I can't

think of anything right away. You read on. I'll think this over and catch up with you later.

- **Personal flaws.** The nasty, unpleasant angels of a character's nature. Need I list them all?
- **Family relationships.** Jerry's and George's, which crop up every few episodes.
- **Mysteries.** Kramer's first name.
- **Hobbies, careers or technical interests.** Jerry as a stand-up comic. George's ambition to be a pretend architect. Kramer's creation of miniature art from pasta—art that appears in the background of the set in many an episode.
- **Job relationships.** Elaine's baffling relationships with a variety of bosses. George's continual boss battles.
- **Fears and deep, personal secrets.** Kramer's first name again. Jerry's unwillingness to commit to a woman. George's PIN.
- **Personal history.** Past experiences that bear on the present situation. Cosmo's mother. The Jerry-Elaine relationship.
- **Talents.** Jeez, other than to make you laugh, do those characters have any?
- **The continuing effects of nature and the environment.** Big-city eccentricities and life, such as waiting "on line," form the backdrop of the series and play larger roles in many episodes.

You get the idea. You can see from this illustration that subplots, or *situations* in the sitcom, can often rise to enough importance to compete with or even become the central story. But they can also remain subliminal, occasionally cropping up to remind the reader that they are there.

 I sometimes forget about my subplots because I have so many going at once. How can I keep track of them and see them through to some kind of resolution?

Two things can help you keep track of your subplots: a solid character dossier, often called a concordance, and a subplot tool.

I use character cards arranged in a nifty flip-up folder. I address this technique in detail in *You Can Write a Novel*, and chapter 4 reviews the high points. There I also offer other tools for keeping characters in line.

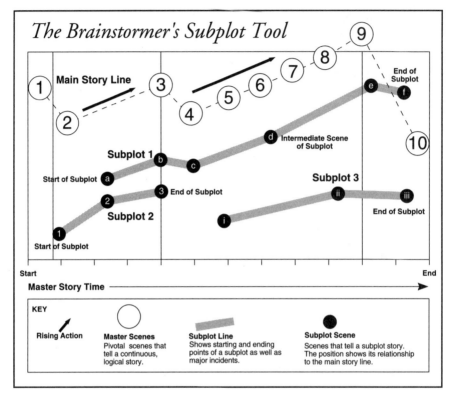

FIGURE 7. The Brainstormer's Subplot Tool.

THE SUBPLOT TOOL

Simple enough, eh?

When you introduce a subplot, label it on the model, indicating the starting point. When the subplot issue is resolved, mark the end of that particular line.

This is not to say you must know all the minor issues you'll plug into your story before you start writing it. It's more a way of keeping track as subplots occur to you. You merely note the starting point and trace its progress as you go.

Two considerations:

1. **Subject your subplots to the same rules of rising action and tension** as your central story line and individual scenes. See chapter 5 for a detailed discussion of this issue. If you can write subplots as "a novella within a novel," the entire story benefits.

2. **Resolve important subplot issues at or near the climax of the central**

story line. If you can work out a number of issues at crunch time in your story, the reader will be enthralled. This doesn't mean your subplots must last through an entire story. In Figure 7, subplot two might involve a meeting between the heroic character and a love interest who is killed by the villain in the point-of-no-return complication. Above all, observe this . . .

CAUTION: Don't throw so many issues into the resolution of the climax that it clutters the story. Better to follow Strategy 6 and simplify than to dilute the effect of your resolution.

 Ideas, plots, subplots—I get confused with so much to keep track of. How can I stay focused on my story?

Thanks for asking. In keeping with Strategy 6—Simplify—try the next tool in the brainstormer inventory.

The Nugget

"Forget the books you want to write. Think only of the book you are writing. . . . Concentrate. Narrow down. Exclude."
—HENRY MILLER

Here's a great tool to help you keep your focus.

In forty words or so, write down what your story is about. Here's an example from one of my own tales:

> Love Busters, Inc.
>
> *A romantic thriller*
>
> *A con man breaks up a marriage on the wedding day. Inspired, he starts up Love Busters, Inc., gets rich wrecking relationships for hire, loses all to a ruthless woman, and risks life, limb and heart to get even.*

That's thirty-nine words, not counting the title and category.

HOW TO KEEP YOUR FOCUS USING THE NUGGET

- Type or print your idea onto 3″ × 5″ cards.

- Carry one in the pocket of your blouse or shirt.
- Put one in the place where you'll be writing your novel. Put another on the visor of your car.
- Carry one in your planner.
- Keep this nugget before you as a reminder of your novel and the story you have committed to telling.

Any time you feel you're drifting from the story you set out to write, you can do one of two things:

1. Get back on track.
2. Write another nugget that describes your new focus.

> **"I always do the first line well, but I have trouble with all the others."**
> —MOLIÈRE

CHAPTER 3

Brainstorming the Story's Nuts and Bolts

Thirty-plus problems and one-hundred-plus solutions in getting off on the right foot

 our puzzlers to start you thinking before you undertake problems dealing with:

- Firsts and lasts
- Titles
- Point of view
- Basic mechanics

See if you can identify the well-known works, mostly fiction, in which these first and last lines originate. I tried to arrange them from the easiest to most difficult.

First lines:

Call me Ishmael.

I had a farm in Africa . . .

Let me say this: Bein a idiot is no box of chocolates.

You are not the kind of guy who would be at a place like this at any time of the morning.

Beware thoughts that come in the night.

Last lines:

'Tis.

"Finest kind," replied his father.

You know what I mean?

. . . his heart was going like mad and yes I said yes I will yes.

Don't ever tell anybody anything. If you do, you start missing everybody.

Answers are on page 277. Now that you're warmed up, get ready to deal with perhaps the most critical chapter in this book. Not because the content is so complex or difficult. Rather because the choices you make about your story's nuts and bolts, if they are not sound before you start writing, will dog you until you write the words *The End.*

The first two segments of the chapter, Firsts and Lasts and Titles, deal with choices that will influence whether editors and agents will consider buying and representing your story. The remaining segments, Point of View and Basic Mechanics, will influence your style and capacity to tell the story in the first place.

Firsts and Lasts

Your first and last lines can turn on—or turn off—an agent's or editor's interest. If your first and last chapters can sustain that interest, the general reading public might get the chance to read those first and last words.

Why don't we get started? Go ahead and ask a writing question or state a writing problem, and I'll address it.

 Speaking of firsts. What's the first thing an editor looks for in deciding whether to make an offer on a manuscript?

Intentionally or not, the first thing every editor looks for is an excuse to reject your manuscript—by expending the least effort possible.

He's in a hurry. The burden is on you to compel him to spend more than thirty seconds looking at it, no matter that your novel might have taken a year or more to write. He carries his own agenda for the kind of novel that will boost his career as he works toward that mythical position as publisher. If your project doesn't mesh with that agenda, then it will be turned away.

What kind of novel will boost an editor's career?

As a rule, the careers of editors and agents take off when they consistently take on books that make money. The bigger the money, the faster the career takes off. Critical acclaim can make a career, but big money will make it faster. If editors think your story will make lots and lots of money, they'll fight over it, spending lots and lots of their company's money.

How can they know if they never even look at my stuff? I get so many automatic rejections of my query letters. And the writing samples come back so fast I doubt they were read. Is my material so terrible?

Not necessarily. What's terrible is the sheer volume of demand on editors and agents. They are forced to focus their attention on a limited number of categories to publish or represent. To some degree or other, everyone in the business specializes, so if you aren't pitching exactly what they're looking for, they don't look very far into your pitch.

Next to money, the most valuable resource in the publishing industry is time. Every agent and editor would be swamped trying to read complete manuscripts in the search for the great American novel. That's why they hire readers and screeners. That's why they ask for query letters first. Then synopses, outlines and first chapters before entertaining the full manuscript. No matter how idealistic they were when they entered the publishing world, they come to realize that publishing is a business, not an art. Time is money. Success accrues to those who use their time most fruitfully. So they do not spend precious minutes on projects that do not have the possibility of making money. And if they can't make it big on quality, they'll try to swing quantity, making a bunch of easily edited books. Not too many editors will take on a writer as a project.

So how can I sweep an editor or agent off her feet with my writing project?

Assume that you have successfully pitched your idea in a query letter that contains the minimum essential elements of a salable story, including that quality of *oh, wow!* in your nugget statement. You have been invited to send the complete manuscript. Now, let's stick to the firsts and lasts of the manuscript itself.

 Are you suggesting I can't sell a novel unless it has a first line as memorable as *Moby Dick* and a last line as uplifting as that in *Angela's Ashes*?

Hardly. I selected the puzzlers at the head of this chapter to indicate to you that in both fiction and nonfiction, first and last lines alone won't determine a work's salability or literary permanence. If your first line is a stopper in 10 words or fewer, congratulations. But I wouldn't expect an editor to stop reading after 10 words, either to buy your manuscript or to reject it, no matter how good or awful those 10 words are.

 So what do you mean by first lines?

THE FIRST 100 WORDS

The first and last 100 words of every film, play and novel are crucial to its success. Even at that, an editor or agent who asked to see your work probably won't reject it on the basis of such a small sampling.

 Then how far can I expect an editor or agent to read into my manuscript before deciding to reject it?

RULE OF THUMB: If a publishing professional has asked to see your manuscript, her first critical decision point likely will be at the 1,000-word mark, roughly four to five manuscript pages. If you can't sell your story to her by then, she will most likely reject it.

That's not so bad. According to best-selling author, Dean Koontz, a potential reader in the bookstore probably won't give you even that much attention. As an unknown, you'll be going up against best-selling authors. If it's a toss-up between plunking down eight dollars for John Grisham's paperback or yours, he'll get the nod more often than you.

Even so, the situation isn't hopeless. Editors and agents, especially those on the first rungs of their career ladders, won't have the clout to edit somebody like John Grisham. Instead, they'll be looking for the *next* John Grisham, constantly searching for the talent to give their own fortunes a boost.

 ## What kind of brainstormer magic will help me sell my tale in the first thousand words?

Let's talk about it, shall we?

The Brainstormer's Checklist for the First 100 Words
At a minimum, does this critical segment of the work:
- ☐ Set the tone of the narrative, including vocabulary, attitude and harmony of language?
- ☐ Establish a point of view?
- ☐ Preview the mechanics of the story, including sentence length and density of paragraphs?
- ☐ Sketch in a suggestion of the setting?

A tall order, considering that I used more than that allotment just getting to the end of this sentence—107 words, to be precise.

Test this observation about the first 100 words by picking up any novel, script or play. Count the words. (If the hundredth word falls in the middle of a paragraph, include the entire paragraph in your sample. This gives the writer a fair chance to finish her thought.) Evaluate the material according to my checklist, as I have done with several dozen modern novels. Every one that became popular satisfies each element on my checklist, which is evidence enough that you should consider following examples of success.

Of these qualities of the first 100 words, which is the most important?

Without a doubt, the 10 striking words that create the element of *oh, wow!*

 Give an example of techniques to help me arrive at 10 truly striking words.

Sure. I chose my selections by randomly pulling books from my own shelves. If a selection went longer than 10 words, I let the writer finish the thought. Keep in mind that the opening words don't have to do everything on the following list. If those words accomplish just one of these missions, they are a good start on the road to selling your work.

What Striking Words Can Do
- **Create a powerful sensory image.** In John Grisham's *The Street Lawyer*, you'll find these words in the first paragraph: "I didn't see him at first. I smelled him though. . . ."
- **Open an emotional vein.** Kaye Gibbons did this in *Ellen Foster*: "When I was little I would think of ways to kill my daddy. I would figure out this or that way and run it down through my head until it got easy.

  "The way I liked best was letting go a poisonous spider in his bed. It would bite him and he'd be dead and swollen up and I would shudder to find him so. . . ."
- **Jolt the reader with a sense of dissonance.** In Terry McMillan's *How Stella Got Her Groove Back*, you find: ". . . much as I loved my son, I was glad to see him disappear. . . ."
- **Capitalize on the outrageous.** But always remain wary of being too gimmicky. In Nora Roberts's *Montana Sky*, this is the opening sentence: "Being dead didn't make Jack Mercy less of a son of a bitch."
- **Shape a fresh language impression.** Jay McInerney used this technique in *Bright Lights, Big City*: ". . . you rode past that moment on a comet trail of white powder. . . ."
- **Tantalize with a sense of drama, irony or suspense.** Winston Groom's narrator, Forrest Gump, says, "Probly, tho, I'm closer to bein a imbecile or

maybe even a moron, but personally, I'd rather think of mysef as like a *halfwit*, or somethin—an not no idiot. . . ."

Or, if you are endlessly talented like Alice Hoffman, you can write a first paragraph that contains the entire package, striking words and images one after another, as in *Here on Earth*. A sampling:

> *Fox Hill, where the pastures shine like stars.*
>
> *These woods are best avoided, or so the local boys say.*
>
> *(The boys) walk home quickly. If the truth be told, some of them run.*
>
> *(Boys) pry kisses from their girlfriends.*

And when you can write like the following in your first paragraph, forget about some artificial 10-word/10 percent rule:

> *A person could get lost up here. After enough wrong turns he might find himself in the Marshes, and once he was there, a man could wander forever among the minnows and the reeds, his soul struggling to find its way long after his bones had been discovered and buried on the crest of the hill, where wild blueberries grow.*

Where wild blueberries grow. The striking contrast between the notion of death (foul play suggested), burial, lost souls and that of beautiful, tasty fruit. I have only two words for that passage: *Oh, wow!* You can't learn art like that from any writing manual.

 ### If an editor is willing to read a 1,000 words anyhow, why are the first 100 so important?

You can't afford to waste a single word of the first 100, because those words will help create your *first impression at the bookstore.*

You might not have much to say about your book's title, cover, preview quotes or ad copy, but any potential book buyer who has been motivated by those things to pick up your novel will glance at the first paragraph or two to get a taste of your storytelling ability. Those first 100 words must snag his interest and hold him like a Velcro-captured cotton ball, so that the only time he dares relax his grip on your novel will be to lay it on the counter to get his wallet.

THE FIRST 1,000 WORDS

 What is the function of the first 1,000 words then?

Obviously, to create a lasting first impression on an editor or agent. The word *compelling* gets a lot of mileage in lines pulled from critical reviews, but here I mean it quite literally:

> *Your first 1,000 words must compel an editor or agent past the milestone where she would normally reject a manuscript. The deeper you can force a publishing professional to read into your novel, the greater the likelihood she will eventually be invested enough to buy or represent it.*

REALITY CHECK: Publishing professionals will often reject a work even when they don't dislike it. Take a look at the following list (not based on scientific study), which I invented merely to illustrate my point:

An editor or agent might have one or a dozen reasons for rejecting your query. Here are a few.

- She hates it—your style, your approach, your story. And you.
- She hates your topic, although she might like your writing.
- She likes your writing potential, but it'd take too much work to develop it to salable standards.
- She loves your writing, but she never takes on fiction.
- She loves your fiction, but never deals in romances.
- She loves your romance, but already has an author engaged in an identical project.
- She loves your project, but your topic went out of vogue two years ago—try again two years hence, when it makes a comeback.
- She's never even looked at your stuff. After six months, it's time to clean out the office and send back everything with SASEs and trash everything else.

- She's in the middle of a failed relationship and hasn't liked anything for months.
- She's got you confused with somebody she hates.

And the point I wish to illustrate? Hey, sometimes you get rejected for reasons you nor anybody in the business can understand. Do your best and keep on submitting until somebody learns to love your work.

Write the first 1,000 words to compel a publishing professional to fall in love with your work. Utterly. Nothing less will do. Those first four or five manuscript pages must compel an agent to forget about the ten to fifty clients he represents. They must divert him from any book deal now in progress unless it is six figures or more.

They must compel an editor to ignore the dozen or two projects she is now shepherding through any stage from acquisition to second printing. She must forget about any author she edits with a status less than that of Stephen King.

Your first 1,000 words, for at least the five minutes it takes to read them, must occupy the world of the publishing professional so completely that an editor or agent actually visualizes high-six-figure deals and Stephen King status for the writer of those words.

And, of course, they must compel the publishing professional to read on.

 ## What are the minimum daily requirements of the 1,000 words?

The Brainstormer Checklist for the First 1,000 Words

Use the following checklist to evaluate your work's crucial first 1,000 words. The functions of the first 1,000 words are:

- ☐ **Introduce the heroic character** and give clear signals about his personality, appearance, flaws and strengths. In other words, begin to characterize him, a process that will continue throughout the novel. Force your reader to care about this character.
- ☐ **Introduce, or at least allude to, the heroic character's worthy adversary.** Characterize her as well.
- ☐ **Present or strongly suggest the surpassing conflicts of the story.** You may have several—you should have several—but certainly the most impor-

tant should come into play early in the story.

- [ ] **Deliver evidence of the danger, suspense or dramatic irony** you might have hinted at in the first 100 words.
- [ ] **Remain true to the tone and mechanics** of the first 100 words.
- [ ] **Foreshadow crucial scenes** to come in the first 50 to 100 pages to the point-of-no-return complication.
- [ ] **Foreshadow the climax** in some way, however mysteriously.
- [ ] **Flesh out the setting.**
- [ ] **Demonstrate your ability to write** at least one scene filled with action, conflict, imagery and dialogue. You might find it artificial for me to suggest using part of your novel like a resume just to prove you can write certain things. Not at all. If your first 1,000 words simply used narration and exposition—explained the background, described people or settings and philosophized about action that will come in later chapters—you haven't a prayer of escaping the inevitable rejection.
- [ ] **Establish a clear central story line** (what I call *singularity*) so the reader knows, or thinks she knows, where the story will go.
- [ ] **No matter how serious your drama, elicit a couple of smiles and at least one hearty laugh** from your readership.
- [ ] **Create the taste of *oh, wow!*** at intervals, at least once on every other manuscript page or so.

 Of these qualities of the first 1,000 words, the most important is that last one, the *oh, wow!* thing again, right?

Nope. Your first 1,000 words should contain each of these elements, without exception. If I had to choose only one objective for you to accomplish, I would say:

> *Demonstrate your ability to write at least one scene filled with action, conflict, imagery, and dialogue. Done properly, that is, maintaining singularity, such a scene would accomplish all the other objectives, including making the editor or agent believe your project could make money.*

Give examples of how each of these techniques is accomplished.

I will do so in the upcoming chapters as we address individual elements in much more detail.

 You're saying that if I can write the most gripping, powerful 1,000 words in the history of literature, I can sell my novel, guaranteed?

Not on your life. In fact, if you try too hard, you'll likely end up being guilty of one of the *over* sins. Senior editor Jack Heffron of Writer's Digest Books cautions against "overhyping the opening in a vain attempt to hook the reader." Not to put words into Jack's mouth, but the attempt becomes vain when you drive a reader away rather than hooking him by trying too hard—like a breathless suitor.

The last thing I want to do is create the impression that all you have to do is write an opening alone. In fact, your best creative effort should appear in the climax of the novel. Otherwise, you run the risk of writing an anticlimactic story, one in which the climax and ending do not deliver on the promise of the opening.

By definition, a novel's opening cannot be as good as the climactic scene because the climax delivers a degree of resolution and redemption that's simply not possible to give away in the opening pages.

Still, your opening lines must be powerful without straining. They must promise without overselling. They must create a sense of curiosity without relying on bizarre voyeurism. Try to seduce your reader, not proposition him like a cheap prostitute. Captivate your editor with finesse, not by overpowering her as if you were a mugger.

 So far all you've talked about is first words and first lines. What about first chapters?

Don't think in terms of chapters. I've never understood the value in using chapters as measuring sticks. You might be one of those writers whose chapters is each no more than four pages long. Or maybe each chapter is fifty pages long. Either way, a publisher's directory that contains a guideline telling you to submit the first two to three chapters is useless.

But if you write the first 100 words to seduce readers and the first 1,000 words to captivate publishing professionals, chapter length won't matter. And if you are invited to send sample chapters, the first fifty pages will be about right.

FIRST 10,000 WORDS

Assuming that your first 1,000 words have accomplished the seduction of your target publishing professional, here's the . . .

Mission of the Writing Sample
*To engage an editor or agent so strongly he will read the entire sample
and commit himself to asking for the complete manuscript.*

Reading an entire manuscript from an unknown is a significant investment of that publishing professional's second most valuable resource: time. That's why they often ask for the sample first.

Granted, an associate editor or intern might be the first one to read the full manuscript after you submit it. She will probably have rejection power if your story does not live up to its promise of the first 10,000 words. In that case, you'll want to create enough doubt in the mind of that reader to force her to pass along your novel with a long list of positives and as few negatives as possible. Make those 10,000 words count. Get that editor to invest in reading the full manuscript.

 What elements must I include in the first 10,000 words (fifty pages) to compel a publishing professional to ask for the complete manuscript?

The Brainstormer's Checklist for the First 10,000 Words

☐ **Maintain those qualities of writing and storytelling** you established in the first 1,000 words.

☐ **Force the reader to fall in love with your heroic character,** creating the feeling that the reader will personally share in any of his joys, perils and griefs.

☐ **Create a cast of distinctive minor characters and unforgettable major characters.**

☐ **Maintain singularity,** that continuous central story line, while texturizing with relevant subplots. By page fifty, you should have set up every piece of action that is to come, especially the climactic scene.

☐ **Entrap your main character in the central conflict** of the story so firmly that he has passed a point of no return. By the time your story has reached fifty pages, the titanic clash between the heroic character and his worthy adversary should be inevitable. That a struggle will occur is no longer a question—only its timing, the extent of its violence and its outcome remain in doubt. For you, the writer, what's left is the suspense and art you employ in compelling your audience to the climactic moment of your story.

- ☐ **Every now and then, relieve the dramatic tension** with an occasional smile or laugh.
- ☐ **Firmly establish the expectation of that sense of** *oh, wow!* once every few pages.

 What is the most important element I must achieve in writing my first 10,000 words?

A no-brainer. The most critical element of the first 10,000 words has everything to do with your heroic character. I'll list three things distilled from the checklist above. We'll talk more about these subelements in the next chapter.

The Three Indispensable *E*'s for the First Fifty Pages
1. **Establish your heroic character** unequivocally as the focal point of the story, no matter how complicated your plot.
2. **Endear your heroic character** inseparably to your readership, even if she is cursed with a flawed personality.
3. **Entrap that heroic character inextricably** in the central conflict.

That about does it for firsts. If you can satisfy yourself that each item in the previous checklists has been accomplished, odds are good that a publishing professional will invite you to submit the complete manuscript.

LASTS

Your success in getting a publishing professional to look at your completed manuscript depends upon how well you accomplish the firsts. Getting an editor to buy your manuscript, an agent to represent it or a book buyer to talk it up to her friends depends on how well you accomplish your lasts.

To me, the last 10,000 words are so important that I recommend writing the climactic scene of your novel first, at least in sketch form. No scene is as important as your climax. Every scene that precedes the climax must logically build toward it, and every scene that follows to the end of the story must be a logical result of it. So writing it first is one way to assure that all scenes that come before are directed toward the climactic moment in some way.

The Brainstormer's Checklist for the Climactic Scene

☐ **Is this scene a titanic final struggle?** Blow away your readers. Simple as that. No scene that precedes the climax should be more exciting. This is the payoff for your fiction.

☐ **Does the heroic character confront the worthy adversary?** Absolutely mandatory. No exceptions.

☐ **Is the conflict resolved in the heroic character's favor?** Not mandatory, but usually the most popular choice.

☐ **Does the heroic character learn an important lesson?** The most dramatic events of our lives teach our characters—and us—something of lasting value. Our scars cost us something, perhaps innocence or purity, but we also wear them as badges of learning. A reader who walks away from the novel with a so-what attitude will kill you in the word-of-mouth department.

☐ **Does the scene avoid coincidence or divine intervention?** Your heroic character's decisions and actions must decide the story's most crucial battle.

☐ **Does the scene introduce new material?** It shouldn't. Everything that appears in the climax should have been set up earlier in the story.

☐ **Does the scene rely on flashbacks?** Avoid them at all cost in the climax. Keep the story moving using action and dialogue.

☐ **Does the climax use exposition?** Explanation causes this vital scene to drag.

☐ **Is the conclusion logical?** Just as all that goes before should point to the climax, even if many signposts have been artfully concealed, all that flows from the climax should be reasonable. An ending with a twist is fine, but no tricks.

☐ **Does the climax leave us feeling a sense of wonder?** Contrary to the conventional wisdom about impressions, your novel will be judged by its final impression, not its first. What will readers tell their friends after they put down your story?
That's the ticket.

THE REST OF THE LAST 10,000 WORDS

 Do you have a checklist for the last fifty pages of my story?

Certainly. I have distilled everything into this one:

Elements of the Last 10,000 Words

Create a climactic scene that surpasses any other scene in the novel in terms of action, conflict, imagery and dialogue. Blow your readers away with the height and depths of emotions you achieve. Tattoo the outcome of your story on their brains and hearts forever. Leave them feeling disadvantaged that they might never again meet your heroic character unless you write another novel featuring her.

 That's it? You tell me to do this without telling me how? I'm supposed to write fifty pages with that level of intensity?

Relax. Here's a list of do's and don'ts that might help clarify your task.

The Brainstormer's Checklist for the Last 10,000 Words

☐ **Don't necessarily write a single scene fifty pages long.** But do, in those last fifty pages, travel as directly as possible to the climactic moment of the novel when the titanic struggle between the heroic character and his adversary is resolved.

☐ **Don't introduce any new characters or subplots.** Don't introduce *any-thing* new. Any appearances within the last fifty pages should have been foreshadowed earlier, even if mysteriously.

☐ **Don't describe, muse, explain or philosophize.** In chapter 5, I recommend minimizing all these practices. In the last fifty pages, you should prohibit them altogether. Remember the master story model's setup, complication and resolution phases. By this point in the story, setup is done, complication is wrapping up and resolution should be entirely uncluttered so you and the reader can make an unimpeded dash to the finish line.

☐ **Do, as a corollary to the last bit of advice, distill every word,** sentence and paragraph into action that leads to the climactic scene without detours.

☐ **Do create that sense of *oh, wow!*** once or twice on every page; if possible, more frequently.

☐ **Do enmesh your reader so deeply in the outcome** of your story that she cannot put down your novel to go to bed, to work or even to the bathroom until she sees how it turns out.

THE LAST 1,000 WORDS

Whether you adhere to the rule of placing the climax that close to the end or not, be aware that once the central conflict is resolved, there's not much point in rambling on.

The Brainstormer's Checklist for the Final 1,000 Words

In the last four to five pages:

☐ **Resolve the central conflict** in favor of the heroic character, if you please. You don't have to provide a happily-ever-after ending, but do try to be uplifting. Readers want to be uplifted, and editors try to give readers what they want. So should you.

☐ **Surprise your reader.** Again, I'm not suggesting a quirky *Twilight Zone* twist or trick ending. No "And then my alarm went off, waking me up" or "Why are you asking me? I'm just a dog" jerk-the-reader-around finishes. Nothing cute or stupid. However, even if your resolution has been foreshadowed so that your reader would have predicted it if she had read the clues properly, inject some element of surprise, even if only on a minor issue.

☐ **Afford redemption to your heroic characters.** No matter how many mistakes she has made along the way, allow the reader—and the character— to realize that, in the end, she has done the right thing.

☐ **Tie up loose ends of significance.** You don't have to establish a Kodak moment, that rare snapshot in time where every minor contentious issue is neatly solved. But every question you planted in a reader's mind earlier should be addressed, even if the answer is to suggest that a character will address that issue later, after the book ends.

☐ **Inject a note of irony, however mild.** Give your audience something to smile about, if only wryly.

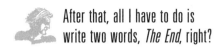 After that, all I have to do is
write two words, *The End*, right?

Strictly speaking, yes. But really striking stories always find a way to add an extra measure of audience satisfaction in . . .

THE LAST 100 WORDS

Perhaps it's in the last line of dialogue or the last image you create. Or maybe the heroic character comes to a realization about a secondary problem he has not solved but will reconcile himself to living with. Often it involves revealing a critical, redemptive decision of the heroic character. Quite often that decision involves a love interest and the issue of a romantic union is resolved. Often enough those words perform a sales function, indicating that a sequel is in the works.

Whatever it is, writers can pack a lot of word-of-mouth buzz into the final 100 words of their fiction. So use your last lines to deliver the ultimate *oh, wow!* After the reader puts down your book, his reaction ought to be: "I can't wait to tell somebody about this story."

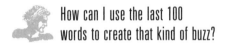 How can I use the last 100
words to create that kind of buzz?

You can't tack even the most powerful, memorable ending onto a boring story. Your audience will abandon you in the boring parts and will never see the ending. If you can write powerful, memorable endings, you must do the same for the beginnings and middles of your story, which will carry them through to the final pages.

With that abiding guidance in place, here's a little checklist of do's and don'ts you can use when considering how to put together the last few lines of your stories.

The Brainstormer's Checklist for the Last 100 Words

☐ **Foreshadow early on what your final words will be.** Remember Strategy 1—Begin at the end? When you begin a journey of writing already having established a destination, it's much easier to make calculated detours, twists and turns in your storytelling tactics. When you know the ending, your complications will point to it. That doesn't require you to telegraph the finish, but merely create a feeling that the final words hearken to an earlier moment in the story.

- [ ] **Don't change voice, tone or attitude in the last 100 words.** An ending will feel tacked on if the voice of the narrator suddenly sounds alien to the voice that's been consistent for the previous 80,000 words.
- [ ] **Don't press too hard.** This is no place for breathless, suspenseful writing. That should already have taken place in the preceding climactic scenes. Now that your audience is catching its collective breath, show the nice people out of your story gracefully.
- [ ] **Above all, it's important enough to repeat, do *not* introduce cute endings,** visual or language clichés, laborious descriptions or mysterious, unresolved outcomes. The last impression you want to create is a positive one. Don't leave an audience feeling tricked or cheated.

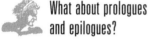

What about prologues and epilogues?

Excellent question.

PROLOGUES

A prologue literally contains information that comes before the telling of the story, a kind of prebeginning. As with forewords, dedications, acknowledgments and credits, readers often skip them. So I recommend against prologues.

In *Screenwriting*, Richard Walter quotes Aristotle to tell us that the beginning of a story is "that part that comes first, and before which is nothing." Then he writes:

> *Yet in my experience . . . the single most common error is screenwriters' failure to begin at the beginning. . . . All too typically they commence* before *the beginning.*

Note his emphasis on *before*. Start with the first piece of action that an audience needs on the path toward your ending. Don't spend dozens of pages setting up settings or situations. And don't bother with a prologue. Get on with it. When you do that, stories take care of themselves.

I don't care what you say. I just *have* to use a prologue in my story. Tell me how to handle it.

Fine.

How to Handle a Prologue

Write your prologue, if you must. Reveal all the prestory information you want. Then label it chapter 1 and set your story in motion without delay in chapter 2.

No matter what you call it, keep the prologue brief. One or two pages is ideal. Five max. Keep reminding yourself: *If my readers skip this prologue, they might be confused when the story actually begins.*

Then, in the revision process, try one last time to find the courage to cut out the prologue.

AND NOW FOR EPILOGUES

The word *epilogue* literally means an addition to the story. You shouldn't need one if you have delivered a satisfying ending to your story. Even so, I frequently use epilogues in writing category fiction where word limitations prevent me from creating a dozen or more scenes to tie up complications that can't be addressed in a fast-moving narrative. After a suspenseful climax, I prefer taking readers to the end of the story with a feeling of mission accomplished.

 Don't readers skip epilogues, too?

Yep. Happens all the time. But I figure, if somebody likes the book well enough to get to the end of it, odds are good they'll peek at the epilogue. Besides, I always finish the central story before beginning an epilogue. I also leave a mystery unsolved on an important issue. Then I unveil the solution in the epilogue.

If you decide to use an epilogue, try this checklist on for size.

How to Handle an Epilogue
- [ ] **Keep it brief.** Don't exceed a thousand words.
- [ ] **Try using a checklist format,** with short paragraphs and extra space between each. I often list characters and matter-of-factly tie up loose ends

about unresolved issues for each of them.

☐ **Don't try to address critical plot issues in the epilogue.** You should satisfy yourself that, if they do stop reading after your last regular chapter, they will not have missed anything of importance. Should you run up against an important unresolved issue, don't try to fix it in an epilogue. Go back and revise your central story, no matter how much rewriting you have to do.

☐ **Don't get artsy-crafty with your epilogue.** Speak to your audience like a narrator in a documentary. Just let them know what happened after the story ended.

☐ **Don't take yourself or your work of fiction too seriously.** Now is not the time to climb up on a soapbox and preach. If you haven't taught your lessons within the context of the story, anything you say after the story ended will have little value to your audience.

☐ **Give your reader one last wisp of a smile** or a gentle parting *oh, wow!*

☐ **Don't ramble on.** Impart your after-story information, then stop!

Titles

The very first words a publishing professional or consumer audience will see about your work almost certainly will include the title words. If your novel, play or film is remembered at all, the title will be the handle by which everyone carries its memory. Most important, *titles sell.*

Here's a list of alternate titles, some of them spoofs, for works whose popular titles you should know. (See p. 277 for the real titles.)

Romeo and Ethel, the Pirate's Daughter
War, What Is It Good for?
Lost Moon
Horsemen, Pass By
American Hero

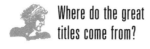 Where do the great titles come from?

I have two theories.

First, somebody discovers a great story and the title assumes greatness by feeding off the story. The publishing phenomenon, *The Bridges of Madison County*, whatever you feel about its literary greatness, was an enormous commercial success. I suspect the title itself did not cause the book to fly off the shelves. But once word of mouth gained momentum, all you heard was that title in the discussions about loving or hating the content of the novel.

Second, a great title draws attention to a great story. Just hearing the title causes a reviewer, reader or viewer to find out more about the work of fiction. *Divine Secrets of the Ya-Ya Sisterhood*, *The Horse Whisperer*, *Midnight in the Garden of Good and Evil*, *Jaws*, *Jurassic Park*, *Cool Hand Luke*, *The Coffin Dancer* and almost any title from Anne Tyler, Stephen King and John Grisham are good examples. A famous author's name might well be the deciding words on the cover, but many authors always seem to have captivating titles anyhow.

No matter how you cut it, **a great title is of no value without a great story behind it.**

 What elements should I consider in creating a title?

QUALITIES OF TITLES

A great title is endowed with the elements of this checklist:

☐ **Stopping power.** Usually meaning it is short and snappy. One to three words. You could name a thousand exceptions. Even so, between multiword best-selling titles like *Midnight in the Garden of Good and Evil* and *Divine Secrets of the Ya-Ya Sisterhood,* you will find hundreds of three-word titles. Until a publishing professional examines your story in full and passes judgment on its greatness, be brief. Think in publisher's terms. A short title lends itself to ease of handling in reviews, advertising copy, and cover typography. One or two words can be printed larger on the cover or poster than fourteen. Examples:

    Cheaters

    Hannibal

    The Edge

☐ **An ability to position the work.** This is especially important in category fiction, if that's what you're writing. The selection of a title should indicate whether the intended readership is primarily men or women. Beyond that, is this novel a western, a romance, a science-fiction tale or what?

Dangerous Kiss

Hannibal

The Girls' Guide to Hunting and Fishing (not that this novel is so much a guide to the outdoors, but that it's a title that makes an open, if ironic, appeal to women)

☐ **Word images that suggest cover art.** Does your title conjure a picture that ought to go on the cover? For instance, do you remember the image on the cover of *Jaws*? *Jurassic Park*? *The Silence of the Lambs*? *Memoirs of a Geisha*? *King Kong*? Of course you do. (Jaws, T-Rex bones, death's-head moth, geisha and gorilla, right?)

☐ **Simplicity and directness.** It is usually not obscure, bizarre or made up. Once again, you can find dozens of exceptions. Just remember, you're selling. You wouldn't intentionally write a million-dollar advertisement for a spot during the Super Bowl that didn't tell viewers the product you were trying to peddle. Granted, an obscure title might not prevent a reader from checking out the first line of your synopsis to find out the topic of your novel. But why make a mystery of it?

 Do you have a brainstormer tool for coming up with a title that fits these qualifications?

You know I do.

THE BRAINSTORMER'S 1,001 TITLE TOOL

Phase 1: The First One Hundred Possibilities

1. **List at least twenty titles off the top of your head.** Set down every title that has occurred to you in noodling with your story idea. Even bad titles might later prove to have possibilities. This first brain dump will clear your mind for what is to come. Twenty is the mandatory minimum for this part of the exercise.

2. **List at least ten existing titles** that you might bend, borrow or steal from books, plays, shows, films, commercials or advertisements. This is an exten-

sion of the brain dump, helping to further clear your mind of the obvious.

3. **List ten distinctive place names or settings** from within your story. If you don't think you have that many, invent them for later use. Name cities, streets, rivers, topographical features, buildings, districts, houses. Ten should be a no-brainer. (A wonderful side effect of this part of the exercise is to encourage you to avoid using commonplace names.)

4. **List ten distinctive character names, hobbies or careers.** If necessary, invent them. If you must, check out chapter 4 where the topic of names is addressed. No James Smiths or Mary Joneses, if you please. Remember— distinctive.

5. **List ten moods, situations, distinctive pieces of hardware, software, machinery, animals, plants or natural phenomena** from your story.

6. **List fifteen pertinent, distinctive, message-bearing words** from your story.

7. **List fifteen pertinent phrases** of five words or fewer from your dialogue or narrative.

8. **List ten possibilities for cover art.** Describe each image in five words or fewer. What pictures would you like to see on the cover or posters for your work of fiction?

Done? You should now have one hundred title possibilities in rough form among eight groups. It isn't necessary to refine them or even to limit them to three words or fewer. Just get down ideas for titles.

Phase 2: Expanding the Possibilities for Titles

Get out your legal pad. On the left-hand side, write each of the following categories. Then create several columns on the page.

Photocopy this page because you'll need a supply of blank forms to arrive at more than one thousand possible title entries.

Literal interpretation: _____

Alliterative or rhyming: _____

Numerical: _____

Mysterious or psychological: _____

Ironical or humorous: _____

Spiritual: _____

Romantic or sensual: _____

Scientific or medical: _____

Criminal: _____

Oxymoronic: _____

Modify each of your hundred or more choices from Phase One. Add an adjective or noun to the choice, or substitute a synonym that transforms your title into one of the categories listed.

For example: Suppose you have written a mystery in which the heroic character is a professional wrestler, a woman whose muscular appearance belies her docile nature and love of classical music. Under the category of names and careers, one of your ten choices was *female wrestler.* Let's work with that, deriving a possible title for each of the connotations suggested.

Literal interpretation:	*Woman Wrestler*
Alliterative or rhyming:	*Deadly Lady Lacey*
Numerical:	*One, Two, Three, You're Dead*
Mysterious or psychological:	*The Final Fall*
Ironical or humorous:	*The Queen of Lumps*
Spiritual:	*Angel of Death*
Romantic or sensual:	*Wrestling With Ladies*
Scientific or medical:	*Blood Sport*
Criminal:	*The Killer Was a Lady*
Oxymoronic:	*Lady Wrestler*

Phase 3: Selecting the Best Choices

You should now have at least ten new titles for each of the original one hundred titles you conjured up, making a total of 1,100 in one hundred groups of eleven related titles.

Circle the best title within each group of eleven. When in doubt, combine words from two or more titles. For instance, in the example above, let's say the best possibility is *The Killer Was a Lady Wrestler,* a combination of the criminal and oxymoronic categories. If you have a particularly strong group of possibilities, keep two or three for the next step, but do your best to keep the list down to three in each category.

You should now have a hundred or so of the strongest title possibilities from more than a thousand. Your next step will be to brainstorm the best of the best until you arrive at the perfect title for your work of fiction.

Segregate your titles into ten groups. Select the best title, two at the most, within each group, leaving you a dozen or so of the best of the best. Remember, your titles are best if they conform to the standards of brevity, positioning, simplicity and suggestiveness of cover art. Don't throw way any of your previous lists just yet.

Phase 4: Isolating the Perfect Title

The first step in this phase is to reexpand these ten possibilities. You want to be sure that you haven't settled for a title just yet. Even if one seems to jump off the page at you, perform this exercise thoroughly. You can't know if your excellent title is actually second best among the possibilities unless you look behind it to be sure the perfect title isn't lurking there. You don't want to miss anything just because you haven't looked far enough. I repeat Strategy 5—Never settle.

You have performed several operations that should have stimulated your creative juices to bring some strong title possibilities into play. Even so, these possibilities have come from categories and lists that I've provided for you. So far, you have not engaged in any truly open-ended brainstorming. The exercise that follows is a combination of closed-ended searching and freewheeling thinking. This kind of ordered disorder generates your best creative gems.

THE PERFECT TITLE

Use a separate page of a legal pad for each of your remaining possibilities. Write the title candidate at the top of the page. Perform each of these steps on each title candidate. If one of these steps should take you off on a brainstorming detour, follow it, capturing all of the possibilities as you progress down new paths. When you have exhausted those unexpected gifts of eureka, return to the procedure.

STEP 1. Using a dictionary, look up the definition of each word. Write down any new ideas or variations that occur to you.

STEP 2. Refer to entries in encyclopedias, almanacs or other reference books for any proper nouns or terms. Record new possibilities that grow out of your search.

STEP 3. Check references in scriptures, song titles or lyrics that might expand possibilities for your title. Also be wary that your title has not already been used for someone else's work of art.

STEP 4. **At the library, check the words and terms** against *The Reader's Guide to Periodicals Literature.* Record ideas from the entries there or any articles you can access.

STEP 5. **Check the words or terms against entries in a book of quotations** like *Bartlett's Familiar Quotations.* Record any new possibilities.

STEP 6. **Consult a good synonym dictionary for each noun, verb, adjective or adverb,** as well as any possibilities you have developed in the previous steps. Record any title word possibilities that come from this search.

STEP 7. **Perform the same operation using an antonym dictionary.**

STEP 8. **Consult a rhyming dictionary** for your title candidate and each new possibility you have generated. Can you develop new title possibilities out of alliteration, rhythm or rhyme?

STEP 9. **Reduce all title possibilities** that you have developed from this candidate back to three of the very best so the next step won't overwhelm you.

STEP 10. **Visit the Internet.** Using your search engine of choice, conduct a word search and follow the links until new ideas occur to you in numbers that force you to quit or you feel you have exhausted the possibilities.

STEP 11. **While on the Internet, visit amazon.com or bn.com (www.barnesand noble.com also gets you there),** which sell books and films. Run your title candidate and any other strong possibilities through their search engines. This accomplishes two things: It allows you to generate new title possibilities, and it lets you know whether any existing books and films have already used the title you're considering.

STEP 12. **After you have performed each of the preceding steps for each title candidate, reduce all of the possibilities back to one** in each category. Then reduce the remaining possibilities down to the single most perfect title for your work.

Whew!

In looking back over this process of choosing the perfect title, two things stand out. First, you have used almost all ten brainstorming strategies introduced in part one of this book. You have used a dozen techniques in a procedure that is both structured and open-ended. No doubt, new strategies and possibilities occurred to you along the way. Congratulations! That's how brainstorming is supposed to work.

Second, you might be thinking that this process is too laborious, too structured, too formal. Better that you should wait for inspiration and a perfect title to strike you while you're singing in the shower. I acknowledge that such things can happen. Remember, I have accepted the possibility that a title might occur to you that is so perfect you have to invent a novel just to see that title on its cover page. Sometimes you get lucky. But when luck and inspiration fail you, you can always rely on perspiration.

Phase 5: The Final Test of the Perfect Title

Don't forget that you have to have a great story behind a great title. Here's a scale that can help you evaluate this title-story relationship.

A SCALE FOR EVALUATING TITLES AND STORIES

- One to three words is an ideal length for the title on a work of any quality.
- Four to five words in the title won't raise any publishing eyebrows, but the work *should* be powerful.
- Six or more words in the title *requires* that the work be powerful.

Point of View

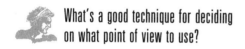 What's a good technique for deciding on what point of view to use?

Return to the ten-scene tool. If you haven't done so, tell your story to yourself in this abbreviated form. Once you've finished, examine the necessary elements of character development that must occur in the telling of your story. Consider the plot developments that you have sketched out in getting to your climax. Then answer the following questions:

1. What kinds of character and plot developments must be known only to the heroic character and his allies, the heroic character's adversaries, and the narrator?
2. How much information do you wish to keep hidden from the reader?
3. Do you wish to have the heroic character present in every scene of your story?

The answers to these questions will help you narrow your choices. You can also examine representative samples in the type of stories you wish to write. In category fiction, you are often expected to follow accepted conventions of the genre, for instance, most action-adventure stories are told in the third person. It seems to me a high percentage of Oprah Book Club selections are told by first-person narrators.

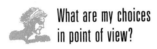 **What are my choices in point of view?**

Let's review them. Without resorting to a grammar primer, you have three overall possibilities.

FIRST PERSON

The *I, we, me, my, mine, us* narrator, often using the voice of the heroic character or a constant companion of the heroic character.

> *There I was, minding my own beeswax when she up and kissed me. I near passed out.*

Advantages of This Point of View
- It feels natural to most writers because we live in an I-world.
- You only have to deal with one mind: the narrator's.
- You can create a distinctive internal voice.
- You can add an element of craft by creating a narrator that's not entirely reliable.

Disadvantages of This Point of View
- You can only write about what the narrator sees or senses.
- The narrator must constantly be on stage or observing the stage.
- You can't go into the minds of other characters.

SECOND PERSON

The *you* narrator. This point of view is rarely successful, and usually only in shorter books. Check out Jay McInerney's *Bright Lights, Big City*. Most publishing experts advise against this point of view.

You're just standing there. She comes along and kisses you, and you nearly faint.

Advantages of This Point of View
- All I can think of is the power to be different, even eccentric, in the way you can speak to the reader so informally.

Disadvantages of This Point of View
- It begins to feel quirky, whether you're reading or writing it.
- It says to the publishing professional: *I'm a Jay McInerney knockoff. Reject me!*

THIRD PERSON

The *he, she, it, they, them* narrator. This point of view appears more often than any other in mainstream and category fiction. It offers you a variety of possibilities for limiting omniscience, or providing information that the narrator and reader are privy to in the telling of the story.

Third person, unlimited omniscience. The author enters the mind of any character. She transports readers to any setting or action she likes.

He stood stiff as a fence post, watching her come his way. What did she want? *he wondered.*

She had decided to kiss him, no matter what. So she did. She could see the effect of her kiss at once. He nearly fell over.

Advantages of This Point of View
- Different points of view offer you more chances to enrich your novel with contrasting characters whom the reader can identify with in turn.
- Allows you and your reader a breath of fresh air as you change viewpoint characters.
- You can broaden the scope of your novel as you move from widely separated settings and conflicting points of view.

Disadvantages of This Point of View
- You can confuse yourself and the reader unless every voice and point of

view is distinctive.

- You can diffuse the flow and impact of your story by switching to too many points of view. Notice how the last two sentences about the kiss jolt you from one observer's mind to the other.
- It's too easy for you to get lazy and begin narrating as the author instead of one of your characters.

Third person, limited omniscience. The author enters the mind of only a limited number of characters.

> *He stood stiff as a fence post, watching her come his way.* What did she want? *he wondered, as she approached. Then he saw the determination in her face.* Good crackers! *She was going to kiss him, no matter what.*
> *She did, too, and he nearly fell over.*

Advantages of This Point of View

- All the advantages of the previous point of view, plus
- The ability to concentrate the story by keeping to major characters' and strategic minor characters' thoughts.

Disadvantages of This Point of View

- None, really. By imposing discipline on your points of view, you minimize all the disadvantages of unlimited omniscience.

Some writing manuals describe three or four times as many point of view choices, including third person, minor character point of view. Don't analyze the topic to death. Choose one and get busy writing.

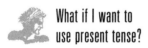 ## What if I want to use present tense?

Knock yourself out. But first study *Here on Earth*, where Alice Hoffman tells most of her story in the present tense, as in:

> *At last, the Judge decides to look down by the Marshes. The sky is already purple; the first few stars have appeared, suddenly, as if someone had thrown a handful of silver across the edge of the world.*

Notice the artful use of "had thrown a handful of silver," which is a form of past tense used to reference action that might have happened before the present moment in the narrative. Hoffman resorts to past tense entirely when she engages in flashback techniques. But often you can find present, past and future tenses used in the same paragraph, as in:

> *It is almost possible for March to catch sight of the ladder her brother, Alan, left beside those sugar maples. That dark shape in the woods may be the bucket Judith Dale used to collect blueberries. And there, by the stone wall, is the boy March once loved. Unless she is very much mistaken, he has begun to follow her. If she slows down, he'll be beside her; if she's not careful, he'll stay for good.*

The elegant simplicity of this selection belies its complexity. In the words and behind the words, so much is going on that only the most disciplined creative writers should attempt it. The fact is, the story in *Here on Earth* is of a complexity that permits such techniques. If you can tell your tale simply and directly, do so in third person, past tense. Don't use present tense or a combination of present and past simply as an experimental gimmick. Any publishing professional worthy of the name will recognize the gimmickry at once.

Basic Mechanics

This is as good a place as any to help you deal with decisions you should make and attitudes you should adopt before any extensive creative writing.

Most of what we've done in this and the preceding chapters dealt with organization and useful exercises. Most of the coming chapters involve techniques you will use in actually writing your characters and scenes. So let's get three rules out of the way, three fundamentals that apply whether you are writing the great American novel or scribbling graffiti on a bathroom wall.

The Three Little Big Laws of Creative Writing
1. Spelling counts.
2. Punctuation matters.
3. Simplicity endures.

SPELLING COUNTS

Spelling Quiz

Circle the misspelled words in the following list. Then write the correct spelling in the blank provided.

Accommodate _____

Cemetary _____

Curious _____

Curiousity _____

Nucular _____

Receive _____

Souvenier _____

Volkswagon _____

Wierd _____

Yield _____

Scoring Your Spelling Test

1. Before going any further, if you are in doubt about any of your corrections, look up the proper spellings in a dictionary—don't bother going to the Solutions section of this book. Circle any word or correction you did not look up.
2. Then, individually reexamine each circled word or correction you didn't look up because you are certain of its correct spelling. Are you positive? Would you bet a hundred dollars on that certainty? If the selling of your work of fiction depended on the spelling of any one of these words, would you dare not look it up? If you are the least bit unsure, look it up now.
3. Finally, use your dictionary to check the spelling of the remaining words, those that you circled because you are certain they are spelled correctly, either on my original list or your corrected spellings. If all are correct, you pass. If any of those words is misspelled, you have just failed the spelling test. If your failure had occurred in a proposal for a piece of fiction, you might very well have been rejected as a penalty.

TIP: For the rest of your writing life, every time you encounter a word that causes you to hesitate, even for an instant, look it up. Ask yourself this question: "If selling my work of fiction depended on the spelling of this word, would I dare not look it up?" If the answer is *yes*, I'm certain you know how to spell that word.

Even if you have cultivated the self-defeating habit of telling yourself, "I cannot spell worth a darn," this tool, used often enough, will break that habit. It will raise your spelling awareness to levels you did not think possible.

 Hey, even if a word is misspelled, why not let the editor fix it. That's her job, right?

No. Spelling counts, and it's your job.

PUNCTUATION MATTERS

Punctuation and Capitalization Test

This quiz addresses some of the most common problems fiction writers encounter. We'll deal with more sophisticated problems in the coming chapters.

Correct the punctuation and capitalization in the following sentences. Don't edit anything else. Other than uppercasing or lowercasing to bring the words in line with the punctuation changes, leave the words alone.

He said "no I won't go! Digging in his heels, and screaming, never!"

"Who wants to know?" She asked.

"Who said, 'I won't go?' she asked?"

He ran away from home, his dad didn't even know he was gone.

Check your responses against the answers in the Solutions section (page 277). Punctuation matters.

SIMPLICITY ENDURES

Strategy 6, remember? Don't worry about themes, metaphors, symbols, history or complexity. Don't try to write great literature, message fiction or meaningful prose. Tell a good story. The rest will take care of itself.

The Elements of Simplicity

Borrowing heavily from *The Elements of Style* by Strunk and White:

- Write short sentences.
- Use the active voice.
- Let specific verbs and concrete nouns carry most of the freight.
- Get to the point in your sentences, paragraphs and scenes.

Respect the concept of singularity: a single idea to a sentence; a single topic to a paragraph; a single purpose to each scene; a single central story line to your work of fiction.

"It is not sufficient to assemble a character by adding characteristics: . . . a big nose, duck-like walk, houndstooth check jacket, taste for Beethoven and the Red Sox, and a foolish fidelity to a faithless wife."

—Oakley Hall

 **CHAPTER 4**

Brainstorming Characters

Ten-plus problems and forty-plus solutions in handling fictional players

ive puzzlers to start you thinking before you undertake problems dealing with:
- Settings as characters
- Fictional characters as real people with distinctive
    Names
    Faces
    Interests
    Motivations
    Dark secrets
- Redemption
- Stereotypes

Here are some titles you should know from film and fiction. Translate, please, and check your answers on page 277.

1. big MAN
2. foslter
3. kacitizne
4. conGverosadtions
5. **NOTICE**

Stories tell about what happens to people, remember? If you accept that argument, you realize that all novels, plays and films depend on the characters to appeal to the various audiences. If you envision a film script crammed with car chases, fistfights, gun battles, explosions and high-tech gadgets (enough to make *Saving Private Ryan* look like a lovers' spat) but forget to include people who an audience can care about, you don't have a chance of selling it.

To paraphrase a political catch phrase: It's the characters, stupid.

So let's deal with them.

Having said that, you may find it contradictory that the first topic in this chapter is . . .

Story Settings as Characters: The Big Picture

No matter where you come from, the setting or environment where you live defines who you are and how you act. It includes the people around you and the possibilities that you can embrace. If you live in one of the nation's cities, certain neighborhoods might be alien to you at certain times of the day, usually because of the types of people you might meet. In contrast, look to the Pacific Northwest, where wilderness areas and the ocean present risks that you dismiss at your peril, as hundreds of unwary hikers and boaters discover every year. Often the lack of people increases this peril because you find fewer chances for rescue or aid in the cases of disaster. Between those extremes, growing up on a farm in Iowa might limit the number of friends and amount of leisure time you can enjoy, and it imposes its own set of hazards, as farming is one of the most dangerous, demanding occupations in America.

Writers who do not factor the setting into the telling of their stories will be leaving out a crucial dimension. That shortcoming will be every bit as obvious as playing craps using dice with blank sides.

Think of your own experiences. How do you feel about the daily grind and press of the city, the noise, the traffic, the crush, the waiting in line, the availability of cultural and entertainment activities and the effort you must expend to enjoy them? These things form so much a part of daily life that to leave them out is a serious omission.

Whereas the first aspect of this issue deals with possibilities for omission, the second aspect addresses opportunity. You don't need to be told how many classics of literature do everything but personify a setting, but I'll mention a few anyhow. The sea in *Moby Dick*. The heath in *The Return of the Native*. The frontier in *Lonesome Dove*. The marshes in *Here on Earth*. Chaotic London and its caste system in *Shakespeare in Love*. The sea again in *The Shipping News*, *Jaws*, *Das Boot*, *Snow Falling on Cedars* and a thousand other novels.

In these works, the setting frames the story and the interactions among other characters. At times, you see a setting dominate the action and act as an adversary to the heroic character. Any story can be enriched by thoughtfully treating the setting as a character.

 I want to set my novel in Hong Kong. Do I have to travel there to make my story realistic?

No, but you do have to transport your audience to Hong Kong. These days, you can effectively research a setting because the tools of high technology, including the Internet, give us almost limitless capabilities. Besides the traditional books, travel magazines, encyclopedias and maps you can find in the library, try the following resources.

RESOURCES FOR RESEARCHING SETTINGS

- **Dig into magazines,** especially those that contain high-quality photographs. The nice thing about *National Geographic* is its availability back to the 1800s. You can get an idea of how places and people looked and acted in decades past.
- **Look for sources on CD-ROM.** In this way, you can own and periodically update a world of information, literally. *National Geographic* is available in this form.
- **Use the Internet.** You can get free information about any travel destination from any number of sources.
- **Buy or rent videos.** Watch travelogues as well as films set in certain locations. You can also find documentary footage on many Web sites.
- **Download free maps and illustrations.** Use your favorite search engine, entering the keyword of your setting *and* the word *map*.
- **Look for university Web sites,** government pages and researchers or news groups with an interest in the area of your setting.

Fictional Characters as Real People

Your fictional world must be peopled. And with distinctive, interesting, realistic characters, even if those characters are Antz and Bugs. Before you get too far in creating your fiction's denizens, you'll want a way to keep track of them. The better organized you are at the outset, the less time you will have to spend finding materials you mislaid.

THE BRAINSTORMER'S CHARACTER PORTFOLIO

In *You Can Write a Novel*, I recommend that beginning writers keep track of each character's characteristics on index cards: $5'' \times 8''$ cards for major characters and $3'' \times 5''$ cards for minor characters. I reasoned that you should do most of your writing in the story rather than devoting a huge effort to creating detailed dossiers for characters.

A true brainstormer wouldn't try to limit fiction writers in any way, especially on a matter of housekeeping. The important thing is to create realistic characters. Whether you write character bios on cards or catalogues or clouds ought to be up to you. Choose from compact cards limited in space for elaboration to expansive dossiers with no end to the room you can devote to preparation. Use any or all or any combination.

This is your treasure chest of information on characters, settings and background for your stories. Depending on the quantity of your research, this might be in a file folder, a document box or an entire filing cabinet. Put books, magazines, videos, downloaded files, CD-ROMs, photographs and whatnot in the treasure chest. Give each character or setting a clearly labeled folder. That way, when you need to isolate a particular aspect of that setting or character, you won't have to turn your house upside down looking for it. If you're like me, the larger references, like books and magazine articles, will blossom with Post-it notes and other bookmarks.

Whatever your method of hoarding story information, I recommend one tool above all others.

Brainstormer flip-up cards. These are the most compact, accessible method for recording essential biographical information and for keeping order in the lives of your characters.

Start with $5'' \times 8''$ cards. On page 119 is an improved, annotated example of one I developed and introduced in *You Can Write a Novel*. You can find the blank card, suitable for photocopying, at the back of this book.

Filling in the blanks ought to be a no-brainer for you. The improvements I've made since my last book appear under the "Goal/Motivation" category, tinted lightly enough for you to write over. I originally encouraged writers to pluck four such motivations from the ether without trying to sort them. Here I suggest differentiating them according to these types of human motivations. Showing how fictional characters are moved to action by a variety of forces prevents you from finding motivations in only one aspect of their lives, which makes them much less one-dimensional. Consider these as motivations and goals for your characters, which we'll discuss a bit later in the chapter.

Character ☐ Master ☐ Major ☐ Minor   Role/Title:

Pertinent Bio	Physical	Distinctive Language
	Ht./Wt. _____	
	Hair _____	
	Eyes _____	
	Nose _____	
	Mouth _____	
	Hands _____	
	Striking Feature	

Goal/Motivation

1. ___Mission-Duty___

2. ___Career-Selfish___   – Fatal flaw

3. ___Romance-Sex___   + Saving grace

4. ___Quirk___

Name: _____   "   " Age: (   )

FIGURE 8. The annotated Character Card.

Keep your cards in a box, if you like. I tape them in an overlapping order inside a file folder. That way I can literally put my finger on the name of a character, flip up the preceding cards and either collect or record a bit of data.

DISTINCTIVE NAMES

What's so tough about names? A character turns up in my fiction piece, and I name her.

Fine. I'd just point out a fistful of cautions that can save you a mountain of problems.

Checklist for Naming Characters

☐ **Brainstorm a list of names before you begin your novel.** Collect last names for every letter of the alphabet. Use a phone book, almanac or other great source. Then build two separate lists of male and female names, one or two first names for each letter as well. With this list at your fingertips, you don't have to stop your story to name a new character that bursts into the tale. You can just pick a name, put it on a character card and keep on keeping on.

☐ **Don't use names of real people.** Even friends and family. If you name a character after your sister and that character flies out of control and kills everybody at the post office, how are you going to feel? You'd have to stop the novel and rename her, right? Or else be prepared never to talk to your sister again.

☐ **Avoid names that begin with the same letter.** Betty, Brandi, Briana, Bobby, Bud? Bad idea because too many such names can be confused with each other.

☐ **Avoid names that can be both male and female.** Pat, Terry, Kelly, Marian, Les, Robin, Bobby and a boy named Sue? Not unless your story confuses the identity to create a twist.

☐ **Be wary of first last names.** Grant, Tyler, James, Kelly, Chase or Terry. Each name could be last or first. I'm not saying not to use them; I'm saying that if you do use them, do so knowingly, so you can deal with the ambiguity.

☐ **Don't overuse alliteration**—first and last names beginning with the same letter. Alice Adams, René Rousseau and Melanie McManus in the same story? Too much.

☐ **Don't use names that sound like half the people in the phone book.** Mary Jones? Bill Johnson? Nuh-uh. Try to be a little creative. And never use Jim Smith—it's way too common already.

☐ **Don't use names that rhyme within the same story**—Mary, Carrie, Barry, Gary, Harry, Larry, Perry and Zarrie (Zarrie?). Too much confusion. And too cute besides.

- [ ] **Be wary of long names.** Typing them can kill you.
- [ ] **Be conscious of names ending in *s*.** This can cause awkward punctuation when you want to show possession. Suppose your heroic character is Regis Jones. Whatever he possesses is Regis's. When two or more members of her family appear in a scene, they are the Joneses. And their house is the Joneses', which is enough to make you avoid such names altogether.
- [ ] **Don't be cute.** Ben E. Hahna? Maybe in a TV sitcom, but nowhere else.
- [ ] **Don't use a name twice.** Remember to cross a name off your list when you name a character.

 I have trouble describing characters. They seem like such vague images in my head. Do you have any help on sharpening that image?

Yep. Here's how to create . . .

DISTINCTIVE FACES

The flip-up character card helps you keep track of key elements that make your character distinctive from every other character in life or in fiction. You can list the physical description on the card, but that's not always enough.

The Brainstormer's Picture Book of Characters

I borrowed this idea from writer Karl Largent. I use photographs for all my characters. You can too. Cut pictures from magazines and catalogues. Keep them in a file. I put them in plastic sleeves to keep them clean. Whenever you're writing a scene, lay out all the characters who play a part in the action. Then you can refer to the picture when you want to add a detail about their appearance to enrich their image.

Use Post-it notes to add name labels. Use larger notes to record extra details that you might not put on the character card.

You can brainstorm ways to dress your characters, too. This trick saves you from wasting valuable brainpower on "thinking up" a character's wardrobe. Use fashion sources such as Abercrombie & Fitch, Victoria's Secret, the *New York Times* and its magazine, Eddie Bauer, Sears, Kmart and others for isolating the distinctive aspects of your character's dress. These specialty catalogues and sources tend to target different demographic groups. Since these retailers and direct-mail researchers have already done their homework, you can capitalize on it. Also, if your character has a sporting or hobby interest that involves specialized clothing or equipment, check out those catalogues.

DISTINCTIVE INTERESTS

Use the library, magazine racks and Internet to identify interesting, individualistic aspects of a character: their hobbies and tastes in clothing, furniture, food, drink, movies, books and so on. Don't dump too much information at once. Create continuing threads and tie-backs that contribute to a feeling of a subplot. Don't be arbitrary about it; never drop details into the story for their own sake. Instead, bring those interests into play as part of the central story line, or at least a major subplot. Be authoritative. You can hardly paint your character as an expert on Central American aborigines if neither you nor she can name a single tribe. Do your homework or avoid the issue altogether. Put the headlines into the space provided on the character card and the in-depth analysis into your character's treasure chest folder.

DISTINCTIVE MOTIVATIONS

Why do fictional characters do the things they do? Motivations, of course. But have you ever asked yourself why certain characters do things that most sane people would never dream of doing? For instance, in a story where the screen is literally bathed in blood after a series of basement murders, why would any movie character, after hearing a strange noise, go into the basement to investigate? And why does a brilliant, competent, sensitive, sensible law enforcement heroine recklessly rush into a fight against half a dozen black-hat, black-belt bruisers without even calling for backup?

Again, the answer is motivation. Except, in these instances, it's the writer's motivation. He wants to pit the character against the basement murderer *mano a mano* (or, often enough, *womano a mano*), so he sends that character into the basement. The sense of unreality in that is palpable. I mean, haven't any of these characters ever gone to the Freddy Krueger movies in their fictional world? Don't they know that you never go into the basement, not even to check the furnace, during a murderous crime spree? And haven't movie cops ever read their own procedures or even police procedural novels?

Naturally, my questions are rhetorical to make a point.

Don't position characters in terrible situations simply to let them demonstrate qualities like heroism, toughness, sensitivity or any other quality. The artifice shows through every time and weakens your story. Anytime a character encounters a terrible situation, the predicament ought to have been logically foreshadowed as an outcome of previous events. More important, the character's response to that situation should be logical, although not necessarily inevitable. No matter what choice a character makes under duress, the audience should conclude without straining that the character has proven himself capable of that decision by his performance in previous, less stressful situations.

 Are you ruling out illogical behaviors altogether? After all, we humans do make misjudgments all the time. Some of us, every day.

No, I am not ruling out illogical behaviors. In fact, the huge mistakes that fictional characters make contribute to the best stories of our times. If Ishmael had heeded a fortune-teller's warning not to go aboard a whaling vessel, the sinking of the Pequod and the story of the white whale would have been reduced to legend and a speculative newspaper article. Without Woodrow Call's obsessive itch to drive a cattle herd to Montana, an entire cast of characters would have lived boring, uneventful lives in Lonesome Dove.

Those decisions, however, really are structural ones, getting us and a narrator together for the telling of a tale. The decision sets the chain of related events into motion, forming the basis of the story itself.

Mistakes frequently form the central issue of conflict within the story. At the outset of the tale, or even before the story begins, a character errs. The central conflict for the remainder of the story is the character's sense of self-doubt and personal struggle to come to grips with that mistake.

In the movie *In the Line of Fire*, an over-the-hill secret service agent played by Clint Eastwood made a prestory mistake. He blames himself for the assassination of President Kennedy, and so do some of his colleagues and superiors. The mistake haunts him throughout the story. Ultimately, though, he earns redemption when another president is threatened and Eastwood's character saves the president's life. Sometimes a character repeats a mistake elsewhere in the story before finally learning a lesson from it.

Problems with mistakes occur when a heroic character, who is otherwise courageous, intelligent, crafty and competent, behaves foolishly at the climactic moment and everybody in the audience knows it. Some very successful, highly popular stories suffer from this problem.

How do I give my character qualities that make him believably motivated?

You may think I'm quibbling here, but you can begin by eliminating terms like "give my character" and "make him" from your writing vocabulary. I'm uneasy with those terms because of an experience I had evaluating another writer's novel. Whenever I pointed out a fictional situation that didn't sound entirely credible, he would respond by saying something like, "What if I give him a heart attack? Wouldn't that give him a reason for being in the hospital?" Or, "I could make him cross the street against the light and get hit by the taxi. I could make it a minor injury, but just enough to get him sent to the hospital."

I've exaggerated for effect, but you can certainly see the attitude that is present when a writer uses such terms. You can see the hand of the author moving characters around, causing things to happen like a deity on high. I don't see how you could keep that sort of attitude from seeping into the construction of your fiction. Avoid it.

Rather, create realistic, distinctive characters with a full range of feelings and experiences. Breathe life into your characters with an attitude that these people existed before you began writing your story. Cultivate an attitude of someone who feels so lucky to be privy to the wonderful, true story that you are obliged to tell it within the framework of a play, film or novel. When you reveal character traits as if they have always existed—as opposed to making them happen because they're necessary to make your story click—your story will work.

Think about it. Haven't you ever met somebody who seemed unpleasant on the surface, who made the first impression that caused you to pinch your nose shut? Then, later, did you discover a brilliant, witty personality underneath that unpleasant exterior? And how many times have you met the all-American man or woman who, in a succession of situations, proved to be utterly treacherous? Of course you have. And that process of discovery should give you a clue to character creation.

No matter what the situation or character, do not feel compelled to immediately reveal everything about it in your story. Don't stop narration or action to tell every facet about any single element of the story. Let situations replete with action, conflict, images and dialogue reveal the element one layer at a time. That's how life works. That's how life in fiction should be portrayed within the framework of dramatic storytelling.

 Rephrasing the question, what are the foundations of believably motivated characters?

Great fictional characters come to life when they are motivated by the same things that cause a given behavior in your own life, even if a character's behaviors are not the same as your own. Even if your life isn't as dramatic as the ones you intend to write into your story.

Psychologists are fond of saying that we are products of both our genetic makeup and the environment in which we are nurtured. Studies of identical twins who were raised apart without even knowing of the existence of the other twin have thrown some astonishing weight into the influence of genes alone. A recent television news magazine featured twin brothers who never met or even knew of each other until they were middle-aged. They demonstrated identical tastes and mannerisms, from the exotic, imported toothpaste they both used to the way they held their coffee cups. Without collaboration, they gave each other their first Christmas gifts after shopping in different cities: identical sweaters.

On the other hand, we commonly think of ourselves in terms of our upbringing in both macro and micro terms. Our grandparents' generation, most likely raised during either the Great Depression or World War II, consists of people who are likely to be loyal to a corporation, patriotic to a fault, frugal and conservative. The next generation, baby boomers, grew up during the Cold War era and tend to move from job to job in a search for the ideal personal fit. They have less faith in traditional institutions and are willing to buy on credit. After that comes what we might call the microchip generation, people whose lives are so influenced by high-tech that, when told their parents were raised in households without televisions, can only wonder: "Then what did you plug your VCR into to watch videos?"

On a more individual level, our personalities are affected by the region in which we grew up; the size of our hometown; and the income, occupations and personalities of our parents, race, gender and friends.

On a strictly personal level, we have developed tendencies, preferences, tastes, likes, fears and a thousand different unmentionables of thought, impulse and shameful indiscretions.

Fictional characters, to be believable, will be motivated in some way, not necessarily predictably, by all of these variables. How a writer reveals a character—a bold slash here, a broad stroke there, a stipple, a dash, a mention, a flash, an image, a thought, a tic, a misstep, an act of bravery, a moment of cowardice, a wink or a smile—contributes to (or detracts from) the fictional reality.

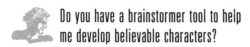 Do you have a brainstormer tool to help me develop believable characters?

Absolutely. Begin with the remaining elements of the character card. I recommend that beginning writers avoid building voluminous dossiers. Stick to the headline elements on the card. Confine your writing of character to the story rather than thick histories full of trivia that you feel compelled to plug into the story just because of its existence.

Character Personality Evaluation Tool

Mission-Duty Motivations and Goals. Our patriotism, honor, loyalty, devotion—the better angels of our nature—drive us in idealistic ways. They're the reasons we stay faithful to friends and lovers, political parties and other associations. They cause us to vote, write letters to the editor and volunteer to feed the homeless one day a month at the city shelter.

If you're worried that the bad actors in your fiction might not find motivations in this category, don't be. Remember, every coin in the realm of the good has its evil side. Neo-Nazis and terrorists take patriotism to an extreme. And nobody claims to be more patriotic than the leaders of a coup d'etat. Republicans and Democrats engaged in bitter political struggles often seek the same lofty goals but differ on the means.

Use the following scale as a tool for brainstorming each of your characters,

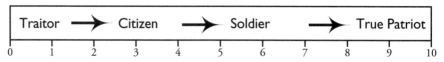

FIGURE 9. Mission-Duty Spectrum of Character Motivations.

properly placing each along this spectrum. Just put a number on the character card (page 119) on the top line in the "Goal/Motivation" section and describe that position in a few words.

Career-Selfish Motivations and Goals. No matter what our mission, we usually have career motivations and selfish considerations deeply enmeshed in it. For instance, a soldier enlists for patriotic reasons, but that doesn't mean he wants to rush into a minefield to give his life for his country. However, in the course of serving, he gets a few promotions along the way, which is usually a strong motivation to serve, too.

On the flip side, somebody who uses despicable tactics, such as extortion, racism or sexual harassment, to climb the career ladder clearly uses unpleasant, if not unlawful, means to achieve his goal.

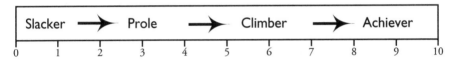

FIGURE 10. Career-Selfish Spectrum of Character Motivations.

Romance-Sexual Motivations and Goals. This involves needing to love and be loved, from the most platonic sense to the most devious. You ought to be able to place your characters somewhere along that spectrum. In a romance, a hero's goal might be marriage to the heroine. And the hero's worthy adversary might be trying every bit as hard, not to woo the heroine, but to take her in a much more sinister sense.

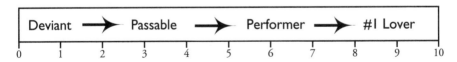

FIGURE 11. Romance-Sexual Spectrum of Character Motivations.

Quirks as Motivations and Goals. I wouldn't want to overstate the case for kinky motivations, but let's face it—everyone you know is an eccentric in some sense, however large or small. Jeffrey Dahmer and Hannibal Lecter fit on one end of the spectrum. Your neighbor, who seems to have a funny gait but only because she refuses to step on the cracks in the sidewalk, fits at the opposite end. I own two golden retrievers who, in turn, own me. Gus refuses to eat while I'm around. Kelly won't eat unless I stand by her side. Each quirk defines an aspect of their personality, making individuals of the dogs. The same is true for your characters.

You needn't stretch everybody's quirk to the bizarre as you populate your story, unless you want it to look like a barroom scene in one of the *Star Wars* movies. Look to real life for a sense of proportion. Although you can name a quirk in anybody, not everybody is ruled by quirks. Most of us keep our kinks under control and out of sight. Those who don't come off as sociopaths because they have so many eccentricities, some of them to the extreme. So I built this last scale based on visibility and severity of the quirks in your characters. Use it to guide your prefiction planning as you brainstorm and build characters.

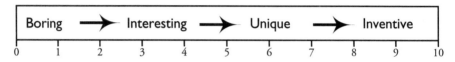

FIGURE 12. Quirk Spectrum of Character Motivations.

DARK SECRETS

Each of us has something in his past. It makes us cringe to think about it. It's something we can't talk about with our lovers and closest friends. Just recalling that we have dark secrets makes us cringe.

You can tap into the uneasy feelings caused by your own dark side. It isn't necessary to make a personal confession in your fictional tale to be effective. All you have to do is create a similar queasiness in your characters, especially if you can reach out from behind your work of fiction and generate the identical feelings in your audience. Two examples come to mind from the same story, Thomas Harris's *The Silence of the Lambs*. One of Hannibal Lecter's intriguing qualities was the ability to identify that humiliating soft spot within other characters he interacted with. He rattled Clarice Starling, the FBI candidate played by Jodie Foster in the film, with his deductions about her upbringing, which she betrayed by the shoes she wore. The more we learned about Starling's secrets and fears, the more we admired her for overcoming that past. Ironically, we learn all of Lecter's most revolting past up front ("I ate his liver with some fava beans and a nice Chianti"). Yet the secret that struck him at his heart was a sense of compassion he revealed near the climax of the story. For a moment, you might have been willing to forget his repulsive past, until he resorted to his vicious, cannibal tendencies, which jolted you back to the fictional reality of his persona.

You can evaluate each of your characters using the spectrum indicated above. Within each category you might find an extreme of behavior, personality or tendency that would lead to a character's dark secret. It might not even be necessary for that character to reveal such a secret—revelations along the way might give your audience enough evidence to form conclusions on its own. To generalize:

> *Don't let anybody off the hook. Your most heroic characters as well as the most villainous have secrets. That alone doesn't make them bad people, only believable people. And isn't that what you wish to accomplish, after all?*

Redemption

Likewise, each of your major characters ought to have a chance at redemption. Your audience should recognize that moment of redemption. Your character should recognize the moment, even if it has passed and can't be had.

 What is this redemption? Define it and give an example of it.

Thanks for asking.

THE BRAINSTORMER'S REDEMPTION CHECKLIST

The notion of redemption literally includes words like these:

- ☐ To recover
- ☐ To set free
- ☐ To buy back
- ☐ To atone
- ☐ To avenge
- ☐ To reward good deeds
- ☐ To punish bad deeds

To those literal meanings, I'd add these literary ideas:

- ☐ To know
- ☐ To be aware (the epiphany)

- ☐ To see the error
- ☐ To correct the error (resolution)
- ☐ To know the difference between right and wrong
- ☐ To vow to do better from now on
- ☐ To *be* better
- ☐ And, if no form of redemption applies, at least to be witty, which we have come to know as the Hollywood wisecrack at the moment of death and destruction.

Let's see how some fictional characters have gotten their redemption. The easy ones first. Hamlet avenges his father's killing at a high cost. Lear sees the error of his ways and at least dies reconciled to the one daughter true to him. Robert Urich's character in *Lonesome Dove* is hanged, but at least he's sorry. Harrison Ford's character in *The Fugitive* proves his innocence, and Tommy Lee Jones's marshal proves he believes in that innocence. These are so easy. The Lone Ranger always puts things right and rides off with a *Heigh-ho, yadda, yadda, yadda.*

Let's look at two tougher cases. Hannibal Lecter escapes to eat again in *The Silence of the Lambs*. That's redemption for him but leaves us feeling a little queasy. He's smart, witty and capable of compassion, but he's got the eating disorder to end all disorders. Macbeth, one of the bloodiest killers in literature, would rather die like a man than yield to a life of ridicule.

As a rule, nearly all Hollywood and most category fiction—romance, horror, action, western, mystery—redeem characters in the endings. The bad guy is punished. The good girl gets the guy. The poor get rich, and the rich get poor. Mainstream fiction often leaves the issue of redemption ambiguous.

No matter what you write, offer redemption. Then let the character accept or reject it. I find this rejection the most powerful option of all. I don't mean those stories where the bad guy, who deserves to be killed, gets his just desserts to the raves of the audience. No, I mean a character, either heroic or antiheroic, who sees redemption at his grasp. He decides to forego it (or he decides not to decide, which loses it for him). Dramatically speaking, these situations—when characters can have redemption but turn their back on it—give us our best dramatic pieces.

The Nazi officer Amon Goeth, played by Ralph Fiennes in *Schindler's List*, might have had partial redemption just by pardoning Jews instead of killing them—although he'd already killed so many. Macbeth considered sparing his king and enjoying his titled status and universal respect, but he went for the gold instead, using a killing spree to win the crown.

In *Fargo*, the smiling villain Jerry Lundegaard, played by William H. Macy, could have called off the scheme to kidnap his wife at any time before the two thugs broke in on her. With a simple phone call, he could have met her for lunch and saved her life. He could have admitted to the crime at almost any time before the kidnapper killed his wife. The combination of his greed, his desperation, his ignorance, his cowardice and his stupidity caused any number of deaths in this film, a tragedy worthy of Shakespeare.

And all because a character refused to redeem himself.

Stereotypes

Or should I say *distinctive stereotypes*, if that's not too profound a contradiction in terms? This is as good a place as any to deal with them. In going against the conventional wisdom, I suggested at the beginning of this book that you could exploit stereotypes.

TYPES OF STEREOTYPES

Stock characters: Ignorant southern redneck. Callous husband having an affair on the side. Know-it-all army officer (or know-it-all police department bureaucrat, academic dean, corporate vice-president, parent, boyfriend, athlete, sorority sister—you name it, he or she knows it all). Drunken, brawling, bawling Irishman. Fashion-forward gay man who acts giddy. Butch lesbian woman with the acerbic wit able to put down any male character with a single quip. These are all stock characters.

Stock character behaviors and reactions: Hostile minority member (whose reason for homicidal hostility is a past racial injustice). Pacifist goaded into a Rambo-like rampage. Beautiful, fun-loving prostitute with Jay Leno's wit and William F. Buckley's intellect. Anti-everything youth whose destructive, boorish behavior is ultimately put to good use in defeating a platoon of criminals and simultaneously solving all adult problems in a story.

Stock character situations: Boy meets girl; girl hates boy; boy and girl fall into bed; boy and girl fall out of love (although it has not yet been established that they were ever in love); boy and girl fall in love after all and live happily ever after. Arguably, this stock situation occurs more often as a central story line or subplot in Hollywood films than any other.

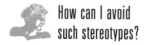

How can I avoid such stereotypes?

Don't avoid them—that alone forces you to use up creative energy. Begin by acknowledging them. Then, out of tired, worn characters, situations and stories, create something fresh.

The Brainstormer's Guide to Working With Stereotypes

1. **Start with a stereotype character and change her in unconventional ways.** Have the character undergo change in attitude and behavior over the course of the story. Unfortunately, this situation is all too commonplace. It's better to add extra dimensions to a character to transcend the stereotype. Perhaps the best example I can think of is Lieutenant Giardello in the television show *Homicide*. He can be demanding, unfair and sometimes even on the far side of scrupulous in performing his job. In these aspects, he isn't much different from any supervisor who ever tried to undermine Dirty Harry. But Giardello isn't a one-dimensional character at all. He can show an entire range of emotions in a single scene. He is as loyal to his detectives as he is demanding of them. He is capable of a broad range of sensitivities. More often than being unfair, he is scrupulous. He fails to get promoted to captain because he has been too honest in the past. Or not honest enough, depending on the other characters' points of view. In other words, Giardello is more than a realistic character; he is human, just like you.

2. **Use the stereotype with only a few, telling modifications to type.** Let your audience know up front that even a one-dimensional character is capable of qualities that can be interesting. Each time a stereotypical character, situation or formula seems to resort to type, add a gentle twist to tweak the audience. In the end, capitalizing on both the predictability of a type and the unpredictability you inject, you create a twist that might have been foreseen but was not.

   For instance, the Force Recon series came to me in the form of a bible. One of the characters is Henry Friel, a kid forced from the streets of Boston to the marines by a judge who offered him a choice to enlist or go to jail.

He's a sharpshooter and wiseacre, a natural born killer. In other words, as one reviewer put it, a type. But a type that transcends even the stereotype in his own mind. You see, he knows he has a reputation as a killer and acts up to sustain that image. But inside, he's torn by emotions that contradict type. As the novels proceed, we see that beneath the body of a cynic is the soul of any kid you've ever met.

More on types in chapter 10 when we discuss the special world of category fiction, which is always open to new authors, new stories and new takes on types.

> "All the fun's in how you say a thing."

—Robert Frost

✳ **CHAPTER 5** ✳

Brainstorming Creative Scenes

Twenty-plus problems and eighty-plus solutions in creating and evaluating scenes

ive puzzlers to start you thinking before you undertake problems dealing with:

- Scenes
- The ACIDS test: Action, Conflict, Imagery, Dialogue, Singularity
- Brainstormer tools: scene intensity, first draft, scene evaluation

Following are some more titles for you to decipher. Check out the answers on page 277.

1. oleander
2. kill kill bimockrd
3. enutrof
4. get т
5. cles cles

Scenes

Before we get into the Brainstormer aspects of scenes, let's get a handle on some terms I use.

DEFINITION OF A SCENE

Here's one that works for me:

> *A scene is the basic building block of a piece of fiction, one that portrays characters in action, moving the story forward by their behaviors, words and thoughts. The essential elements present in almost every scene are action, conflict, images and dialogue—all unified by a singular, dominant purpose.*

When you write scenes, put the spotlight on the characters. Let the reader see and hear them as they act and interact. Scenes carry the novel like pictures, action and dialogue carry a film.

Scenes differ from narration, in which the author does the talking.

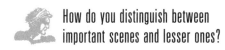 How do you distinguish between important scenes and lesser ones?

It helps me to divide them into types, according to their importance to the story.

TYPES OF SCENES

I identify three types of scenes: master, major and minor.

Master scenes. These form the basis of the ten-scene tool we examined in chapter 2. Your story's most significant events take place as master scenes: the opening scene, the point-of-no-return complication, other pivotal complications (reversals and victories for your characters), the climax and the ending. Remember, you're not limited to any number of master scenes by the ten-scene tool. You can write as many as you want. The ten-scene tool forces you to simplify your central story line by focusing on a finite number of powerful scenes that drive the work.

Use the following criteria as a checklist for your master scenes so you don't overwrite them. You wouldn't want to manufacture the literary equivalent of a diesel tractor if all you plan to do is pluck the weeds from your window box with it.

1. **Always involve heroic characters or their adversaries in conflict.** In the climax, the confrontation between heroic characters and their adversaries is mandatory.
2. **Always portray pivotal action in scenes.**
3. **Always include dialogue,** either spoken or internal monologue. That is,

the character's thoughts as words to herself.

4. **Always mirror the action and tension profiles** of the master story model. Show action rising to a climactic moment, usually near the end of the scene.

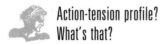 ## Action-tension profile?
What's that?

You can hardly find a writing manual that doesn't talk about the concept of fictional action and tension rising to a climactic moment, then tapering off to an ending. Along the line between the opening scene and ending you'll find terms like *reversal, complication, pacing, moment of truth, denouement, resolution* and the like. Good stuff.

Too seldom do you find a discussion of those terms within scenes, paragraphs and sentences, but you need to consider them if you wish to elevate your writing to the professional level. Think of every scene as a miniature story, complete with its own structure, which includes a beginning, middle, end and all those other terms as well. Here's a picture of the action-tension profile of a master scene.

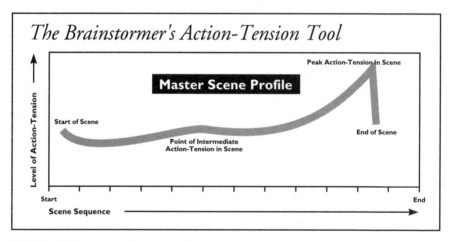

The Brainstormer's Action-Tension Tool

FIGURE 13. Rising action-tension profile in master scenes.

Don't get the idea from the illustration that a scene must have a long buildup and a single intermediate spate of action or tension. All I want to get across is the notion that this profile mirrors the storytelling profile of rising action-tension that you saw in the master story model.

Major scenes. These are important but less than pivotal. They advance the story but don't portray important setbacks or major victories for the novel's central characters. Some criteria for major scenes:

1. **You may include your heroic character or his worthy adversary,** but secondary characters might carry the scene just as well.

2. **Use major scenes to set up coming master scenes.**

3. **You can write action rising to a climax** in the scene, but you don't have to. It depends on the purpose of the scene, which we'll discuss soon. For instance, if you write the scene just to introduce a new character who will help or hinder the heroic character in her quest, you might show tension without overt conflict. This tension might suggest new problems for the heroine without actually requiring her to solve the problems. In that case, the action or tension profile of the scene might look like any of the following:

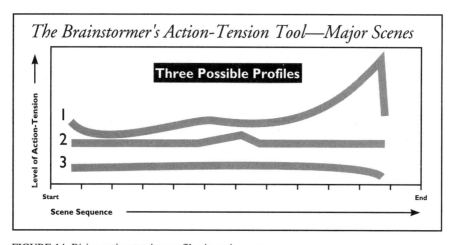

The Brainstormer's Action-Tension Tool—Major Scenes

FIGURE 14. Rising action-tension profiles in major scenes.

Minor scenes. Don't let the name fool you. Treat minor scenes with importance. They add life to a story, even if they're only used to show minor action and small detail. Think of them as brush strokes. They might be so brief as to not even fit into any of the action-tension profiles I've shown you. Still, they should be punctuation marks that stand on their own and, like the other scenes, accomplish a purpose.

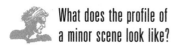 What does the profile of a minor scene look like?

It might have any of the shapes of major scenes.

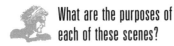 **What are the purposes of
each of these scenes?**

PURPOSES OF SCENES

A scene might fulfill one or more purposes, although one must dominate all other purposes.

First of all, every scene *must* move the central story line ahead. This direction might only seem to lead toward the next master scene in the ten-scene plan, but ultimately, every scene must point toward the climax. All scenes must fulfill this purpose to some extent. Here are some other purposes by category:

Purposes of Master Scenes

- ☐ Introduce or develop master characters acting and reacting
- ☐ Portray a significant victory for a master character
- ☐ Portray a significant setback for a master character

A master scene might also perform any of the purposes below, say, create atmosphere, but any time one or more of the primary purposes is called for, develop the action as a master scene.

Purposes of Major Scenes

- ☐ Introduce or develop secondary characters or develop master characters in lesser ways
- ☐ Introduce or worsen a plot problem
- ☐ Solve a secondary problem
- ☐ Set up later master scenes
- ☐ Create atmosphere
- ☐ Develop the setting

Major scenes might also perform the purposes listed below.

Purposes of Minor Scenes

- ☐ Develop the major characters in small ways or develop the minor characters

- [ ] Create atmosphere
- [ ] Develop the setting.
- [ ] Portray information or data through action

So what's narration and how is it used?
More important, how can I know when to use it?

Good questions.

NARRATION

Remember, narration isn't a bad thing. Recall that selection from Alice Hoffman's *Here on Earth*, the imagery of the setting in which wild blueberries grow. That was prime narration, full of images, implied conflicts and promises of tense moments to come in the story.

Narration is a way for the author to give information, including creating atmosphere, developing the setting or providing data that would take too long to portray in the action of a scene. Like scenes, narration must move the story forward from one scene to another. Narration, being easy to write because the author can empty his thoughts and opinions on the page, is often the main ingredient in amateur fiction. Scenes require work because you have to bring people to life and create realistic situations that speak for themselves.

RULE OF THUMB ON NARRATION: Write your master scenes using the ten-scene tool. Then use other types of scenes to carry the subplots and move the readers between master scenes. Finally, if gaps remain between any two scenes, build a bridge of narration to carry your audience.

As you try to decide between using a scene or using narration to make a point, here's another tool.

The Brainstormer's Narration Test

- [ ] **Use narration when it's the most economical way** to move a story forward and a master or major scene isn't called for.
- [ ] **Never use narration in place of significant action** that affects a significant character.

Have you ever read one of those stories in which the hero hears that the villain was killed offstage while the hero was in pursuit? You feel cheated by the author who didn't show the action but rather told it. Don't do that yourself.

 All of this is nice information, but how do I go about writing a scene? Where do I begin? How do I proceed?

Assuming that you've sketched an outline for your story, either in the ten-scene format or some other system, here's my suggestion.

The Brainstormer's Plan of Attack for Writing Scenes
- ☐ **Tell what happens in the scene.** Identify the action, players and setting.
- ☐ **State the purpose of the scene,** which ought to help you. . . .
- ☐ **Identify the type of scene** you'll write: master, major, minor or narration.
- ☐ **Identify a singular element to highlight:** action, conflict, imagery or dialogue.
- ☐ **Write the scene** according to an appropriate action-suspense profile that seems logical to you. In the writing of it, exaggerate the high points of that profile.
- ☐ **Evaluate the scene** according to one or more systems.

And now a discussion of each step, using a device I've invented just for this purpose—the Brainstormer's Scene Card (see Figure 15).

HOW TO TELL WHAT HAPPENS IN A SCENE
Answer these questions in the corresponding space on the card:
- What will happen in this scene?
- Why will it happen?
- What earlier event caused this scene to happen?
- Whose motives drive the scene?
- Whose motives will those motives come into conflict with?
- Which characters will play out this scene?
- What happens to each of them in the end?
- In what ways do they interact?
- Who is helped and harmed by the outcome?

Scene Card ☐ Master ☐ Major ☐ Minor

Story phase				Setting
☐ Opening ☐ Setup ☐ Middle ☐ End				

Characters in this scene:

_____ _____

_____ _____

_____ _____

The scene's purpose is to:
☐ Move the master story line ahead
☐ Introduce or develop characters
☐ Introduce or worsen a problem (Defeat)
☐ Solve a problem (Victory)
☐ Set up later scenes
☐ Create atmosphere or develop setting
☐ Present information or data

The scene's action-tension profile:

Sketch a profile in the box

What happens in this scene:

ACIDS element to emphasize (circle one): ⟶

Then mark each scale with the intensity of each element in the scene (at its peak):

ACTION	impending	incidental	overt	urgent	frenetic
CONFLICT	tension	passive-aggressive	open hostility	injurious	fatal
IMAGERY	suggested	incidental	telling	active	determinate
DIALOGUE	internal	monologue	debate	argument	imbroglio

FIGURE 15. The Brainstormer's Scene Card.

- Who learned what lessons in this scene?
- Because of this outcome, what consequences will be felt later in the story?
- How does this scene point to the climactic moment of the story?
- What was the element of *oh, wow!* in this scene?
- What detail in this scene ties back to an earlier scene?
- What detail in this scene comes into play in a later scene?

When you've answered these questions, you have probably filled in much of the space provided and maybe even the back of the card.

 Whoa! That's a lot to answer in a very small space.

Do the best you can. Just get down the headlines at first. Then develop the scene in detail, working from this card as your blueprint. Use the card to help you focus until you're done writing, then evaluate your scene by the same standards you used in planning it.

State the purpose of the scene. If you've answered the questions in the first step, all you have to do now is check one or more of the boxes in the lower left of the card. Depending on the boxes checked, you should be able to . . .

Identify the type of scene. Check master, minor or major in the top left of the card.

Identify a singular element to highlight. Circle one of the elements of ACIDS. This will help you focus your writing, putting your scene to the ACIDS test.

 The ACIDS test. It's about time we got to that, wouldn't you say?

Good idea.

Mark the intensity scale of each ACIDS element. This step keeps you honest. If you intend to create singularity in the scene by emphasizing action, this element should have the highest mark. To remind you that the scene will contain all elements to some degree, make sure you mark each one.

The following discussion will be helpful to you.

The Brainstormer's ACIDS Test

By now you've figured out the acronym:

     Action—the level of movement or activity in a scene

     Conflict—the level of argument or contention in a scene

     Imagery—the level of visual cues in a scene

     Dialogue—the level of conversation in a scene

     Singularity—focusing on one of these four elements and identifying a single purpose of the scene

I argue that every important scene must contain each of the first four elements: action, conflict, imagery and dialogue. Further, one of those elements should dominate the scene, contributing to a sense of unity that I call singularity.

 I hear what you're saying about the ACIDS test, but I don't see how it works. Show me.

Sure. Let me give you a few visual examples from the film *The Horse Whisperer.*

THE HORSE WHISPERER

Action as the element that dominates a scene. In one of the film's scenes, the horses lose their footing partway up a slope. Chaotic action dominates the rest of the scene as the horses stagger, fall and slide downhill. Images contribute to the action with many sharp cuts and much jerky handheld camera work. The dialogue is telling—words and screams of panic. The conflict appears as the girls try to control their horses, and the forces of nature prevent them from doing so. In many films, action—motivated by some basic form of conflict such as war or fighting crime—dominates all.

How conflict can dominate a scene. In this film, from the moment the horses and girls fall downhill into the path of a truck, conflict dominates nearly every scene. Grace, the girl whose leg was amputated after the accident, struggles with her disability. Her anger compounds any normal conflict that a young girl might have with her mother. And all is made worse because the horse she loved suffered grievous physical and emotional injury.

Imagery as the dominant element in a scene. One early scene in the film shows two young girls riding horses in the woods. Imagery clearly dominates the scene, giving us beautiful pictures of Robert Frost's snowy woods, two pretty girls and two pretty horses. Action is obvious with the two girls riding. Dialogue is present but is little more than idle chitchat; the director lets you know that it is not important by allowing it to fade into the background of the scene, where it is difficult to follow. Conflict seems absent as the girls ride along the forest trail. But, as anybody who rides horses knows, there's always an element of risk. That is compounded as the scene ends with the girls turning off the trail to take a shortcut up a slope through the forest. If we know nothing else from childhood, we know from Little Red Riding Hood never to take a shortcut through the forest.

Dialogue that dominates a scene. Much later in the film, telling dialogue dominates a scene in which the mother and daughter argue. More important than the conflict between them is the girl's revelation of her fear that no one will ever love her because of her disability.

Arguably, every scene, no matter how fragmentary, contains all four elements. I think I could even argue that dialogue in the form of internal monologue occupies a place in a strictly high-action car chase. But I won't argue that point because such a discussion tends toward the theoretical, which won't help you in brainstorming your writing. So I'd rather recommend you write all four elements into even the briefest of scenes.

You can improve almost any scene by incorporating all four elements of the ACIDS test and, as much as possible, spotlighting one of those elements above all others. This helps give the scene a singular purpose and focus.

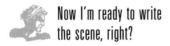 Now I'm ready to write
the scene, right?

You are probably good to go, but I have another brainstormer tool you might find useful before you begin writing. This one will help you decide in advance the level of intensity for each of the elements of the ACIDS test. It can keep you from pressing too hard on elements that should be downplayed.

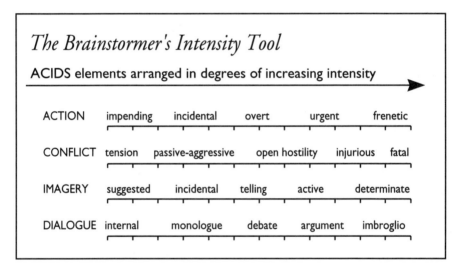

FIGURE 16. The Brainstormer's Intensity Tool.

As you can see, each element is arranged from low intensity to high intensity.

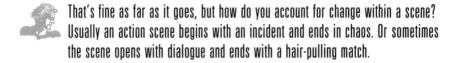 That's fine as far as it goes, but how do you account for change within a scene? Usually an action scene begins with an incident and ends in chaos. Or sometimes the scene opens with dialogue and ends with a hair-pulling match.

Excellent observations. That's why we discussed the rising action-tension profiles in dealing with types of scenes. Refer to Figures 13 and 14 to refresh your memory. You can plot a profile of any shape you please, except that I strongly recommend master scenes be written with a strong climactic moment near the end.

Sketch your action-intensity profile. There's a place to do this on the bottom left scale on the scene card.

 Fine. Can we get on with writing the scene now? Finally?

Yep.

Write the scene. You have planned the scene. You're ready to write. Your way of tackling the scene is probably as good as any, but I have a suggestion. Use the following tool to write your first draft.

The Brainstormer's First Draft Tool

For this tool, we borrow from the world of screenwriters. We simply modify the format of a screenplay and put it to a variety of uses.

Here's an illustration of screenplay format:

EXT. A PRAIRIE BLUFF OVERLOOKING A RIVER—DAY

> LEWIS scans the horizon for signs of buffalo. Suddenly he drops to his belly and calls out to his THREE MEN.

> > LEWIS
> > Get down. Indian camp in the valley.

FIGURE 17. Screenplay format.

That's screenplay format. For our purposes, consider this format as having only three segments:

Setting
Action
Dialogue

SETTING

This segment is always limited to a single line printed in ALL CAPS and containing three elements:

1. The first element on the line is either EXT. or INT., which tells the director, actors and especially sound, light and camera technicians whether the scene is to be shot indoors or outdoors.
2. The second element indicates the setting in which the action will take place.
3. The third element indicates whether the action plays by day or night.

Examples of headings from the film *Pulp Fiction*:

INT. COFFEE SHOP—MORNING

INT. CAR (MOVING)—DAY

INT. LANCE'S HOUSE—NIGHT

EXT. HOLLYWOOD APARTMENT BUILDING—MORNING

Such elegant simplicity. It's a wonder to me that all novelists don't borrow this technique. If you haven't already, I'm giving you the wherewithal to use it now.

ACTION

Here the screenwriter tells what action takes place, always using the present tense, which gives the entry a sense of immediacy. A second example from the *Pulp Fiction* screenplay, which won these best screenplay awards: Golden Globes, Los Angeles Film Critics, New York Film Critics Circle Awards and the Oscar.

In one of the memorable moments from the film, Bruce Willis's character, Butch, returns to his apartment to recover a wristwatch with extraordinary senti-mental value and comes face-to-face with hit man Vinny Vega, played by John Travolta. Here's a segment of the action described in the screenplay after Butch discovers Pop-Tarts heating in the toaster and a submachine gun on the counter. He picks up the weapon.

Then . . . a toilet flushes.

Butch looks up to the bathroom door, which is parallel to the kitchen. There is someone behind it.

Like a rabbit caught in a radish patch, Butch freezes, not knowing what to do.

The bathroom door opens and Vincent Vega steps out of the bath-

room, tightening his belt. In his hand is the book Modesty Blaise *by Peter O'Donnell.*

> *Vincent and Butch lock eyes.*
>
> *Vincent freezes.*
>
> *Butch doesn't move, except to point the M61 in Vincent's direction.*
>
> *Neither man opens his mouth.*
>
> *Then . . . the toaster loudly kicks up the Pop-Tarts.*
>
> *That's all the situation needed.*
>
> *Butch's finger hits the trigger.*

What lessons can novelists learn from one of Hollywood's genius screenwriters and his use of the screenplay format to sketch action in a scene?

Brainstormer Lessons in Writing Action in Screenplay Format

1. **Brevity.** There are no wasted words. No windy explanations. No artificial attempts like multiple exclamation points or adjectives of the superlative degree to add drama or suspense. No shouting lines of dialogue. There's only the slightest intrusion of the narrator, but no emotional commentary. It's mostly facts and circumstances made to unfold in a direct and logical order to create a clean and powerful scene. When we sketch out a first draft like that, we get to the heart of the scene.

2. **Realism.** The passage has a documentary feel to it, don't you think? With so little commentary that a reader (or a viewer seeing it on-screen) wouldn't dare quibble with its authenticity. Think about plausibility. Vega's reason for being in the apartment was to ambush Butch, should he come back. Butch returned for a watch, the only thing of value in his life, that his girlfriend left behind when packing. Neither thinks it likely that the other would appear. What idiot would rip off the ominous character Marcellus and then not vanish immediately? Examine the scene's probability of unfolding any other way in real life than exactly as Tarantino wrote it. Finally consider its impact. I doubt you or I could revise the scene to make it more powerful without damaging it by overstating reality.

3. **An impeccable sense of** *oh, wow!* From Butch's point of view, imagine finding a Pop-Tart heating in the toaster in your home then discovering a lethal weapon on the counter, followed by the sound of a toilet flushing. From Vin-

cent Vega's viewpoint, imagine stepping out of the bathroom with a book in your hand and your gun in your enemy's hands. Having the toaster kick up a Pop-Tart snaps the tension of a dramatic moment and sparks a killing that would not have been as effective if it had been done simply in cold blood.

4. **A sense of the writer's mastery of his story, comfort with the telling of it and confidence in his material and himself.** Tarantino writes with the assurance that the director will share his vision for the tale he is telling (no doubt because he is both the writer and director, a luxury most writers will never be afforded until they reach a certain celebrity status with the appropriate financial resources that accrue to such status). But that doesn't mean we can't emulate the confidence that's so apparent in this screenplay.

5. **Noticeably and necessarily absent from this excerpt are discussions of motivation and lengthy descriptions of settings, characters and actions.** That's because the settings will have clearly been established by the pictures in the film. Earlier in the scene, Tarantino's choice of details include: "a few boxing trophies, an Olympic silver medal, a framed issue of *Ring Magazine* with Butch on the cover and a poster of Jerry Quarry and one of George Chuvalo." These select details help characterize Butch as a boxer who once showed promise, just as the book Vincent Vega held when he was shot told something about him as a reader of pulp fiction.

6. **Novelists can also learn the power of simple, direct language** exploited in this sample to heighten suspense and portray dramatic action in early drafts. Tarantino uses active voice, concrete nouns, and specific verbs. The scene contains no unfamiliar words. You never get the sense that Tarantino strains any muscles in his guts or brains to communicate the intensity of this scene. Naturally, that's because two superb actors get paid big bucks to carry off the writer's and director's vision of the scene.

Therein lies one of the most important lessons you can take from the screenplay format: Create powerful, distinctive characters with all the ability to project reality as well as Willis and Travolta. Do this and you won't have to hyperventilate when you write the situations (scenes) in which characters act and interact.

Write the first draft of your story in the style I've just described. There's no better way to capture the essence of the story line. Then, once you know how the scenes will play out in screenplay format, you can add whatever degree of art, literature, craft or whatever you feel is necessary to tell the story as a novel.

DIALOGUE

I devote all of chapter 15 to writing powerful dialogue, so all I'll mention here is the value of using the screenplay format. There's nothing to it, just the name of the character speaking (in all caps) followed by the lines he speaks (without quotation marks). Here's what a scene looks like, using a segment adapted from my novel *Love Busters, Inc.* I use the heading to tell where the scene takes place, and two lines to describe the action. In the previous scene, Tug agrees to woo a woman on Marty's behalf (to steal a Shakespearean theme).

INT. MARTY'S CAR—DAY

MARTY parks outside the Seattle Nordstrom.

>   MARTY
>   What do you think?
>   TUG
>   I think you're a moron.
>   MARTY
>   Yeah, but what about the plan?
>   TUG
>   I think I'd like it better if it made sense.
>   MARTY
>   Put yourself in my shoes, and it'll make perfect sense.

TUG closes his eyes and crosses the fingers of both hands.

>   TUG
>   I wish I may, I wish I might, I wish I were a moron.
>   MARTY
>   Better?
>   TUG
>   Dear God, I think I am.

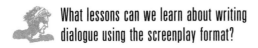 What lessons can we learn about writing
dialogue using the screenplay format?

Brainstormer Lessons in Writing Dialogue in Screenplay Format

1. **Brevity.** Again, no wasted words, no speeches. Any time a patch of dialogue uses more than three lines or three sentences, you should be wary that it's getting too long.

2. **Simplicity.** This prevents clutter between the exchanges of an argument. You don't have room for one character to take a detour of the imagination and remember how his dad used to drop him off at the Nordies when he was a kid.

3. **Power.** The spoken words have to carry the freight. No bizarre punctuation, no adverbs, no adjectives of the superlative degree in an attempt to add drama or suspense, as in: *"I think I'd like it better if it made sense," Tug said sarcastically, putting on his widest sneer.*

4. **Rhythm in the exchange.** You get the feeling of give and take.

That's the screenplay format. The thing I like best about it is the clean form. You can get the story down before worrying about the art of your prose. You don't have to research the accuracy of bear behavior to show a grizzly attacking two hikers on a trail. Set the scene on the trail:

EXT. HIKING TRAIL IN THE FORESTS OF THE ROCKY MOUNTAINS—NIGHT
Put the situation in action format and add dialogue for drama:

RHONDA and BILL walking at dusk when they hear sounds of brush crackling.

RHONDA

Something's coming. There. To the right. A bear?

BILL

No. It couldn't—

RHONDA

Yes. Get up a tree.

BILL

Help. It's got me.

RHONDA scrambles up a pine tree. She climbs frantically, calling out.

> RHONDA
> Bill? Bill? Bill? Bill? Bill?

Nothing but snorting and thrashing on the ground.

> RHONDA
> Answer me, for God's sake, answer me, Bill.

Later, you can research bear behavior to add the telling details. You can flesh out the scene, put it into prose format, add necessary (but not excessive) imagery, quotation marks and so on.

 That's fine for your elements of action and dialogue, but what about conflict and imagery?

I think you can imagine images for this format, can't you? In the film world, the director and cinematographer decide how to shoot the literal images: the pictures. And the actors add their interpretation to the framework prescribed in the script excerpt above: the emphasis of voice, gesture and facial expressions. As you try to convert this screenplay format to prose, here are some tips to help with imagery and conflict.

Screenplay to Prose
IMAGERY

Never write description. That's my credo. Description implies stopping the story to write colorful stuff. In contrast, creating powerful imagery suggests keeping the story in motion using those images to pump up the action, conflict and dialogue.

 Nice advice, but *how* can I avoid descriptions and create telling images?

Brainstormer Lessons in Creating Powerful Imagery
1. **Paint the image in small bites.** Never stop your story to describe. Keep it going. Let's take the example of the bear attack and convert it to prose, incorporating vivid images, enlarging the action and putting the dialogue in context.

A sponge carpet of pine needles covered the trail. It cushioned their soles and absorbed the sounds of their footsteps.
   Rhonda stopped short and whispered, "Something's coming. There. To the right. A bear?"

2. **Incorporate images into the action.** Suppose I had written only:

A million years of discarded pine needles lay on the forest floor, carpeting the trail.

That's description. Static. The author's talking. Can you hear her? The difference in the first version is tying their walking to soundless footsteps. This clears the way for Rhonda to hear and see.

She pointed at a looming hulk, for all the good that pointing would do in the ink of night.
   Bill grasped her arm. "No. It couldn't—"
   But the crashing of brush told them it could.
   "Yes. Get up a tree."

3. **See through the character's eyes.** Hear through his ears. When you can, use the character's senses instead of the author's.
4. **Use the tiny but telling detail.**

She tore free of his grip and leaped off the trail. A spider's web tugged at her face. Any other time she would have screamed. She ran into a tree—a rough pine bough slapped her breasts and needles stabbed at her eyes. Any other time she would have cursed.

The spider's web. Ever ran into one?

5. **Choose action-bearing verbs.** *Cushioned, absorbed, stopped, whispered, pointed, grasped, tore, leaped, tugged, screamed, ran, slapped, stabbed, cursed.* These words do so much more than say what it is. They indicate first fear, then panic.

6. **Choose action-bearing nonverbs.** *Looming* is a verb form used as an adjective. *Crashing* is used as a noun.

7. **Invent fresh viewpoints.**

She climbed blindly. And so quickly. Like a ladder. That was scary. If she could scale this pine so easily, the bear—

> *She drove her head into a branch. But the sound of crying wasn't hers.*
> "Help. It's got me."
> Bill. Oh, God, Bill.
> *The bear had him. Still she climbed, seeing nothing but sparklers of pain in her head.*
> *He shrieked at her from the dark below.*
> *"Bill?" she called, still climbing. "Bill? Bill? Bill? Bill?"*

This is the viewpoint of a woman in panic and pain. When she looks into the darkness, she sees only sparklers. She calls out as if concerned for Bill. Clearly, she's so frightened, she's only trying to save herself.

8. **Create an image without saying so.**

The pine limbs now bent like those of a Christmas tree. A fresh breeze chilled her skin.

> *"Bill," she called. "Answer me, for God's sake, answer me, Bill."*
> *But he did not. All she could hear was snorting and thrashing. She put a hand to her mouth. She thought she might scream but nothing came out of her mouth. Fear of attracting the bear kept her quiet. Besides, the pitch on her hand glued her lips shut.*
> *And, yes, the shame. That silenced her, too.*

The thin limbs bending and the fresh breeze tells us Rhonda has climbed high into her tree. The chill tells us she's been sweating. And the pitch, though she and we didn't notice it in the climbing, is there on her hands and face. We'll look into this technique of saying things without saying them, which I call writing in the white space, more closely in chapter 16.

I hope this imagery works for you. You're almost ready to begin cranking out the first draft of your first scene. First, we have to look at the remaining ACIDS element.

CONFLICT

Conflict appears in this scene in any number of ways. Let's look at some.

Brainstormer Checklist for Creating Conflict

- [ ] **Overall atmosphere.** Walking at night in the forest? That's conflict defined—fear of the unknown, the wilderness.
- [ ] **Simple argument.** A disagreement between Rhonda and Bill about whether a bear was coming at them. That's conflict.
- [ ] **A change in ambience.** The silence followed by the crashing of brush. That's conflict, too.
- [ ] **An attack on the senses.** The creepy feeling of running face-first into a spider's web. Getting hit by a pine bough. The sight of the bear. The sound again. The silence of not hearing Bill's voice. The darkness. The stickiness of pitch on her face.
- [ ] **Personal emotions.** Fear that grows to terror. She hears thrashing but no sound of Bill. Shame.
- [ ] **Action.** The bear attacking. If that's not conflict, nothing is. Rhonda climbing the tree in terror. She's running away, leaving her friend. She is certain the bear will follow. She climbs as high as she can. All action suggestive of conflict.
- [ ] **Word choice.** Most of the verbs show conflict.
- [ ] **Statement of a problem.** Although it's not mentioned, it's certainly implied. Can she get down?
- [ ] **A mystery.** Implied, not stated. Can a grizzly climb a tree? And what happened to Bill? Not knowing creates tension, anxiety and conflict.

That's how to write a scene, starting with a plan, putting it to the ACIDS test, writing it in draft and converting the draft to prose.

Let's evaluate our work, shall we?

The ACIDS Test Redux

Let's use a new brainstormer tool:

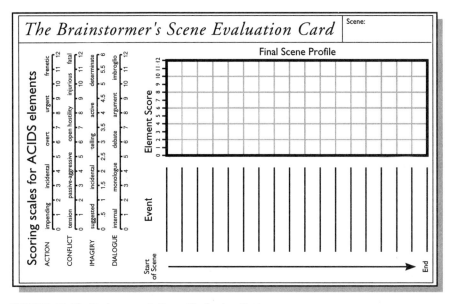

FIGURE 18. The Brainstormer's Scene Evaluation Card.

THE BRAINSTORMER'S SCENE EVALUATION CARD

How to Evaluate a Scene

1. For the record, label the scene card in the upper right corner. Then turn the card on its side.

2. Under Event, list the incidents of the scene in the order they happen from beginning to end.

3. Referring to the brainstormer's intensity tool, evaluate the action of the first item on your Event list. Compare the appropriate adjective with the event and make a light pencil mark on the Final Scene Profile at the corresponding point on the scale. On the example on page 157, I evaluated the scene from *Pulp Fiction*. The first event was "Butch picks up the gun." I gave it a 2 on the scale.

4. Evaluate the conflict in the same way. As before, I referred to the intensity tool and gave it a 2.

5. Evaluate the imagery in the same way. *Note:* The values on this scale are half that of the other ACIDS elements because imagery is simply not as important as the other elements. I gave the event a 3.5.

6. Evaluate the dialogue. Since there is none, I didn't consider dialogue.

7. Using a bold dot, I marked the highest score of the three elements for this event: 3.5.

8. Move down the Event list until you evaluate all that happens.

9. Connect the dots on the graph. Turn the card a quarter turn to the left and read the scene's action-tension profile.

 Your scene evaluation card might work fine for you, but my idea of the elements of ACIDS are way different from yours. I guess I can't use it, huh?

Wrong-o!

I can see your problem with my system if you're writing romances where the action and conflict are less physical and more a test of will, and all of your struggles might be internal as characters contest issues of conscience. No problem. Create your own intensity tool using different adjectives. For instance, your conflict scale might consider only tension, passive-aggressive and hostility. Fine. Eliminate injury and fatality, move hostility to the extreme end of the scale and insert intermediate levels.

How to Interpret the Results

ANSWER THESE QUESTIONS:

☐ Does the scene do what I planned?

☐ If not, how can I improve it? Or should I modify my purpose?

☐ Does any one element of ACIDS rise to a singular height?

☐ If not, should I pump up any element to increase the drama of the scene?

☐ Or should I diminish a competing element?

☐ Or should I downgrade the scene to simple narrative and move on to writing the next scene more powerfully?

THE BRAINSTORMER'S SCENE EVALUATION CARD IN ACTION

When you turn the card (in Figure 19) on its side, you'll see how this scene, a master scene in the film, closely mirrors the profile of the master story model.

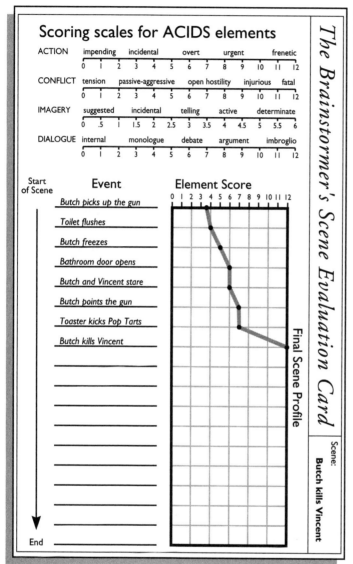

FIGURE 19. Using the Scene Evaluation Card to evaluate a narrative scene from the script of *Pulp Fiction*.

BRAINSTORMER REMINDER: This tool doesn't presume to tell you how to write. It gives you the ability to evaluate your own writing and make reasoned, logical revisions to your writing.

" 'When *I* use a word,' Humpty Dumpty said, in rather a scornful tone, 'it means just what I choose it to mean—neither more nor less.' 'The question is,' said Alice, 'whether you *can* make words mean so many different things.' 'The question is,' said Humpty Dumpty, 'which is to be master—that's all.' "

—LEWIS CARROLL

Brainstorming Word Choice

Ten-plus problems and fifty-plus solutions in working with a style that becomes you

ive puzzlers to start you thinking before you undertake problems dealing with:

- Word choice
- Specificity
- Embracing clichés
- Attitude

Solve these seemingly impossible but utterly simple word problems. Consult a dictionary if you like—the answers can be found on page 278.

1. What is the one word that almost everybody pronounces wrong?
2. On the other hand, can you identify at least four words that anybody can pronounce right?
3. In what dictionary does fiction begin with an *f* and end with an *e*?
4. Can you list two words that contain every letter of the alphabet?
5. What's the commonplace sentence of only nine simple words that uses every letter of the alphabet and duplicates only a single consonant?

Word Choice

Successful—that is, *published*—storytelling involves two essentials: having a great story and telling it beautifully. Word choice lies at the center of beautiful storytelling.

 What's so difficult about word choice? You refer to a thesaurus, pick the right word and move on, right?

That's a strategy, certainly. Far too many writers neglect even this most basic process. They try to tell a story at the cost of careful word choice.

 So I should use a thesaurus on every word, right?

Not necessarily.

When you find yourself emptying a thesaurus entry of all its choices on a single manuscript page, you've probably gone too far. Amateur writers, for example, tend to wear themselves out finding synonyms for *said*. You see dialogue exchanges like this:

> *"You seem like a nice girl," he said. "Only you don't smell nice," he continued. "My eyes water when you come around," he added.*
>
> *"Well!" she snorted. "I never."*
>
> *" 'Never' about says it all," he countered. "You never bathe," he argued.*

The word *said*, used twice at most, would have worked just fine. Even better would be just the one *said* in the first bit.

I went into this in much greater detail in *You Can Write a Novel*, where I strongly urged writers never to *sneer, grin, snort, joke* or *argue* their lines of speech. But the essential point is not to be afraid to repeat a word. In fact, repetition can be effective in both tie-backs and transitions. We'll talk more about that in chapter 7.

For now, let's look at two qualities of words: specificity and attitude.

Specificity

Here's Question One for your word of choice: *Mechanically speaking, is this word specific enough to identify exactly what I want the reader to see as a mental image?*

An example will illustrate this notion of specificity. It will also allow me to introduce another writer's tool.

Take this sentence, which might well be a first-draft, brain-dump creation:

The man, thin as a rail, jumped into the car as it sped away.

And this context, which will prevent this brainstorming exercise from feeling like something right out of a high school grammar book:

The story is narrated from the point of view of a character, Ray Hammersmith, a retired homicide detective. The tall, thin man had been standing on a city sidewalk, leaning against the detective's apartment building, reading a newspaper. As the detective approached the door, he reacted by instinct to a sudden movement, ducking away from a knife blade wielded by the man, falling to the sidewalk. Again by instinct, the detective reached for his service revolver, which wasn't there. Meanwhile, a parked car lurched away from the curb, and . . .

The man, thin as a rail, jumped into the car as it sped away.

And apply this tool to each word, word pair or word cluster. Feel free to elaborate on the action and borrow from the context, but don't invent entirely new information. Try to work with and improve on the words I've given you, even if you have to use a longer phrase to get the job done. Fill in the blanks for the words I've indicated.

The Brainstormer's Specificity Tool

AUTOMATIC	LITERAL	CONCRETE	SPECIFIC	INVENTIVE
_____	man	_____	_____	_____
jumped into	_____	_____	_____	_____
_____	car	_____	_____	_____
sped away	_____	_____	_____	_____

Finished? Before discussing my responses for comparison, let's examine each of the categories of this tool and revisit the notion of writing drafts and revisions.

AUTOMATIC

I suspect that most agents and editors would tell you that the most common sins found in rejected manuscripts wouldn't be ordinary misspellings, common punctuation errors or tired clichés.

No, misspellings and punctuation problems can be detected by most word processors. And clichés, which we'll deal with later, tend to jump off the page during the editing process.

Most writing suffers from ordinary words, common language and tired expressions—automatic language. Writers who borrow expressions from the popular culture—television shows, films, celebrities and opinion leaders in current events—expose themselves as unoriginal. When they steal the language of politicians and business leaders, they reveal themselves as downright hacks. If any of the following expressions sound familiar, it's because they have become part of the lexicon of automatic language. Be wary of using such language, even in quotes and on first drafts. As a rule, try to avoid using automatic language.

Dawn of the new millennium

Living la vida loca

Y2K bug

Hasta la vista, baby

So not comfortable (so *not* anything)

Right

Trust me on the sunscreen

I'm so sure

As if

Shag

LITERAL

Words in this category identify general classes of objects, actions and emotions. Words like *little, colorful, animals, people, food, lodging, transportation* and so on include so many individual possibilities that they tend to be useless. Even more specific categories like *tiny, greenish, dog, woman* (and even *young woman* or *girl*), *breakfast, apartment* and *car* aren't particularly helpful in creating images that bring stories to life. Except as necessary shorthand, minimize your reliance on literal language in writing even your first draft. Instead rely on the next two categories.

CONCRETE

Writing with concrete words takes you from ordinary writing to creating imagery. The instant one of your written words plants a picture, you become a creative writer, if only for that instant. Let's work with the selections from the literal category. As you see the comparison in each case, you cannot help visualizing an image as well. Observe.

> Little—half-inch
> Greenish—olive
> Dog—golden retriever
> Woman—Oprah
> Food—sushi
> Breakfast—eggs and grits
> Apartment—cold-water flat
> Car—Corvette

SPECIFIC

Use specific images to elevate your art. Add character. Distinguish individuals from every other individual within a category. Create distinctive pictures that stand out even from other concrete images. If you can use words from this category in the draft stage, it will make your revision process that much more creative. Let's take the concrete examples and turn them into specific images.

> Little—half-inch—dime-sized
> Greenish—olive—olive drab
> Dog—golden retriever—matted golden retriever
> Woman—Oprah—Oprah without the smile
> Food—sushi—sashimi
> Breakfast—eggs and grits—fried eggs and boiled grits
> Apartment—cold-water flat—windowless cold-water flat
> Car—Corvette—Corvette convertible

INVENTIVE

Here is where you transcend all other writing. For illustration's sake, let's continue improving upon the word choices in our exercise

> Little—half-inch—dime-sized—olive pit
> Greenish—olive—olive drab—martini olive drab

Dog—golden retriever—matted golden retriever—golden retriever matted in
its own drool

Woman—Oprah—Oprah without the smile—Oprah without the money

Food—sushi—sashimi—cooked sashimi

Breakfast—eggs and grits—fried eggs and boiled grits—raw eggs and un-
cooked grits

Apartment—cold-water flat—windowless cold-water flat—barless cell

Car—Corvette—Corvette convertible—Corvette convertible stripped to the
frame

The Brainstormer's Checklist for Creating Inventive Language

☐ **Look for the unusual**—an olive pit used as a dimension.

☐ **Add another, more specific dimension**—a martini olive pit suggests the
notion of an alcohol-related frame of reference.

☐ **Try for a gut reaction**—a golden retriever matted in its own drool.

☐ **Go for irony**—Oprah without the money.

☐ **Reverse a concept**—*cooked* sashimi? (Tuna casserole? Ugh!)

☐ **Reverse a literal image**—grits and eggs.

☐ **Create an extreme**—a cold-water flat described as a jail cell.

☐ **Strip the image bare**—as bare as a Corvette frame.

After this discussion and before we discuss your solutions to
the thin man problem, I want to take another run at it.

Be my guest. Meet you back here when you're finished.

Back? Good. Compare your responses to mine. Finding a "right" answer is not
as important as pushing your brainstorming capacity to find the one best word that
creates exact imagery for your story.

AUTOMATIC	LITERAL	CONCRETE	SPECIFIC	INVENTIVE
guy	**man**	attacker	slasher	perp

I think the context, especially the notion of a retired homicide detective as
narrator, would demand the use of either slasher or perp, don't you? By the way,
here's one of those instances where it would be pointless to use a thesaurus to find
a synonym for *man*.

AUTOMATIC	LITERAL	CONCRETE	SPECIFIC	INVENTIVE
jumped into	entered	dived into	crunched himself into	high-jumped into

For the specific and inventive categories, I relied on the context. If you've ever seen a tall person fold himself into a small car, you'll know what I mean by crunched. And if that car is a convertible, somebody on the run would high-jump into it. This possibility puts a literal twist on the automatic version and creates an active image, especially if the slasher flops onto his back in the rear seat.

AUTOMATIC	LITERAL	CONCRETE	SPECIFIC	INVENTIVE
sedan	car	Chrysler convertible	LeBaron convertible	

Notice that I did not supply a response for the inventive category. That's simply to make my point again about overwriting. Good writing often has a factual, even documentary quality to it. You can't always improve a sentence by taking poetic license with every word in it. You would want to choose words that reflect the personality of the character in this situation. For instance, if our homicide detective had grown rusty after a long retirement, he might notice only a blue Chrysler convertible. If all his police instincts were intact, he would probably get a license number, identify the LeBaron's model year and notice how the trunk latch had once been jimmied.

AUTOMATIC	LITERAL	CONCRETE	SPECIFIC
sped away	accelerated	squealed	nosed into traffic

INVENTIVE
touched off a cacophony of squealing tires and honking horns, leaving behind a symphony of noise conducted by finger-waving drivers as the convertible weaved its way through the afternoon snarl

Even if that last one is a bit overdone, you get the idea. Certainly you can see the image I tried to create. Try putting your new sentence together. Now that you have brainstormed several possibilities, from the concrete to the inventive, feel free to embellish on the basic sentence. Here's mine for comparison.

The perp, thin as a rail, vaulted into the convertible, flopping onto the rear seat as the LeBaron nosed into the afternoon traffic creating a snarl of tires squealing, horns honking and fingers waving not-so-fond farewells. The Hammer lay on the sidewalk, peering between the ankles of passersby. Tears pooled in his eyes from the pain of a one-point landing on his left elbow. A lard-ass woman squatted in his face to— what? Kiss his ouchie? *The tears and her calves covered with the purple welds of varicose veins kept him from getting a make on the license number. As if that weren't bad enough, the woman decided to make like a Samaritan.*

"Somebody call an ambulance," she screeched. Hammersmith thought she looked and sounded less than sincere in the way she gawked around for the video camera that might put her on America's Best Rescues.

"This poor man is talking nonsense about three of Adam's dogs." She cradled his cheeks in her hands, kneading his face like pizza dough.

For a second there, he thought she might kiss his pooched mouth. That did it for Hammersmith. He pulled his face away and swore that he could hear his lips slam shut. He regained his feet and limped off without so much as a thanks. He didn't necessarily want to be brusque, but he'd got a partial on the license number and didn't trust it to his retired cop memory: Three Adam Dog—Three Adam Dog.

Granny Samaritan misinterpreted the brusqueness. She back-shot him with a stream of names that would just have to be bleeped out of America's Best Rescues.

Did you do better? Great. Certainly almost anything you wrote would be an improvement over . . .

The man, thin as a rail, jumped into the car as it sped away.

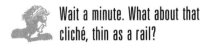 Wait a minute. What about that cliché, thin as a rail?

Nice catch. Let's work with it. Remember one of my outrageous suggestions from chapter 1?

Embrace Clichés

Take the cliché, *thin as a rail*, and rag it around awhile. Fill in the blanks in Column A only.

COLUMN A	COLUMN B	COLUMN C
Thin as (a) _____	_____	_____
Thin as (a) _____	_____	_____
Thin as (a) _____	_____	_____
Thin as (a) _____	_____	_____
Thin as (a) _____	_____	_____
Thin as (a) _____	_____	_____
Thin as (a) _____	_____	_____
Thin as (a) _____	_____	_____
Thin as (a) _____	_____	_____
Thin as (a) _____	_____	_____
Thin as (a) _____	_____	_____
Thin as (a) _____	_____	_____
Thin as (a) _____	_____	_____
Thin as (a) _____	_____	_____
Thin as (a) _____	_____	_____
Thin as (a) _____	_____	_____

Finished? Before we grade your performance on this creativity quiz, I'll pontificate awhile. You follow along until, finally, I make my point.

If you reread my Strategy 3 (act a little crazy) remarks, you will notice that I did not say to use clichés in your writing or conversation. I chose my words carefully, asking you to *embrace* clichés because I don't believe you should eliminate any creative possibilities as you make writing choices. Rather I suggest you should evaluate the meaning of clichés. Use clichés as a starting point for your creativity journey. Consider creative alternatives to clichés. Play on clichés, twisting and turning them, giving them new, fresh meaning.

Instead of pearls, string raisins and wear them like pearls. Instead of carving expressions in stone, do it in wax. Used in these ways, clichés become valuable creative tools.

You see, as with writing rules, the problem with clichés is that they are automatic. We say them, write them or interpret them as a kind of verbal and mental shorthand. If somebody says, "His beard was white as snow," we think, *very, very white*, and stop right there without any further critical analysis. We don't even have to assume any negative images, gradations or exceptions, such as, *no Dalmatian-like black spots, no salt and pepper, no gravy stains.*

If I correctly interpret *How the Mind Works*, a brilliant and accessible book by Steven Pinker, our minds create a generic picture, probably a Santa Claus–like image dressed in red with a blinding spotlight focused on his sparkling white beard. The notion of snow doesn't even enter the mind of the speaker (or writer); her words are automatic, too. If you are the listener or reader, you're not thinking snow, but white. With clichés, there's no need for a mental detour that creates a blinding white snowstorm, which is then superimposed like a snowdrift on a man's face. Somebody says, "white as snow," and the receiver of that communication automatically processes just how white, either stores the image in temporary memory or dismisses it altogether, and tries to anticipate the substance and connections (if any) yet to come in the communication.

Right about here in the discussion, the conventional wisdom would dictate: Eliminate clichés from your writing and find inventive ways to create fresh images.

Good advice, as far as it goes. Seldom do English teachers and writing manual writers give you the substantive advice you need to comply with their dicta. That's where Strategy 5—Never Settle—comes in. Let's put it to work on clichés.

First, subject every cliché to a few moments of critical analysis. In Montana, where I hail from, and in other western states, white as snow is a concept both dazzling and dangerous. Nothing defines white better than the noon sun reflecting off a fresh blanket of snow. So brilliant is this white that sunglasses or snow goggles are mandatory equipment in the survival kit of anybody who spends time outdoors. Those who disregard the dazzle are subject to the condition known as snowblindness. Imagine pyrotechnic sparklers going off continually in each of your eyes, making it impossible to see anything, including grizzlies attacking from the flank or chasms opening at your feet. That's snowblindness. In the extreme, that's what white as snow can mean.

So, when you hear or read a cliché, or when one automatically pops into your head as you are writing, put it to the test. Ask yourself, "What does this expression mean, literally?"

I used to take a carpenter's tape measure to my writing seminars. At this point in the discussion of clichés, I would bring up the notion of a ten-foot pole and begin playing out the steel footage until the concept became reality. Then with that ten-foot measurement in my hands, I would literally create an expression in the shadow of the cliché. For instance, I might point the tape and say, "I wouldn't touch that floor with a ten-foot mop," instantaneously creating a fresh image out of a cliché.

See how that works? If I constructed that last paragraph correctly, you projected a picture of a ten-foot mop handle onto the retina of your own mind's eye. Once you understand a cliché literally, you can work with it in other configurations. That's how you begin to build your bridges from the automatic to the creative.

BRACKETING CLICHÉS

If you haven't done so on your own, let's revisit the brainstormer's bracketing tool (see page 20) and put it to work on our cliché. I've created a new set of adjectives for handling the problem of word choice.

As before, begin by purging your mind of the two extremes indicated in the tool. I entered *thin as a rail* to cover the automatic answer, putting it out of your mind so you could work on the other possibilities. As an over-the-top response, I suggested, *thin as Australia*. And I have only the vaguest idea as to how the expression might be used in a piece of fiction.

But that's not the point, anyhow. When you're stumped in any writing situation, the idea is to cleanse your mind, opening it up to all the possibilities that lie between the extremes. For instance, if you didn't use the bracketing tool to solve this puzzler, you might have generated a whole family of clichés such as *thin as a* dime, whip or stick. Or you might have extended the coinage image to *thin as a* penny, nickel, quarter and so on through pesos, dinars and drachmas. Congratulations on your ability to generate quantity. You needn't feel abashed. You did what I asked you to do. Now let's add some useful detail to this problem and give you the tools to generate a considerable improvement in quality. Here's a twenty-one-choice spectrum, ranging from Automatic to Over-the-top.

Automatic	thin as a rail (stick, broom stick, twig, whip)
Obvious	_____
Commonplace	_____
Literal	_____
Labored	_____

Interesting	_____
Unusual	_____
Obscure	_____
Odd	_____
Opposite	_____
Inventive	_____
Creative	_____
Magical	_____
Amusing (grin variety)	_____
Amusing (belly-laugh variety)	_____
Amusing (slapstick variety)	_____
Outrageous	_____
Ridiculous	_____
Obscene	_____
Preposterous	_____
Over-the-top	thin as Australia

Why don't you take another run at the puzzler on page 160 with this tool in hand, putting your newer, fresher responses in Column B. And why not add new responses for Automatic and Over-the-top? I'll do the same and meet you back here when we're both finished.

Back already? Wait a sec, I'm not finished yet.

Okay, here's my solution. Let's compare answers again.

Automatic	thin as a stick (broom stick, twig, whip)
Obvious	thin as a dime
Commonplace	thin as paper
Literal	one millimeter thin
Labored	thin as the space between two rails of a railroad track
Interesting	thin as dishwater
Unusual	thin as a railroad tie
Obscure	thin as a two-micron garbage bag
Odd	thin as a rattlesnake

Opposite	thin as molasses (rhinoceros skin, crocodile skin)
Inventive	thin as vinegar
Creative	thin as e-mail
Magical	thin as angel skin
Amusing	
(grin-variety)	thin as a television plot
Amusing	
(belly-laugh variety)	thin as day-old roadkill
Amusing	
(slapstick variety)	thin as month-old roadkill
Outrageous	thin as Rush Limbaugh's skin
Ridiculous	thin as mud
Obscene	thin as baby urine
Preposterous	thin as a Stephen King novel
Over the top	thin as Austria (and you thought *Australia* was stupid)

How did I do?

If you'd like to argue with my responses, go ahead. I don't blame you for thinking that none of my *amusing* answers is all *that* amusing. But you must understand that this creativity tool doesn't evaluate answers as right or wrong. Rather, it stimulates you to generate a range of answers, increasing the opportunity for you to strike a creative spark.

After you've finished criticizing my responses, go back to work. Yes, again. Remember Strategy 4—Imagine Impossible Standards—and Strategy 5—Never Settle. Repeat the exercise, filling in Column C. On your own, please. I'm taking a break.

TIP: As I've suggested in chapter 1, you can set up a scale of your own with the brainstormer's bracketing tool. Just replace my adjectives with useful gradations that fit more into your genre or line of work. You might choose terms like: business, spiritual, biblical, journalistic, poetic, musical, math-related, academic, scientific, gibberish. Whatever moves your creativity quotient.

Keep in mind that the tool can have dozens of uses in your writing beyond this simple application to clichés. It can be used to evaluate ideas, characters, scenes and settings.

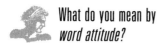

What do you mean by word attitude?

You must continually ask yourself this question in choosing words for your writing:

Artistically speaking, is this word well enough charged with energy and emotion to communicate the precise attitude that I want the reader to feel?

Take the example in which a slasher attacks retired detective Hammersmith. Here's the original sentence:

The man, thin as a rail, jumped into the car as it sped away.

Although I wrote the line according to the customary rules of good writing (active voice, declarative sentence, sufficient verbs and nouns) and can interpret it perfectly, I cannot find a single discernible image in it. But, heck, forget imagery. Review the context I gave you for the sentence, then read the sentence again. Do you hear it? That's not the street-hardened, retired-detective narrator speaking to you. It's the author cutting out all the middlemen—narrator and characters—to tell you what happened in a voice that's entirely devoid of energy and feeling.

Compare it to the reworked scene after we embraced the cliché and remodeled it. By our choice of words, we let the character-narrator speak and keep the author offstage where he belongs. We see images. We participate in the action because we see and feel events as they happen through the senses of the characters.

But there's more. Many of our words and sentences have a quality that goes beyond imagery, concreteness, specificity and inventiveness. I call that quality *word attitude*.

Word Attitude

Question Two to ask when testing words before you use them: *Does this word transmit the emotions and energy I want to communicate?*

Words can do that, depending on their intrinsic power, their context and placement, their speaker and his state of mind. The higher the emotional energy, the stronger the word attitude.

Let's examine each of these elements of word attitude.

ATTITUDE DERIVED FROM THE WORD'S INTRINSIC POWER

A precise word can sell a precise degree of detail or emotion. First, the detail:

esthetically challenged

This is a politically correct way to describe somebody who is ugly. Increasingly harsher are these word choices:

plain
ill-favored
unattractive
ugly
vile
god-awful

Now the emotion:

"You thoughtless person."

This is a gentle way to chide somebody who drank a pony keg of cheap wine before getting behind the wheel and racing home in reverse gear. Other words can portray harsher censure.

"You reckless driver."
"You fatuous numbskull."
"You jerk."
"You moron."
"You +#@%#@!" (You fill in the letters for symbols)*

Words can convey more than a degree of detail or emotion. They can also be judgmental without seeming to be. Take the word *said* and its synonyms, for instance.

"I have a headache," she said.

Straightforward enough. The word *said* simply helps attribute the quotation to its speaker without adding emotion or energy. Compare that to:

"I have a headache," she claimed.

Or:

"I have a headache," she admitted.

The words *claimed* and *admitted* ascribe emotions, motives and suspicions to the words in quotes. It's almost as if the writer has added snide remarks to comment on the quotation, as in:

"I have a headache," she claimed. (Although we're not going to be fooled by that assertion, are we?)

Or:

"I have a headache," she admitted. (Aha! We knew she was lying about feeling fine all along, didn't we?)

Not to promote the use of synonyms for *said*, but look at the attitudes that come across in the following:

"I have a headache," she announced. (As usual, making herself the center of attention.)

"I have a headache," she argued. (Adamant that she'd never give in to his advances.)

"I have a headache," she disclosed. (So that's what was making her so crabby.)

"I have a headache," she conceded. (I just knew there was something wrong with her.)

ATTITUDE DERIVED FROM PLACEMENT

Look at what happens when one word is repositioned in the following sentence. Read each sentence aloud and you'll hear what I mean:

Only you can write the novel you feel.

You only can write the novel you feel.
You can only write the novel you feel.
You can write only the novel you feel.
You can write the only novel you feel.
You can write the novel only you feel.
You can write the novel you only feel.
You can write the novel you feel only.

Hear how the placement forces a change in meaning and emphasis when it's read for the ear? Each change forces a shift in word attitude and sentence emphasis.

ATTITUDE DERIVED FROM A SPEAKER AND HIS ATTITUDE

Unlike the journalist, fiction writers like you have license to editorialize. When you do, it's useful to keep track of whose opinions you're spouting. Words that speak to a reader originate from one of three sources: the author, the narrator or a character.

AUTHOR ATTITUDE

If you have an attitude, unless you're writing an autobiography, keep it to yourself. As a rule, the hand of the author should never visibly pull strings from offstage.

You're probably familiar with ancient literary examples, like *Dear reader,* in which the author spoke to her audience. Modern writers sneak themselves into the picture in a number of ways:

- ☐ **Stepping into the story.** Don't stick your nose into the fictional world with expressions like: *If she only knew what was waiting for her on the other side of that door;* and *he was wrong;* or *little did she know.*

You probably consider these examples so elementary that it's an insult to your intelligence for me to list them, so let me give you some of the less obvious ways for an author to intrude.

- ☐ **Tired expressions,** like ones right out of sitcoms, movies or even the day's news. Using them is like putting a Post-it note in the margin of your manuscript: *Hi, I'm the author, and I watch too much TV.*
    Hell-OH-o, as in any sitcom
    Fancy a shag, as in the film

The bridge to the new millennium, as out of any corporate or political goon's mouth

☐ **Goofy gimmicks and grammatical gadgets!!!** such as alliteration—writing with words that begin with the same letter—and odd punctuation like multiple exclamation points.

☐ **Cute quotation marks.** *She had never met an author so tall—seven-feet, an authentic "literary giant."* Do you see the quotes? That's the author's signature. He's winking at you from behind the narrative, telling you he's made a funny, wanting you to notice it. Take off the quotes, and the irony works just as well.

☐ **Preaching from the mouth of a character.** When I hear a novel's heroine use a tired expression like "male chauvinist pig," whether the language comes in quotes or not, I feel offended. Not because of the politics of radical feminism fresh out of the seventies but that the writer couldn't find a more artful, less preachy way to say the same thing.

☐ **Brand-name revelations.** I like concrete detail, research and accuracy in the things I read as well as the next reader. But after the tenth new vintage wine is described, dated and delivered, it's clear to me that the *author* is showing off his oenological prowess.

☐ **Politically correct assumptions and observations.** Not that some characters shouldn't be written as politically correct. It becomes offensive, though, when the author takes liberties outside of character to push a theme. Even if a reader might not detect the offense, you should. Avoid it.

Even when an author has kept out of his stories by avoiding the intrusions I've mentioned so far, he's not out of danger. Intrusions can be as subtle as a baby's breath. Be alert to these offenses:

☐ **Wink and nod.** This often involves phrases like *of course* and *naturally,* as in this example:

Of course, he didn't say word to influence her decision to get an abortion.

This is a tricky situation to judge. Sometimes it's a character narrator who uses the word or phrase in the sense of: *He knew better than to try.* But it's also possible the author was saying: *We both know it'd be none of his business.* To me, this is the film equivalent of an actor looking to the camera and grimacing at you, the audience.

☐ **Out-of-character narration and descriptions.** Remember the exercise from above, where the man, thin as a rail, jumped into the car as it sped away? Now, remember this selection in one part of the drill?

. . . touched off a cacophony of squealing tires and honking horns, leaving behind a symphony of noise conducted by finger-waving drivers as the convertible weaved its way through the afternoon snarl.

I didn't use it because our hard-bitten character wouldn't use words like *cacophony* and *symphony.* His choice of words for the finger salute would have been more gritty, too. What's the conclusion? That the author is showing off his big vocabulary. Tricky, huh? I'd like to have a dime for every time I've committed this sin.

☐ **Naked clichés.** When a writer uses them stale out of the box, he's annoying his reader just as surely as chewing gum with his mouth open. The reader is thinking: *Can't this guy come up with language a bit more inventive?* Thus, the author intrusion.

☐ **Awkward constructions.** Any time a reader stumbles over your words, you have broken through the facade of fiction to announce your presence behind the page. Take this example, which has to be reread at least once to get the meaning—a meaning not worth the trouble to know:

That's the kind of nonsense up with which she had not put before and wasn't about to begin putting up with now.

Can you imagine how you'd feel if that sentence occurred in the middle of an argument that might end in divorce for a couple? About the third time you read it, you'd have used up all your emotions—not from being worried about the outcome of the scene, but from being angry at the author.

☐ **Static situations and lengthy descriptions.** What Elmore Leonard calls the stuff readers skip. When readers skip, the writer has allowed his presence to be felt. Unpleasantly so.

☐ **Pontificating,** including philosophizing, musing, wandering and other subtle forms of pontificating.

☐ **Repetition.** When you repeat a pet phrase or even an odd word in a story, it calls attention to itself. When you use it more often, it calls attention to the author. As in: *Don't you own a thesaurus?* My wife hates it when I use the phrase, *state of the art*, even once. And in the film *There's Something About Mary,* devotee as I am of the absurd, some of the gags went on too long and too often, even for me.

☐ **Anything too, *too* quirky.** I like quirky writing, other writers' quirks and my own. But sometimes they can destroy the ambiance of a piece of writing. I hate to confess it, but I lose a lot in the reading of Chaucer when it's written in the original Middle English:

Thing that is seyd is seyd; and forth it gooth.

You can forgive Chaucer those quirks because it was his English before we made it ours.

There's a line in Tom Wolfe's *The Bonfire of the Vanities*:

Heh-heggggggggggggggggggghhhhhhhhhhhhhhhh!

This is an odd cackling laugh set in type. That kind of quirk could get old fast, like the handheld camera technique used in some films, especially when the camera circles an actor half a dozen times at high speed.

When should an author's voice be heard? Never. Keep yourself out of the story altogether unless you're writing one of those fictional memoirs or whatever they call them.

NARRATOR ATTITUDE

Your narrator chooses words throughout your story, depending on qualities you assigned to her at the beginning.

The narrator can be neutral or involved. In the Detective Hammersmith example, you probably sensed the attitude of the ex-cop, who is certainly not a neutral observer of the story. Let's look at the degrees of involvement of narrators.

The Neutral Narrator. Should you work with a neutral narrator, simply try to be balanced. Don't use editorially charged words. Don't gush over good guys or condemn the bad guys. Don't sneak the author's opinions into the narrator's point of view. Move the story along by transporting readers from one scene to the next, where character actions and dialogue carry the freight. Most importantly, maintain your neutrality from the opening of the story to its close. Let the reader get her opinions from your character's subjectivity. Read this example, in which the narrator remains neutral, reporting only what goes on:

> *She shot him a look of disgust.*
> *"I'm sorry," he said. "I can't stop drinking. It's a disease. I'm sick. I'm—"*
> *She turned and stalked out of the room.*

Now compare it to this version, in which the narrator lets her neutrality slip:

> *He was a disgusting mess, a hopeless drunk.*
> *"I'm sorry," he said. "I can't stop drinking. It's a disease. I'm sick. I'm—"*
> *Hopeless. She turned and stalked out of the room.*

Does that mean the second version can't work? Not at all. You can read version two as if reading the mind of the woman in the scene. You might even argue that it's superior to the first point of view. I'm simply saying that the narrator in version one stands above the fray and reports what's going on in the scene. In version two, she participates in the scene. She's . . .

The Judgmental Narrator. The judgmental narrator offers endless possibilities for telling a story artfully just in the choice of her words. The narrator wears her opinion on her sleeve so readers can identify with her. Or even disagree. And, in some of the most magical stories, the reader discovers that the narrator cannot entirely be trusted, adding a measure of uncertainty to the reading experience. Often the judgmental narrator tells the story from a first-person point of view of one of the characters, usually the heroic character. This gives the story an air of personal intimacy.

CHARACTER ATTITUDE

To me, the best stories are always stories with characters opposed to each other on attitude rather than circumstance alone. For instance, the conflict between cop and criminal relies on adversity between their career choices. But that conflict always benefits tenfold when they have strong attitudes toward each other as well. No good story can exist without characters with attitude.

By attitude, I don't mean bad attitude. I mean words, characters and narrators who evoke a response, either attracting or repelling us in some way. When such characters come off as distinctive personalities, you're on the way to planting your pennant on Mount Creativity.

Here's an edited selection from my second Force Recon novel, in which three main characters react to a bomb attack their team has directed. You'll find three character attitudes about the same event:

They braced for a pounding. Each had picked a spot clear of rock slides. Each clutched his weapon and buried his face into the crook of one arm to save his night vision. Each spent his next few seconds alone with his soul.

Night Runner felt the earth move. It slapped his back like an old friend after a clean kill of a five-point buck in deer season. Even with earplugs he could hear the shrapnel singing by overhead. The concussion sucked his lungs empty. His skin prickled, both from the shock in the air and in his thoughts. On the other side of the ridge behind him lay a cauldron of hell he had helped create. He had turned his enemy to ash and dust. Worse yet, he'd killed the enemy's animals. Times like this he worried for mankind. He wished high-tech had not come to this. For by making the killing impersonal, new weapons had shrouded the face of death. What if men had to kill each other face-to-face with knife and fist instead? The raw intimacy of such murder might make men shrink from it. He weighed the idea a moment. No, probably not.

Gunnery sergeant Delmont Potts reckoned it a square deal that men who lived by the bomb died by the bomb. You put your biscuit hooks into the fire and start playing around, you better damn well expect to have your butt blistered now and again. Thing was, this was way better all the way around, anyways. Better than a kangaroo trial where the only ones that get anything out of it was the lawyers sucking at the taxpayer's money tree. Better than a firefight, where a decent Marine might get hurt.

This way was clean. One minute a gaggle of terrorists is diddling around a campfire like a bunch of Girl Scouts roasting marshmallows. Next minute they are the marshmallows, flying straight up to terrorist heaven like they're always ranting and chanting they want to do.

Friel wished he could watch. Just once he'd like to see the last look on one of the cheese-eating bastards that killed sixty-three kids in the city streets not so long ago. He came off the streets himself. Could have been him in another time. Or one of his family any day now.

But the captain shot him down when he asked to watch the impact at the briefing. Later on the chief told him to check out the story of Lot's wife in the Bible next time he wanted to get up close and personal with fire and brimstone. He didn't remember too many Bible stories, no matter how hard the Jesuits tried to bongo them into his head. But he remembered the ones where God kicked butt like he was a Force Recon Marine his own self. And he remembered the Bible chick that didn't listen and got her own butt turned to a block of Morton's best.

Just one little peek-a-boo. It'd be better'n Wile E. Coyote handing over a stick of TNT to the Road Runner. And what he wouldn't give to see that.

But the captain says nooo-uh!

Officers. He'd never met one that didn't need an enema.

"A simple style is like white light. Although complex, it does not appear so."
—ANATOLE FRANCE

Brainstorming Style and Writing Mechanics

Ten-plus problems and forty-plus solutions in working with a style that becomes you

ive puzzlers to jump-start your thinking before you undertake problems dealing with:

- Writing the best-seller—*guaranteed!*
- Sentence structure
- Paragraph structure
- The basics of transition and tie-backs

Identify the common phrases hidden in these puzzlers—you'll find the answers on page 278.

1. i an an an an i

2. = old fool

3. statement / credwhatanible

4. habirdnd = butwosh

5. i l w8 u u u u ever ever ever ever

In chapters 2 through 5, we discussed some of the macro issues in writing fiction like ideas, plots, characters and scenes. Then we devoted chapter 6 to a seemingly microcosmic issue: word choice. This chapter will help you fill the space between the extremes.

The Brainstormer's Guide to Writing a Best-Seller! Guaranteed!

Isn't that what everybody wants? The lazy man's way to riches? And, if you don't mind, riches without raising a sweat. No effort. No risk. Complete with a money-back guarantee.

Here is just the gimmick for you. If you use this tool faithfully, it could take you down the path toward writing riches. Try this technique for learning to write like the masters:

TIP: Copy your favorite best-selling author's novel word-for-word. By hand. Longhand, that is.

Don't groan about being tricked. Give it a try.

WHAT COPYING A BEST-SELLER CAN TEACH

- **Simple mechanics**—things like punctuating dialogue.
- **Publishing conventions of the genre**—chapter length, narration, story structure.
- **Writing action, conflict, imagery and dialogue** in the category of books you want to write.
- **How to economize on your novel's first draft.** Do this exercise long enough and you'll see how every word serves a purpose in a best-seller, carrying the freight without detours. In short, you'll learn how not to waste your own time and words.

A BRAINSTORMER'S CONSIDERATIONS WHEN COPYING A BEST-SELLER

- **Be wary of plagiarism.** You can't sell the words of another person. This exercise should help you master the *techniques* of the masters, not the exact words.
- **Don't transcribe mindlessly.** Pay attention to what the writer was doing and why.
- **Take notes as you copy.** Jot down the lessons you learn.

- **Don't copy an entire novel at once.** If you want to write breathless action like Dean Koontz in your climactic scene, select one of his novels and copy a suspenseful scene. Then write your own climax. Need your character to develop a distinctive identity? Pick up an Anne Tyler novel and follow one of her creations for a few scenes, copying every word Anne wrote about him.

Sentence Structure

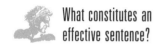 What constitutes an effective sentence?

In a word, comprehension. No matter how creative and poetic your writing, if nobody understands it, it might as well be a diseased elm falling in an empty forest. So let's focus on comprehension as we talk about writing style. Comprehension begins with choosing comprehensible, precise words, which we've already discussed. How you put those words together is called effective writing.

THE SINGLE MOST IMPORTANT LESSON IN WRITING EFFECTIVELY

One factor affects sentence comprehension more directly than any other: Simplicity. And nothing contributes to simplicity like brevity. The shorter a sentence, the greater the comprehension. Period.

When I taught basic reporting to military journalism students for the Department of Defense, I came across a different kind of comprehension scale that measured the ability of newspaper readers to understand sentences of varying length. I don't remember the source of the study and haven't been able to dig it up in my research, but because it had such an effect on me, I can reproduce it here with no trouble. Take a look at Figure 20 on page 184.

At one extreme, the scale tells you that reader comprehension of one-word sentences was 99 to 100 percent. At the other extreme, readers comprehended one-hundred-word sentences at the 1 percent level or less. I know what you're thinking.

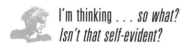 I'm thinking . . . *so what?* *Isn't that self-evident?*

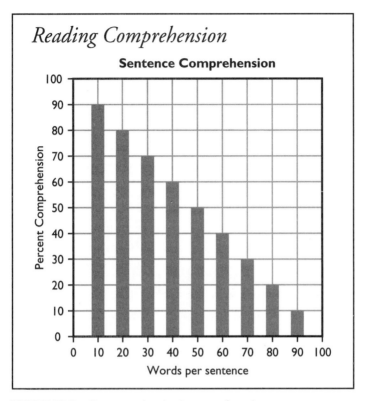

FIGURE 20. Reading comprehension in terms of words per sentence.

Perhaps, but don't stop there. Hold the illustration at arm's length. Notice the nearly straight line formed by the ends of the bars indicating that the longer the sentence, the less the comprehension. You don't often find correlations as direct as this outside of mathematics.

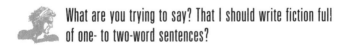 What are you trying to say? That I should write fiction full of one- to two-word sentences?

Hardly. I'm giving you a tool that you can forever implant in the photographic memory section of your fiction-writing brain. From now on, every time you write a sentence, call up that picture. If the sentence you write comes to twenty-five words, you can assume, as a guide, that your readers will comprehend 75 percent of your communication. If you write fifty-word sentences—all other things being equal—expect readers to comprehend only half of what you write. If you dare to write seventy-five-word sentences, you know the percentage of comprehension you can expect to achieve.

 What about that writing adage that says: Write to suit yourself and not some fictional "reader"?

You have a point, and I subscribe to it, as far as style is concerned. Once you start writing to satisfy a potential editor, an actual agent, your Aunt Rita and that demographic slice of stay-at-home women ages twenty to thirty-five, the compromises you make will dilute your writing style to less than ordinary. But right now we're talking about comprehension. You can't afford to alienate readers who can't decipher your message. I give you these basic comprehension tools as a starting point for simplicity of style, which leads to greater understanding of your words and ideas among the greatest number of readers. Don't forget: The greater your readership, the more books you will sell.

Popular novelists do write sentences of forty words or more, but rarely back to back. In the next chapter, I take great pains to show you the value of familiar words, short sentences, pithy paragraphs and stuff like that.

 Besides word count, what other factors affect comprehension in sentence structure?

SINGULARITY

A sentence works best when it expresses a single idea using no more words than necessary to express that idea.

Sentences come in a variety of shapes and forms. Using brainstormer grammar definitions, here's a sampling and examples to demonstrate how singularity can be maintained.

In high school, you learned the terms *simple*, *complex* and *compound* in defining sentence constructions. Brainstormer grammar redefines these terms because we're more interested in writer functions than sterile definitions.

The brainstormer writer needs to know about these types of sentences: simple, embellished, doubled and convoluted.

Simple sentences. Remember, we're talking brainstormer terms and not grammar as you learned it in high school. The effective simple sentence states a fact, portrays an act or paints an image. The writer adds only minimal but relevant clarification. As always, the first job of such a sentence is to somehow move a story forward. Remember the grizzly attack in chapter 5? Here are a couple of simple sentences from that selection:

> *A sponge carpet of pine needles covered the trail.* (nine words)

> *Bill grasped her arm.* (four words)

> *A fresh breeze chilled her skin.* (six words)

Simple sentences send direct messages. And directness helps you maintain singularity. What's more, the message usually involves only one subject—the fact, act or image—and often only one verb. These single-function constructions prevent lengthy explanations and awkward detours. Finally, simple sentences usually contain fewer words to get in the way of that single idea you want to communicate in each sentence.

 How many words do you recommend for a simple sentence?

I wouldn't dream of legislating word count, but I do have this . . .

BRAINSTORMER RULE OF THUMB: Write simple sentences of fewer than 20 words. An average of a dozen words is best.

Write longer sentences as you must, but keep this rule of thumb in mind. Later we'll refer to it in another brainstormer tool.

Embellished sentences. I use this term instead of *complex* because, for our purposes, complexity is a negative. You begin with a simple sentence and add one or more verbal clauses to expand or clarify the fact, act or image of the single idea you want to communicate. Grammarians call these clauses dependent because they depend on the simple part of the sentence (independent clause) for meaning and cannot stand alone. I call them verbal clauses because, to my mind, the simple sentence part of the construction depends on them for additional meaning. A few grizzly examples will demonstrate:

It [the carpet of needles] cushioned their soles and absorbed the sounds of their footsteps. (eleven words)

She pointed at a looming hulk, for all the good that would do in the ink of night. (eighteen words)

Notice that the first part of each sentence (the first line in each pair) stands alone. The second part depends on something in the first part for meaning. Forget about exact grammar definitions. Just consider all the possibilities available to you. Then, because you are a disciplined writer, no matter what form of sentence you write, keep the following principles in mind.

Two Principles for Using Embellished Sentences

1. No matter how complicated your embellished sentence, remember the concept of singularity. Keep to a single idea. If you want to add a second idea, write a separate sentence.

2. Watch your word count. You can often lose control of embellished sentences, especially in early drafts, by adding redundancies, nuances and explanations that weaken your writing.

RULE OF THUMB: Be wary of embellished sentences that exceed 20 words.

As I said, I wouldn't dream of legislating word count in your writing. I am sensitive to this problem because it is a flaw in my own writing of early drafts, especially when I use continuous speech recognition software. No matter how much discipline I try to impose upon myself, I tend to blabber. If you stay attuned to the problem in your own writing, you'll have much less work to do during the editing and revision process.

Doubled sentences. Your English teacher called these compound sentences. A writer uses conjunction junctions or punctuation sleight of hand to form compound sentences out of what could just as easily be two or more separate simple sentences.

From the grizzly attack, here's a doubled sentence with two distinct ideas, connected by *and*. Both ideas point to a singular problem. Each could stand alone:

A rough pine bough slapped her breasts, and needles stabbed at her eyes. (13 words)

And here's a doubled sentence, connected by *but*, amplifying a single idea:

She thought she might scream, but nothing came out. (9 words)

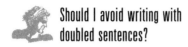

Should I avoid writing with doubled sentences?

Of course not. I use them myself; no doubt I use them *too* much, but they often work well, and they don't have to be lengthy. For example, the preceding sentence is built from four simple sentences but is only 23 words long. A semicolon connects two phrases. And the conjunctions *but* and *and* connect two more.

But doubled sentences, as the brainstormer name implies, tend to increase word count and multiply the numbers of ideas you address. Apply the same two considerations to doubled sentences as you do to embellished sentences.

RULE OF THUMB: Be wary of word counts that exceed 25 words in doubled sentences.

Convoluted sentences. This is any sentence that violates singularity by addressing two separate ideas, adding excessive nuance or explanation, or rambling. For example:

Lord Smith-Piper had mandated that peasants could not hunt stags on the estate, which nestled like a caress between the meandering rivers, but Avery and his band didn't like rules and never abided by them. (35 words)

You might think that a high word count alone would indicate the convoluted sentence. However, it isn't the number of words. It's the number of ideas, nuances and explanations that will confuse a reader. Here we have one lord mandating, two rivers meandering and three peasants not abiding.

Remember that selection by Alice Hoffman in chapter 3? If you like, reread the sentence on page 87, which is 53 words long. A single idea, beautifully amplified.

What about that word-count comprehension scale? If I read it correctly, her 53-word sentence is only 47 percent comprehensible. Am I right?

In my opinion, Alice Hoffman's superb choice of words, the flawless logic and flow of embellishments to her single idea and an altogether elegantly simple style overcome every obstacle to understanding. Her 53 words hang tight while the measly 35 words about Lord Smith-Piper fly apart.

Word counts don't matter when you can write words as she does in that selection. So, if you haven't achieved Alice Hoffman's level of competence, use a meager word count.

 ### What about art? What about craft? What about writing beautiful sentences for their own sake?

Writing that sells in a brutal marketplace begins with telling a good story, which begins with choosing words carefully and crafting singular sentences. Worry about writing one sentence that sticks to a single point as it advances your story. Then write the next sentence, and then the next as we move on to construct paragraphs. Don't even consider art, craft and beauty. These are not objectives for your writing; they are by-products of artful, well-crafted storytelling.

Brainstormer Exercises

Exercise No. 1. Edit this convoluted sentence so it makes sense. Don't rewrite it except to add a word that prevents the change from sounding like nonsense. Strike words when you can. Rearrange sentences. Add punctuation to create a combination of simple, embellished and compound sentences. Before you check out my solution to the exercise, read yours aloud and make final adjustments. Try not to expand the word count. The answer is on page 278.

> *Lord Smith-Piper had mandated that peasants could not hunt stags on the estate, which nestled like a caress between the meandering rivers, but Avery and his band didn't like rules and never abided by them.* (35 words)

 ### Am I reading you right? You're suggesting I use all simple sentences?

Not at all. Look at the next drill.

Exercise No. 2. A reversal of the previous exercise. Read this paragraph aloud before you edit. Notice how ten simple sentences, although easy to comprehend, become monotonous. Combine sentences and use parts of one sentence to embellish another until it reads better. Cut where you can. Give the paragraph direction. See page 278 for one possible solution.

> *Deena decided to catch his eye. She would do it with style. Any woman could attract a man. All she had to do was drop a hanky. Or other article of dress. But not Deena. She would use finesse. She would let him believe it was his idea. That's how you got a man. Make him think the seduction was his idea.*

Paragraph Structure

Writing effective paragraphs requires that you apply many of the same principles you did with sentences and words, so I won't repeat those concepts except when I must amplify the notion of singularity, which is larger with paragraphs.

Paragraph singularity refers to more than a single topic dealt with in a single paragraph. It also refers to a consistent attitude, a single direction and unity of focus. As you might guess from that last exercise, a well-written paragraph also uses a variety of sentence forms in varying lengths. And one paragraph is often tied to other paragraphs in scenes and stories with the use of tie-backs and transitions.

Don't worry that I'm about to launch into a grammar lesson. I think the best way to deal with all these features is to give you a new checklist.

THE BRAINSTORMER'S PARAGRAPHING CHECKLIST

Paragraph length. Evaluate your paragraphs for length.

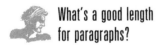 What's a good length for paragraphs?

I don't prescribe paragraph lengths, but you ought to be aware if they go on too long or if they're all too uniform.

Using one of the readability scans, determine the number of sentences in each paragraph of a scene. When paragraphs are all the same length, a sense of monotony sets in. Very likely you need a boost in the scene, varying paragraph length by one of the elements of ACIDS. For example, as you boost action, conflict and dialogue, you'll often find yourself writing shorter sentences and paragraphs. The problem will take care of itself.

Paragraph density. Hold your manuscript at arm's length and go through a scene one page at a time. Do you see any white space on the page? If you're writing one paragraph on each page, the story looks gray, feels gray, probably is gray. Can you use dialogue to break up the huge blocks of type just by adding white space? That's a trick that helps move a story along.

 Cool. I can juice up a boring paragraph just by adding a few carriage returns or some quote marks here and there?

Nah. If the material is boring in huge blocks, it'll be boring in small bites, too. But adding some breaks can relieve the gray.

The topic sentence. One sentence or idea in a paragraph usually identifies what the paragraph is about in nonfiction writing. For instance, in this paragraph, the first sentence fragment does double duty: It is the topic sentence and confesses to it in those very words, with bold type for emphasis. Fiction writers often do the same thing, especially in longer sentences. Rather than write an example, I'll refer you to the paragraph on page 201 that begins, "Swayne hated. . . ."

When you read that sentence, you see that it's the topic of the paragraph, which goes on to explain all the things he did hate.

Next, look on page 208 at the paragraph that begins "Swayne kept quiet." When you get to the end of this paragraph, you find that the information has built up to the last sentence, "It wasn't enough for Swayne," which becomes the topic sentence by summarizing the effect of the paragraph's information.

Either technique unifies the paragraph by telling you the topic of the paragraph or summarizing its impact. The topic sentence also lends a sense of direction. The paragraph's data either flows from the topic sentence or toward it.

Transitions and tie-backs. This subject is so important that I've devoted chapter 13 to it and dubbed it the fifth habit of highly effective writers. In that chapter, I discuss large-scale techniques over the course of an entire story. Here I'll give you a quick review of small-scale transition techniques.

Transition and Tie-Back Review

- **Outright phrases** such as *later, last week, next day, then, soon after.*
- **Direct references.** Often using pronouns like *he, she* and *it* to refer to nouns in previous sentences and paragraphs.
- **Reflections of images and ideas** from one part of the scene to the next.
- **Repetition of words or synonyms** from one paragraph to another.
- **Cause and effect.** Something happens in one paragraph, and its result is seen in the next.
- **Contradiction.** Something is stated or supposed in one paragraph but is reversed in the next.
- **An overall dominant atmosphere to which references are made.** This is tricky to talk about but easy to see. I set the grizzly scene in the black ink of the forest at night. From then on, any reference to darkness or blindness is a tie-back to that atmosphere. Cool, huh?

"In composing, as a general rule, run your pen through every other word you have written; you have no idea what vigor it will give your style."

—SYDNEY SMITH

CHAPTER 8

A Brainstormer's Guide to Revision and Editing

Nine problems and one very huge solution in polishing your story

How would you like to brainstorm with the likes of John Grisham, Stephen King, Terry McMillan, Anna Quindlen and Danielle Steel? Congratulations. You're about to do so.

You are also about to tackle your writing in a way you never dreamed possible—mathematically.

Honest. In this chapter, I'll give you brainstormer tools to help you look at how well your words, sentences, paragraphs and scenes function, so you can plan a strategy to revise and edit without even reading those words, sentences, paragraphs and scenes. Crazy, no?

While tossing around some crazy ideas for ways to look at how to revise and edit manuscripts, I decided to study success. And not just a single case of success or success in only the things I read, but success all across the board. I chose my favorite author and my least favorite. I chose women and men, current selections and works out of the past short of going back to my high school English classics. Only one thing mattered: The writers had to be best-selling authors.

I'm devoting this chapter entirely to my findings, which have changed my writing life forever.

Let's tackle some puzzlers before we begin the discussion of my methods and madness.

FOUR RELEVANT PUZZLERS BASED ON THIS STAR-STUDDED LIST OF WRITERS AND SELECTED WORKS FROM EACH

Fannie Flagg (*Fried Green Tomatoes at the Whistle Stop Cafe*), Kaye Gibbons (*Ellen Foster*), John Grisham (*The Street Lawyer*), Jan Karon (*A New Song*), Stephen King (*Misery*), Elmore Leonard ("Hanging Out at the Buena Vista," a short story), Terry McMillan (*How Stella Got Her Groove Back*), Anna Quindlen (*One True Thing*), Danielle Steel (*Star*) and Wallace Stegner (*Angle of Repose*).

Puzzler No. 1—What decisive trait can you find that is common to the listed writing of these authors? As a rule, the writers share this quality with each other but not with unpublished amateurs, government writers and at least one published writer who has not yet consistently hit the best-seller lists. (That would be me.) Thus, the trait might be your key to unlocking best-seller status. Of these, which is it?

- ☐ Low passive voice usage
- ☐ Short words
- ☐ Short sentences
- ☐ Short paragraphs
- ☐ Short tempers
- ☐ Short literary agents

Puzzler No. 2—The Microsoft Word manual says you should try for a score of 60 to 70 in readability on the Flesch Scale (0-100 possible). My chosen writers averaged:

- ☐ 50 to 59
- ☐ 60 to 69
- ☐ 70 to 79
- ☐ 80 to 89
- ☐ 90 to 99

Puzzler No. 3—The same manual says that standard writing averages a seventh- to eighth-grade level on the Flesch-Kincaid Scale (grades one through sixteen possible). My chosen writers averaged grade levels of:

- ☐ 1-3
- ☐ 4-6
- ☐ 7-9
- ☐ 10-12
- ☐ 13+

Puzzler No. 4—The best way to increase readability in your writing is to follow the advice of Strunk and White and "Omit needless words."

☐ True
☐ False

The answers to these puzzlers follow.

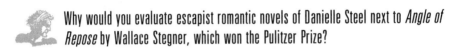

Why would you evaluate escapist romantic novels of Danielle Steel next to *Angle of Repose* by Wallace Stegner, which won the Pulitzer Prize?

To be honest, I don't know why I put them side by side at first, except that *Angle of Repose* is my favorite novel and I wanted to compare it to something less favorite. I admit I've never become a fan of Danielle Steel, but I know she is popular and successful. I respect her success, and I wanted to learn how and why she earns it each time she puts out a new book.

So I took that pair of writers and eight more. I turned three writing samples from each into text files on my computer. The samples ranged from 1,500 to 2,000 words, except for the Elmore Leonard short story, which ran fewer than 900 words. I used all of it. As a form of impartial control, I took the first one-third of each sample from the opening paragraphs of each novel. I also took a second sample beginning at the first full paragraph on the center page of the novel. For the third sample, I went to the back of the book in each case and tried to find a selection with high emotional content. If I had any personal bias, I expect it would show up here.

Before comparing best-selling authors to each other, I also took selections from some not-so-best-selling authors. For sample 11, I found a manuscript an unpublished author sent to me. Sample 12 came from a government manual. It's not fiction, but I used it because it describes combat actions that any credible fiction writer could have turned into high-energy writing. Medal of Honor stuff. Sample 13 comes from me. I chose my second Force Recon novel, which had yet to be revised and edited by my editor at Penguin-Putnam-NAL-Dutton—whatever they call themselves these days.

All told, I transcribed and studied more than 20,000 words, a file about a fourth the size of a conventional novel. If you were to conduct the same study, you would probably choose a different set of best-selling authors or titles, but I'll bet you would get the same results.

 And those
results were?

The pros often used short words, short sentences and short paragraphs. But you probably expected that. You probably also expected their tendency to use passive voice sparingly. In that, you would not be entirely right. In reverse order, let's look at each element and see how it comes into play.

The Winning Qualities of Best-Selling Novelists
PASSIVE VOICE

Passive voice is not a key factor. As Figure 21 shows, the pros varied widely in the averages. John Grisham's sentences scored 13 percent in each sample, and so averaged 13.43 percent overall. Stephen King's worst-case sample scored only 2.94 percent of passive sentences, and his overall average came in at 2.3 percent, by far the best. Meanwhile, one selection from Danielle Steel at 22.7 percent exceeded even the government sample, although her average was much less. My own best case tied Kaye Gibbons with no passive constructions.

The final word on passive voice is this: Unless you are using the passive voice with purpose—that is, to mellow out a passage, to avoid giving responsibility for an action or to slow down the pace of your novel—*don't use it*. Like most writing coaches, I urge you to use the active voice most of the time. But by itself, use of the passive is not an issue that separates the amateurs from the pros.

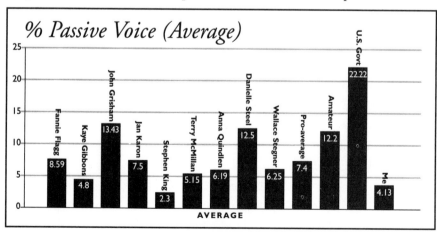

FIGURE 21. Average percentage of passive voice in selections of best-selling authors.

SHORT PARAGRAPHS AND SHORT SENTENCES

Nothing stands out in these areas except for one huge sentence by Terry McMillan, which ran 171 words. In general, the pros average a sentence length of fourteen words. Danielle Steel goes to sixteen, and Terry McMillan averaged eighteen, the same as the government sample. But because of that one hefty sentence, McMillan's average is skewed. Besides, every good writer varies sentence length, so I found such averages of little use in making writing comparisons.

 That leaves short words. I suppose you're going to say that using short words is the key to putting my novel on the New York Times best-seller list.

I wouldn't go that far. But I would say that no other trait ties these authors together more strongly. And when those writers are put up against not-so-best-selling authors, the difference is striking. Take a look at Figure 22 for the average characters per word of the opening sample of each writer's work.

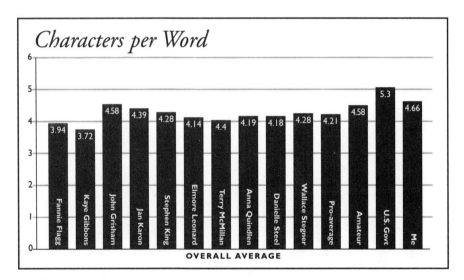

FIGURE 22. Average characters per word for each author's selection.

 You said striking. I see in Figure 22 that the professional average (pro-average) is 4.21 characters a word. The amateur, the government writer and you average only about a character more. You call that striking?

As a naked number, you might think it's trivial. Only when you begin working with the words that make up that number do you realize its importance in revision and editing. So I'm going to talk a lot about tiny differences that matter. But first, let's look at readability.

READABILITY

Look at Figure 23. Notice how the professionals average 83.1 in readability (see the "Pro-average" column). Apparently, best-selling writers have decided that they will not be content for their writing to score in the 60 to 70 range. Of course, using short words contributes to success on this scale. When I began brainstorming using these writers, I expected to find high readability in the Fannie Flagg and Kaye Gibbons novels because of their first-person narratives, one tale told by an elderly woman character, the other by a child. Sure enough, these novels use short sentences and familiar, conversational language. I also expected the lowest readability from Wallace Stegner, the Pulitzer Prize winner, and, to my mind, the most literary of the selections. Not so. Stegner beat out John Grisham and Jan Karon, both wildly popular novelists but hardly literary.

One more thing. Frankly, I expected my draft to score better than it did. Not that I see myself as a better writer than any of my chosen novelists. It's just that I have always paid attention to readability. I've always tried to keep my writing

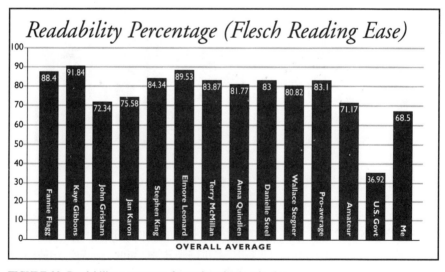

FIGURE 23. Readability percentage for each author's selection.

scores in the recommended range for standard writing. What an idiot I've been in striving for the 60s and 70s when I should have been shooting for the 80s and 90s.

GRADE LEVEL

This one blew me away. See for yourself in Figure 24.

My chosen writers averaged grade level 4.4. The highest levels, Grisham and Karon, only went to the sixth-grade level. Stegner, the literary giant, wrote to grade level 4.9, not much higher than Stephen King at 4.52. Once again, I had to whack myself on the forehead. All this time I've set a goal to write to the seventh grade level. Wrong, wrong, wrong. All wrong. Even the unpublished amateur's instincts proved better than mine.

Silly as it sounds, the writers who sell most of the books in this country aim their work at a level between the second and sixth grades.

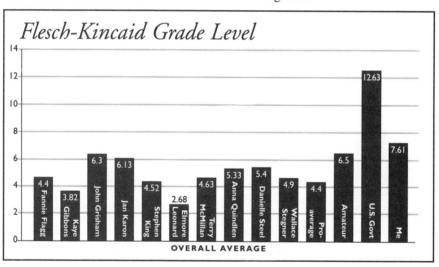

FIGURE 24. Grade level for each author's of selection.

The Ideal Editing Technique

If you truly want to write like the pros, you should take this advice: Omit needless words. But the one editing step that increases readability more than anything else you can do this: Replace big words with smaller, more familiar words. Strive for an average of 4.25 characters a word in your writing.

What about changing passive voice to active? Cutting words? Shortening sentences and paragraphs? Other editing steps like moving words and sentences around? Don't those things count for anything?

Yes, but not as much as cutting word size. I tested a variety of editing steps in a way that you would never use except in setting up a test. Here's how.

Based on my study of the ten novelists, I set an ideal for myself.

THE IDEAL WRITING STANDARD

From now on when I edit my work, I want to arrive at:

☐ **No more than 4.25 characters a word in any scene** and fewer in high-energy scenes.

☐ **No more than 5 percent use of the passive voice** and 0 percent in high-energy scenes.

☐ **No less than 80 percent readability** on the Flesch scale and no less than 90 percent in high-energy scenes.

☐ **A fifth-grade reading level** on the Flesch-Kincaid scale and lower in high-energy scenes.

Next, I chose a writing sample from my own work. These are the opening lines of my second Force Recon novel, totaling 569 words.

"Bingo Brutus."

Merely by muttering the words into the voice-activated boom mike suspended within kissing distance of his lips, Swayne touched off the attack phase of the fourteenth mission for his Force Recon Team.

As it had unfolded so far, the perfect mission.

Somewhere over the horizon to the southwest, a brace of F-117 Stealth fighters should be accelerating to Mach two, should be responding to his words by repeating them.

"Spartan One, this is Pave Nail Seven-Niner, confirm you have a visual on target Brutus."

Leave it to the Air Force to get chatty, using more than ten words when two would have done. So much for perfection.

"Bingo Brutus," Swayne growled, letting his tone add the dammit,

reconfirming that he was eyeballing Imani Abboud Dahni, the scourge of the Western world, leader of a terrorist faction that had set off car bombs on Wall Street, Pennsylvania Avenue, Downing Street, and Champs De Elysee. All on the same day less than a month ago, killing more than five hundred innocents.

Swayne hated repeating himself under tactical conditions. Wouldn't the weenies in cockpits and operations centers ever get it? A dirt-eating Force Recon Marine belly-crawling within rock-chucking range of the enemy couldn't afford the luxury of meaningful personal sharing on the occasion of every fart and giggle. Any time hostile ears might jeopardize an operation, the last thing a field trooper wanted was some console commando "going Alvin," to use Lance Corporal Friel's expression, referring to the hyper-chattering cartoon chipmunk. A single extraneous communication would be fatal if an enemy listening post heard a strange voice whispering in a strange language.

Meanwhile the lead pilot in his Stealth fighter felt no such inhibitions. "Pave Nail Seven-Niner," he droned. "Roger Brutus. Stand by for express mail delivery."

"Roger." Swayne visualized the two fighters streaking upward in a climb of sixty degrees, accelerating through Mach two toward three. Mentally he saw the pilots jerk their craft to the vertical, simultaneously releasing two bombs apiece on a trajectory toward Swayne's team of four. The violence of the maneuver supplied the power necessary for a toss that would carry the winged bombs another half-mile into the air and send them on a gliding trajectory for a distance of thirty miles.

"Spartan One, this is Pave Nail Seven-Niner. Be advised as to bombs-away *in five seconds. Stand by to paint Brutus and his boys in thirty seconds, on my mark." A pause of three seconds. "Mark. Express mail delivered, and Pave Nail is on the way home to the barn. Good luck."*

Swayne gritted his teeth. Fine and dandy, *he thought.* And what do you hear from the little lady? Wanna fill me in on your plans for the evening? The vintage of the wine you'll be drinking at the Riyadh O–club?

But he didn't respond, either sarcastically or tactically. Didn't have to. Four smart bombs away, now in free-flight. No amount of conversa-

tion could countermand the laws of gravity. The best that anybody could hope for now was that the bombs would reliably capture their individually programmed laser beams that would be turned on and directed by three members of the Force Recon team in—Swayne checked his watch—twenty-four seconds. Then the computer brains in each bomb would fire their on-board propulsion jets to make final course corrections, and home on their specified targets. Two of them set to capture Swayne's laser designation.

Here's the result of the readability scan—569 words with an average of:
- [ ] 2.92 sentences in each paragraph
- [ ] 14.92 words in each sentence
- [ ] 4.95 characters in each word
- [ ] 2.63 percent passive constructions
- [ ] 62.16 readability level
- [ ] 8.26 grade level

I used to be proud of numbers like that. Knowing what I now know, I have only one word to say. *Ouch!*

No wonder the reviewer from *Publisher's Weekly* remarked that my first Force Recon novel tended to be wordy at times. The minute I made that discovery about the second novel, which had already gone to the printing plant, I asked my editor to return it so I could revise it to my newer, less wordy standard. I did, and it is.

But when you revise, what works? What steps improve readability? I'm happy to report some helpful results.

THE EFFECT OF CHANGING PASSIVE VOICE TO ACTIVE ONLY

On my first pass, I changed only the passive sentences to active voice. I left all the other words alone except to make minor changes so the opening made sense.

You can see the results on Figure 25. There's not much change, and no change at all in the area where I wanted to see it—average characters in each word.

THE EFFECT OF CUTTING WORDS ONLY

I went back to the original sample and took the advice of Strunk and White and omitted needless words. Once again, to be realistic, I made edits so the sample

Brainstormer's Editing for Readability Exercise

Edits using combined techniques

	Original	Ideal	Passive Fixes Only	Cut Words Only	Punctuation Fixes Only	Shorten Words Only	Edit #1	Edit #2	Edit #3	Edit #4	Edit #5
Word Count	569		555	402	559	552	473	488	532	529	552
Avg. # Sent/Graf	2.92		3	2.62	3.57	2.71	3.93	3.13	3.43	3.36	3.36
Avg. # Words/Sent	14.92		14.23	11.82	11.18	14.53	10.15	10.38	11.8	11.26	11.26
Avg. # Char/Word	4.95	4.25	4.95	4.88	4.95	4.53	4.45	4.38	4.34	4.32	4.15
% Passive Voice	2.63	0-5%	0	1.47	2.63	2.63	0	0	0	0	0
% Readability	62.16	80$^+$%	63.26	69.4	66.3	78.37	84.76	88.32	87.74	87.69	92.86
Grade Level	8.26	4-6	7.93	6.47	6.8	5.9	4.6	3.46	3.73	3.63	2.89

FIGURE 25. Editing exercise on the *"Bingo Brutus"* sample from *Force Recon #2*.

continued to make sense. You will be happy to see that taking out 167 words did improve the sample on both readability scales. Cutting words does help. But not enough in that key area of characters in each word.

THE EFFECT OF SHORTENING SENTENCES ONLY

I went back to the original sample again. This time I cut the length of sentences by using punctuation. Again I saw a nice jump in the readability scales, but no change in characters in each word.

THE EFFECT OF USING SHORT WORDS ONLY

This time I replaced long words with short ones in the original, and for the first time saw a telling drop in characters per word. Although no other factors changed, both readability scales exceeded the ideal I had set. More than anything else, this affected readability.

THE EFFECT OF COMBINING ALL EDITING METHODS

I expected magic the first time I put all my editing tools to work on the sample, but I did not create magic at all. Yes, the readability scales improved over my ideal, but the characters-per-word factor began to show just how stubborn a factor it can be. The result is shown in the column labeled "Edit #1." A big change, but still short of the ideal.

THE EFFECT OF REEDITING YOUR WORK

I decided to go after the characters-per-word factor with a vengeance. Starting from my first try using all the editing methods, I reworked the writing sample.

And went on reworking it. On the fifth try, the factor tumbled to well below the ideal, and the readability scales moved well past the ideals I had set. That's as far as Figure 25 goes.

But now that I had beat the factor, I decided to experiment further.

Finally, after eight edits, the scene fell into focus for me. You can read the results and statistics at the end of this segment in the revised Force Recon sample. Readability scales remained high. And, of all things, the characters-per-word factor continued to slide.

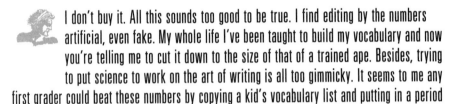 I don't buy it. All this sounds too good to be true. I find editing by the numbers artificial, even fake. My whole life I've been taught to build my vocabulary and now you're telling me to cut it down to the size of that of a trained ape. Besides, trying to put science to work on the art of writing is all too gimmicky. It seems to me any first grader could beat these numbers by copying a kid's vocabulary list and putting in a period here and there. How can we trust these tests in the first place?

I know, I know. I had doubts myself. It does sound too good to be true. But think about it. The readability tests didn't choose the novelists or writing samples. I did. Whether you trust the tests or not, samples from best-sellers passed those tests in a way that lesser writers could not.

BRAINSTORMER REALITY: Best-sellers share two traits: a huge readability rate (expressed as a high percentage on the Flesch Reading Ease Scale or as a low grade average on the Flesch-Kincaid Scale) and a low count of characters per word.

You can't argue with that. It's a fact.

 You might say you could run a spell check on the samples as well. Just because my writing sample had no misspellings doesn't mean I'm in the same class with Stephen King, John Grisham, Danielle Steel and Wallace Stegner.

True. But I would say that to have hope of ever being in that class, you and I both have to submit work with no misspellings. And it wouldn't hurt to have the same kind of scores on readability and characters per word either.

As to the size of our vocabularies, that was the hardest pill for me to swallow, too, because I've tried to build my vocabulary all of my life—until I went back to check the tested selections. Nobody could accuse Wallace Stegner of using a fourth-grade vocabulary. Or any of the chosen authors, except for Kaye Gibbons, whose Ellen Foster is the child narrator of her novel.

Turns out that it's not the vocabulary you own that matters. It's the vocabulary you use. You *can* use big words in your fiction. You should use them when no smaller word fits the precise meaning you want to achieve.

But what this exercise teaches me—and I hope it teaches you—is that you should not fire off your vocabulary in shotgun style. When only one longer word will serve the purpose you intend (the five-syllable *vocabulary*, for instance), use it. If smaller words will work just as well, use them. (For example, instead of *vocabulary*, you might try *word list*. That would work in some situations.)

As for punctuating a vocabulary list, yes, you might beat the test. But that's where your common sense comes into play. Surely you wouldn't try to market a word list to editors and agents. Would you?

I wondered about this notion of beating the system and decided to put it to the test. I chose one more author, Jack Torrance. You remember Jack Torrance, don't you? In Stephen King's *The Shining*, Jack took a job as the winter caretaker of The Overlook mountain lodge. How could you forget Jack Nicholson's portrayal of Jack Torrance going mad as he sat at his typewriter tapping out a novel? And how could you not feel chills when you found out that hundreds of pages contained only these words, over and over?

All work and no play make Jack a dull boy.

So I put together a sample of Jack Torrance's fine novel, the same sentences arranged into paragraphs of different sizes. Then I put the sample to the test. The results? 700 words and an average of:

- ☐ 2.8 sentences in each paragraph
- ☐ 10 words in each sentence
- ☐ 3.3 characters in each word
- ☐ 0 percent passive constructions

So far it looks like Jack Torrance beat the test, but not after you read the remaining statistics.

☐ 112.9 readability level (on a scale of 0-100)

A nonsense result to a nonsense novel.

☐ .11 grade level

Also an absurdity.

It seems the people who invented these tests built some controls into them to keep us from making them look stupid.

I don't doubt that you could take a writing sample from the dic tion ary, add stra teg ic punc. Tua tion and break words into short nons ense seg ments and beat the test.

But why would you? (That goofy sentence, by the way, has 3.8 characters a word, an 87.55 reading ease score at a grade level of 5.39. Corrected, it doesn't come close to my ideals. It contains 4.93 characters a word, a reading ease score of 54.1 at a grade level of 12.42. But which is better, do you think? So much for beating the test.)

Finally, here's the result of the editing work—a dozen passes at the opening of my second Force Recon novel. The improved version cuts only 25 words net. But look at these 59 words and a trite expression or two that I took out to make room for shorter, more telling words:

muttering	language
voice-activated	inhibitions
suspended	express mail delivery
kissing	visualized
distance	accelerating
unfolded	mentally
somewhere	simultaneously releasing
horizon	trajectory
southwest	violence
accelerating	maneuver
responding	necessary
repeating	gliding trajectory
re-confirming	for a distance
terrorist faction	sarcastically

luxury	tactically
meaningful personal sharing	conversation
occasion	countermand
jeopardize an operation	reliably
expression	individually programmed
hyper-chattering	propulsion
extraneous communication	corrections
enemy listening post	specified
whispering	designation

This is the revised selection.

"Bingo Brutus."

Jack Swayne spat the words at the boom mike at his lips. Two words to set off the kill phase of his Force Recon Team's mission. The perfect mission, too, so far.

From Iraq's no-fly zone to the south, the lead pilot of two F-117 Stealth fighters was to say—

"Spartan One, this is Pave Nail Six-Two, confirm you have a visual on Brutus."

Leave it to the Air Force to get chatty when the two words would work just as well. So much for perfection.

"Bingo Brutus," Swayne said. He let his tone add the Damn you, *listen up.*

Bingo *meant Swayne was eyeballing the target of Event 14.* Brutus *stood for Imani Abboud Dahni. Why didn't the guy just say* Bingo Brutus?

Would the weenies in cockpits and ops centers never get it? A dirt-eating grunt in spitball range of the bad guys didn't want to spill his guts after every burp and giggle. And he didn't like some console commando "going Alvin" in his ears, either, to use Friel's words for it.

But this pilot just had to go chipmunk: "Pave Nail Six-Two," he said. "Roger Brutus. Stand by for e-mail."

"Roger." In his mind's eye, Swayne saw the jets streak up at sixty degrees and pass through Mach two. As the pilots hit their time hacks they would jerk their jets vertical. And cut loose two bombs apiece at

once. The high-G toss would fling the winged bombs into an arc a half-mile high. The arc would ease into a glide of thirty miles right to Swayne's team.

"Spartan One, this is Pave Nail Six-Two, be advised as to bombs-away *in five ticks. Stand by to paint Brutus and his boys in thirty ticks, on my mark." A pause of three seconds. "Mark. You have e-mail, and Pave Nail is on the way home to the barn. Good luck and good night."*

Swayne ground his teeth. Fine and dandy. And what do you hear from the little lady? Want to fill me in on your plans for the night? How much wine to suck down? How many two-stars to suck up? *Why was it the combat troops did their talking at the mission de-brief? While the armchair grunts did theirs on the radios and in their chat rooms, bars, and beds—and all their fighting in their dreams?*

Swayne kept quiet. Why bother with more talk? The four smart bombs were away, now in free-fall. The law of gravity had taken over. It would hand off the bombs to the team once they lit up their laser beams in—Swayne checked the LED digits of his stopwatch—two-four seconds. The brain in each bomb would ID its own lasers and fire on-board jets to make final course changes. Each would home to a kill. Swayne's IR laser would direct two of the bombs, both at Abboud Dahni. To be on the safe side, the idea was to kill him twice. It wasn't enough for Swayne.

Abboud Dahni's boys had set off car bombs on Wall Street, Fleet Street, and Champs De Elysee. All on the same day less than a week ago, killing more than five hundred and setting a packed school bus on fire. Payback time was now only—one-niner seconds away.

And here, after eight painstaking edits, are the final readability stats. 569 words with an average of:

- ☐ 3.36 sentences in each paragraph
- ☐ 11.62 words in each sentence
- ☐ 4.14 characters in each word
- ☐ 0 percent passive constructions
- ☐ 92.56 readability level
- ☐ 3.36 grade level

Does it sound as if it were written down to a third-grade level? Or, worse, by a third grader? Not to me. You may not read the genre or agree with my style, but I like it. I feel more tension in the scene, more realism. Swayne's agitation comes through more clearly, and his attitude has picked up an edge. The scene owes its success to that edge. The grunt in the field eating dirt and waiting for smart bombs to go off nearby ought to be testy. He should be nervous, even when things seem to be going perfectly. And he shouldn't be thinking about a looming combat in five-syllable words. That just slows down the action.

I also like the way the last paragraph works in the revision. The more I worked with the scene, the more I wanted to keep unbroken contact with Swayne. In the early versions, this important information about Abboud Dahni got in the way. If you reread the original, you'll find it has the feel of the author putting in his two cents to tell you that this terrorist is really a bad guy for killing hundreds of innocents. In the new version, we see him through Swayne's eyes. It's payback time, and by now you don't doubt that Swayne is in just the state of mind to direct two bombs right into Dahni's Fruit of the Looms. The author pulls back and does a better job of staying out of sight. The scene works better.

What This Tool Can Teach You About Editing Your Work

Even if you argue that readability and characters per word are artificial devices, I counter that forcing the ideal on myself has raised my awareness to conventional revision and editing techniques. This brainstorming tool forces you to:

- **Focus on a clear, measurable standard.** You can measure your editing progress with it. When your readability falls to 50 percent in a high-action scene, you sense that it drags. When you pep it up to 79 percent, you give it legs. When you pump it into the 90s, you know it sings. You don't have to rely on some vague scale like, *It sounds good to me.*
- **Cut out your darlings.** If you can't hit your ideal readability marks without deleting a lovely purple phrase, you will, as Paul Verlaine said, "Take eloquence and wring its neck" in the end. Odds are, you'll improve the passage, too.
- **Elevate your awareness of pacing.** When two characters plan to ruin somebody's marriage and sit around drinks talking about how to set up the tricks and traps of their plot, you know you can ease off on word length and allow

a few more passive constructions. When a couple gets into a dog fight, you know you must tighten the action. This tool acts as a guide. Once again, you can measure your progress.

- **Explore word choices.** When words like *dependability* and *extrapolations* grind your scores into the dust, you will find precise, shorter words. Or else you will cut out the monsters from the page.

- **Identify detours and asides.** When either the writer or a character flies off on a tangent, this tool will shine a light on the sin. Once you see it, you can fix it.

- **Manage word count.** I don't know if you have this problem, but when I rewrite, I always blow the word count off the charts. To me, editing means adding. Improving means filling in the blanks. But with this tool, I tend to fix things, not fatten them. You'll have to try it to see if it affects you the same way.

- **Write with economy on first drafts.** This might be the best effect of all. The pain and shame of seeing how fat my early drafts are make me want to write leaner prose the first time around. I can already see the improvement in my writing.

- **Create distinctive characters.** On second thought, maybe this is the best effect of all. You can apply the scan to various characters and allow the college professors and lawyers in your stories to speak at a better readability level. But the kid from an East LA gang isn't going to have the same score. (Is she?)

 I feel better about this characters-a-word thing, but I won't be positive until I've tried it myself. My software doesn't even have a readability function. How do I go about trying it without spending hundreds of dollars on new programs?

If your word processor doesn't have a readability test, no problem. Millions of computers do have them, and you can carry your novel around on disk looking for one to rent or borrow. It's worth the effort.

 How should I go about conducting the test? What tricks and tips did you find in your own experiment?

Good questions. I assure you, I have made enough mistakes to be able to answer thoroughly.

Adapting the Characters Per Word Test to Your Own Writing

1. **Do not run a readability scan on your entire novel at once.** The software will give you overall readability statistics but you will find them a waste of time. Entire sections of your fiction might be boring dreck full of passive constructions and a readability at the Ph.D. level. These might be followed with crisp scenes of high-energy dialogue and fast action. The two might average out to meet the ideal standards you set for yourself, but the dreck will earn rejections for you. So work with one scene at a time. Set a standard similar to the one I used earlier in this chapter. Depending on the importance of the scene and the energy level you wished to achieve, edit your work either to meet or exceed that standard.

2. **Evaluate your own favorite writers in the type of fiction you plan to publish.** As you saw, my chosen writers and their novels came from different genres and varying literary acclaim. You might select two novels apiece by five romance writers if you plan to sell romances. Or you might choose five thrillers by the same author. Just make sure they are best-sellers. Scan their work. Use the results to set a standard for yourself. I'm not saying you should copy another writer, just adopt the tools of his success to your own fiction.

3. **Caution: Create a master file of the original version of your fiction** *before* you work your editing magic on a copy. That way if you cut too deeply, you can refer to the master and restore selections.

4. **Some readability software lets you turn off spell checks and grammar checks.** Do so, except for the feature that checks passive constructions. That way the scan will work faster.

5. **Create a log like the one in Figure 26.** Enter your results each time you edit and rerun your own scan. This lets you chart your progress with each version and make needed adjustments.

6. **Above all, don't rely on readability and mathematical results alone.** Use all the standard editing tips you learned in school, on the job, from your own research and from writing seminars. As a final step, no matter what method you use, check the average number of characters for each word in the selection and the readability stats.

Brainstormer's Editing for Readability Log

Selection: _____

	Ideal	Original	Edit #1	Edit #2	Edit #3	Edit #4	Edit #5	Edit #6	Edit #7	Edit #8
Word Count										
Sentence Count										
Graf Count										
Avg.# Sent/Graf										
Avg.# Words/Sent										
Avg.# Char/Word	4.25									
% Passive Voice	0-5%									
% Readability	80$^+$%									
Grade Level	4-6									

FIGURE 26. Brainstormer's Readability Log.

Part III
ADVANCED WRITING
THE SEVEN HABITS OF HIGHLY EFFECTIVE WRITERS

Y ou're going to like this segment. I've collected tricks and gimmicks for years, ideas that have helped me in my own writing. Fun ideas, wild ideas and stupid ideas. All of them are ideas that I have used or intended to include in an advanced writing seminar and text.

I've put a variety of chapters into the mix, some short, some long, some detailed, some fragmented. You can put some of these ideas into practice in your writing today. Others you might save for later, for instance, the next one, which will only be helpful to you after you invest in the necessary software.

> "If I chance to talk a little wild, forgive me."
>
> —SHAKESPEARE

CHAPTER 9

The First Habit of Highly Effective Writers

Using continuous speech recognition software to dictate fiction

A s I've said, I'm writing this book by talking to my computer using a killer program called Continuous Speech Recognition (CSR) software. I speak into a microphone at about the same speed you'd use in reading this paragraph aloud, and my words appear on the screen as text. It's like writing with both hands tied behind my back, which my wife forbids me to do anymore.

Instead, I gaze out the window, creating, talking, writing, occasionally warming my hands by wrapping them around a hot cup of coffee. It'd be a shame to call this work, but it's how I do what I do now that I have CSR.

If the computer does make a mistake in understanding me, I can correct it with spoken commands. If I want to keep up my dictating momentum, I can go back to mistakes later and revise.

Besides giving dictation, I can boss my machine around by giving it word processing commands. For example, when I want to start a new paragraph, I simply say the command: *New paragraph.*

To italicize those last two words, I told the computer: "Select *New paragraph.*" After the words appeared as highlighted text on the screen, I simply said: "Italicize that." No pointing and clicking through menus and dialogue windows.

When I'm done formatting text, I can resume dictation without giving any special commands, or typing, or mousing around. I merely speak my next creative thought. The computer knows that I've changed gears, although I haven't told it so outright, and faithfully transcribes my words. Technology groupies are always gee-whizzing about virtual reality, but I'm easily as impressed with this remarkable, if elementary, illustration of virtual intuition. To me, CSR technology is just on the near side of miraculous.

What's the catch to this CSR technology? I suppose you're thinking the software must be expensive. Or complicated. Or hokey. Not at all.

- **As to expense,** several workable CSR programs are available for $100 or so. If you own a PC-compatible computer manufactured anytime after 1997, it's likely you won't have to add memory; the power necessary to run the software was probably standard issue. If you must upgrade, the expense probably won't exceed a couple hundred bucks. CSR is now available for the Mac, too.

- **As to complexity,** you can train yourself (and teach the computer your personal speech patterns) and be up and running in an afternoon. The only manual you'll need for refreshing your memory about formatting and other commands is a reference card only four (*count them: four*) pages long.

- **As for hokey,** you can read this book (and the two novels I've written with CSR) and decide for yourself. I'll just boast that anything you can do when you sit down to write something at a keyboard, I can do in half the time, simply by *talking* to my computer.

Maybe a brief anecdote will impress you.

I put on my headset microphone and handed off the mouse to August, a lawyer friend of mine who is both computer literate and most difficult to impress. I threw down this challenge: "August, I can highlight and italicize any word or phrase visible on the screen before you can even point to it by moving the cursor with the mouse."

To make it a fair start, August's wife, Cassie, was to tell us which words to format.

I put the first pages of this very manuscript on the screen. To give him even the ghost of a chance, I also agreed to wear a blindfold and have my hands tied behind my back. Honest.

The signal was a flip of my head. Without hesitation, Cassie said, "hold onto your joystick."

I said, "Select *hold onto your joystick*" and "italicize that" before August could even find the phrase on the screen, let alone click, drag and use either the keyboard shortcut or formatting menu to italicize.

As you might have realized, the blindfold was no handicap at all for me. In fact, it gave me an unfair advantage—*I didn't have to visually search for the words as my lawyer friend did.* All I had to do was repeat the phrase as Cassie spoke it.

Was my hard-to-impress friend impressed? You bet. The thing was, Cassie couldn't wait to get him out of my house. Not because I had cheated him but because they wanted to go out and buy their own version of CSR software. That's what my little demo meant to them.

What it meant to me was that I had to wait for my wife to come home from work to untie me and remove the blindfold. I'm still not sure she believes my earnest explanation as to how I got into my predicament.

You can understand why I don't write with my hands tied behind my back anymore.

What Can CSR Mean to You?

In the long view, CSR's rudimentary intuition suggests that true computer intelligence is possible. We can now foresee a day when complete voice interaction with a computer will be a reality. We'll be just like the characters who talk to their starship computers in science-fiction thrillers such as the various *Star Trek* series.

But look at the more practical and immediate advantage for the brainstormer:

> *The capability to create by speaking rather than typing removes one*
> *of the last bottlenecks to your ability to express brilliant ideas as words.*

Think of it. CSR technology allows you to sweep your creative atmosphere free of mechanical obstacles such as the keyboard and the mouse. It permits you to cleanse your mind of static interference such as remembering keystrokes and word processing commands. And it lets you double or triple your normal typing speed, no matter how fast you now type. With CSR, you will be able to dictate words on screen at 50 words per minute or better—in only an afternoon of training. Just try to learn touch typing that fast. Surely you remember getting nowhere near 50 words a minute until you had been typing for months, maybe years. Maybe you'll never get there—until you put CSR to work for you.

Finally, consider this: When you become proficient with CSR, probably in fewer than forty hours of dictating, you'll sometimes hit top speeds of 150 words a minute, something so rare in typing that it's usually a television event.

But CSR means so much more than leaving your typing-challenged friends in the dust. You will achieve something dramatically powerful in terms of creative expression.

> *With CSR you can express floods of creative ideas—all you need do is speak them. Your creative energy and productive output are no longer limited except by your own creativity and productivity.*

"It took me fifteen years to discover I had no talent for writing, but I couldn't give it up because by that time I was too famous."

—ROBERT BENCHLEY

CHAPTER 10

The Second Habit of Highly Effective Writers

Knowing when to package material for a series of "smaller" books

Nobody on the fiction side of publishing wants to handle midlist books. Everybody wants either a best-selling collection in one of the categories or a mainstream best-seller. So in many ways, it's easier to break into publishing in one of the genres. Editors will throw $5,000 to $10,000 apiece at ten romances if they show the promise of being a strong, popular series. But they won't spend $500 on any mainstream novel that doesn't figure to be a sure thing at making the big time.

At many houses, the midlist only exists because novels acquired as potential best-sellers either did not perform in the marketplace or were outdone by other titles. You might consider launching your career as a package, aiming for category fiction.

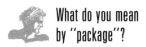 What do you mean by "package"?

Rather than a story idea in a category such as romance, think of a literal package, an attractively wrapped Christmas present. Think of it as a distinctive idea kit that an editor can use in reselling to an identifiable reading audience.

First, imagine yourself as an editor, then sell the package to yourself.

 How does an editor think?

She thinks like anyone else trying to do a good job from day to day while building a record that will help establish her on a career path to the stars. Let's talk about an editor responsible for making a package successful within the house. She knows she will need to buy more than an occasional $5,000 romance to establish her career. She will need to do more than break even on half a dozen novels in a row. Each successful novel must make a profit, and as the novel series grows by word of mouth, readership should grow for each new book—and the backlist besides.

Give her what she needs. Give her a package that shows such promise, and you increase your odds dramatically.

The best way to describe a package's contents is to give you an illustration. Remember the various series by R.L. Stine? The horror books for young adults and children? Think of those as packages and you come up with a raft of characteristics that you can use in formulating your own package.

The Contents of a Package

☐ **A concept recognizable to readers of category fiction.** Young people who pick up novels written by R.L. Stine expect to find a scary read.

☐ **A concept that lends itself to functional artwork.** The covers of R.L. Stine's books tell you at a glance, "This is a scary book." The colors and illustrations suggest suspense, fear and danger.

☐ **A concept that defines its own audience.** The Fear Street series targets young adults. The Goosebumps series aims at a younger set of readers, and parents who buy these books understand that the stories will be less graphic than the young adult series.

☐ **A concept that publishers can serialize.** Within the Fear Street series, you find a collection called "Cheerleaders," and within the collection, the stories are numbered: The First Evil, The Second Evil and so on, leading to . . .

☐ **A concept that permits a continuing cast of characters and settings.** Corky Corcoran, the cheerleader at Shadyside High School, for instance, in the "Cheerleaders" series.

☐ **Perhaps most important, a concept that is fresh.** When R.L. Stine's series began catching fire, horror as an adult category had been in decline for years. His books went against that trend and parental resistance besides. But when his novels took off with kids, they were unstoppable.

What's missing in this checklist? Any discussion of individual stories or plot lines. The editor you're trying to reach is less interested in any one story than in an overall concept in which all of the stories will be written. For instance, in the case of R.L. Stine the overall concept of the collection of near-graphic horror stories for young adult readers has heroes and heroines who are always kids solving violent crimes in which the villains are almost always kids.

 How can I make any money thinking small, selling limited-appeal stories in cheap books?

Think about it. Think R.L. Stine. He was to young adults what Stephen King is to adult adults. Think: Huge success can come in small packages.

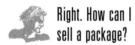 Right. How can I sell a package?

That's the attitude. First decide on a category and study it, either in the trade press, by going to bookstores or by searching the electronic bookstores.

Some Things to Look for in Category Research

1. **Identify the top three superstars within the category.** How many books do they publish with their names on them each year? Do their books make the best-seller lists for category fiction regularly?
2. **Find out how the best-sellers are alike.** Can you spot the similarities in those books using the checklist for a package?
3. **Discover what stands out as unique.** How does each package differ from author to author and book to book? Can you identify other distinctive features of each of the top writers?
4. **Resolve not to emulate any of these top sellers,** either in their writing or their story lines. If you give the appearance of creating a knockoff, you're buying an express ticket to rejection.
5. **Develop a package that's fresh, distinctive, inviting,** capable of making an editor's career (and, not incidentally, your own), yet is recognizable as a package that will sell to the readership of the leading authors.

HOW TO DIFFERENTIATE AN IDEA
- Take the idea either into history or the future
- Combine two categories
- Incorporate technology
- Reflect the headlines
- Reflect established trends in the popular culture

CAUTION: Those last two bits of advice invite you to tread thin ice. Headlines and trends fade fast. Publishers routinely take a year to get a book out after you deliver a first-draft manuscript.

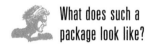 What does such a
package look like?

Editors don't get enough attractive packages from the world of authors like you and me, so they develop their own and canvass agents, looking for authors to write stories for the package. These editors send packages out to the field as bibles. Prospective authors compete for the privilege of writing individual novels within the package. Think of how much work you can save an editor if you submit not just an individual $5,000 novel, but a proposal for a package of a dozen novels. Not to mention those novels might earn you $5,000 to $10,000 apiece in advances and a lifetime's supply of royalty checks.

Here's how you adapt the two previous checklists into . . .

The Brainstormer's Essential Package in Eleven Simple Steps
STEP ONE: INVENT A KILLER SERIES TITLE

Indicate the audience, the level of action or emotion and the category. If possible, strike a familiar chord. Check out chapter 3 again for tips on writing a killer title.

I recently read a publisher's bible for a series called The DREAM Team. It's a package from NAL in the military action-adventure category. The title by itself doesn't tell you the genre, but the cover art will reflect it, you can be sure. I mention this title because it will remind any sports fan of our gold medal Olympic basketball team featuring the superstars of the NBA. The editor who developed this series is smart enough to know that sports fans are likely readers of action-adventure series. Thus the title. Good thinking.

You should do the same kind of thinking. If you are wondering whether that title is a disadvantage because it was also applied to O.J. Simpson's team of lawyers, I wondered about that as well. The bible indicates that the potential series title will be Surgical Strike. Maybe the editor in charge of the series had the same doubts. In any case, one glance at the cover art and the next little item will remove all such doubt.

STEP TWO: COME UP WITH A SUBTITLE THAT COMPLEMENTS THE TITLE

If you already have a killer title, you may not need a subtitle. But the NAL package title does need one. Why?

Besides the questionable O.J. Simpson reference, the letters in DREAM beg a question, don't they? And the Jeopardy answer is, What is Direct Response Emergency Attack, Mobile? Now you cannot doubt that this is a military action-adventure story.

STEP THREE: WRITE A ONE-PARAGRAPH OVERVIEW OF THE CONCEPT

Describe the category in which the series will be placed and distinguish it from all other packages in the category.

The DREAM Team bible begins by saying the title does not refer to either O.J. Simpson's lawyers or the U.S. Olympic team. A waste of words. But the overview paragraph does its job superbly in every other respect. I've edited it for you:

> The ultimate military special team. Unlike Delta Force. Not primarily a hostage rescue team, nor are the members exclusively drawn from Army personnel. A Navy SEAL. A Force Recon Marine. An Army Green Beret. A member of Air Force Airborne Rescue. Three top-flight civilian specialists. Amazing physical shape, can run for miles, swim for miles, parachute, handle weapons. Each knows the basics in demolitions, navigation, flying an airplane, piloting a boat and emergency medical treatment.

You see, the publishing industry has found that a military action-adventure series can attract a strong readership. Until this package, authors competed by selling the idea that "My military special operations unit is the best in the Department of Defense, and my guys can kick your special operation unit's tale." (Pun intended.)

The NAL series promises to take the best of all the military services and combine them into the ultimate fighting machine. That's a one-of-a-kind approach you should look for in the category where you want to make your mark. Notice how the writer of this NAL bible hasn't tried to invent an entirely new category. The editor stuck to the conventions of military special operations units fiction while creating a new, improved niche.

STEP FOUR: ADD A DETAILED OVERVIEW

Make it one or two pages, double-spaced. In this bible, each character in the cast gets a sentence or two of elaboration. A discussion of weapons, enemies, operating instructions and general ground rules follows.

STEP FIVE: WRITE A SIZZLING SUMMARY PARAGRAPH

This segment is wrapped up in a summary paragraph. Here you should give some of the mechanical details. I've included the paragraph in the sample bible, word for word, because I think it is one of the most effective I've ever seen.

> *The plots will be ripped from today's headlines and underscore the need for a small, effective, highly mobile tactical force as the large-scale wars of the past become obsolete. Each book will be about one self-contained action. Rescue a hostage. Blow up a building. Capture a terrorist. Each book will be filled with as much pulse-pounding excitement as can be packed in a 60,000- to 80,000-word manuscript. The villains can be real-world characters, such as Saddam Hussein.*

STEP SIX: INCLUDE A PROCEDURAL PAGE

Write a list of conventions for each story in your package. This allows an editor and agent to understand the limits and procedures under which a story will play out. For example, take vampire stories. In some stories, a necklace of garlic keeps the bloodsuckers away. They operate only at night. They avoid mirrors. A stake through the heart. Fly like bats. Sleep in coffins. All these are rules or conventions. In the NAL package, two somewhat prosaic rules for DREAM teamers, are:

> *5. They report directly to the Joint Chiefs of Staff.*
> *9. No ranks within the team.*

While another rule sets a broader framework for writers in this series:

13. The DREAM team and their U.S. government contact are unambig-uously the good guys. There are no double agents involved, no govern-ment scandals. They always wear the white hats.

STEP SEVEN: SHOW THE FORMAT YOUR STORY WILL TAKE

Or more to the point, story formula, which is not a bad word in packages. This segment sets down the rough structure that all of the stories within the package must conform to. In the DREAM Team bible, one or more paragraphs is devoted to each of these segments:

Prologue
Assessment
Training
Infiltration
Mission
Exfiltration
Epilogue

That's a format.

STEP EIGHT: WRITE BRIEF CHARACTER DOSSIERS

These should be one page maximum for each of the major continuing characters in your package. These pages work best if they look something like a resume. You don't write a full biography here. You simply reveal the headlines of the character's life, especially those things in a person's past that can give clues about her personality. You might cover these areas:

Special skills—10 words
Role in the story—10 words
Age
Personality—20 words
Physical description—10 words
Background—about 100 to 150 words
Pertinent data—religion, language skills, hobbies, youthful indiscretions

You might have as few as six or as many as ten characters you want to highlight in this way. Fewer than six characters suggests you might not have enough substance for a package. More than ten risks boring the editor or agent with too much detail. Even if you have thirty superb characters, limit this part of the package to the best eight or ten.

STEP NINE: CONCOCT SOME SCINTILLATING STORY LINES

Or plots. Consider developing a dozen story situations and describe each on a half page. Here's a chance to use that ten-scene tool to huge effect. Don't get into subplots, repetition of material that appeared earlier in the proposal or extravagant developments in characters. In keeping with the format you already described, tell what's going to happen—in about one hundred words—in a collection of exciting dramatic stories. Fewer than ten story situations might indicate you haven't given enough thought to the series or that your material is too thin to sustain the package. More than a dozen story lines is simply overkill. And remember, these plots must sizzle.

STEP TEN: WRITE YOUR AUTHOR BIO

More than anything else, you have to establish that you can complete a package that you begin. This is where writers with established credits will have an edge on the beginner, especially if they have already completed novels within a series.

STEP ELEVEN: OFFER FOLLOW-UP MATERIALS

You can take care of this in your sales letter to the editor or agent. Established novelists proposing a new package can offer to send published books as writing samples. Beginners can offer sample chapters, but I would recommend being prepared to send the entire first novel of a new series.

In fact, even established novelists should have 10,000 words or so already written. Not that you have to prove you can write. Your published materials should establish that. But you do have to give editors and agents a taste of the characters, plots and tone of the package your proposing. Not to mention that it will give you the feel for the quality and quantity you can deliver.

That's the package—twenty to thirty pages packed with promise, and a writing sample ready to send upon request showing that you can deliver on that promise.

> "You write a hit play the same way you write a flop."
> —WILLIAM SAROYAN

CHAPTER 11

The Third Habit of Highly Effective Writers

Knowing when you have the right stuff for a big book

I can describe the elements I see in a big book, but can't necessarily tell you how to get those elements into your own fiction, especially since you can find categories of big books even in mainstream novels. For example, take Oprah's Book Club. By definition, when Oprah selects a novel, it's going to become a big seller. Anything by a big hitter is destined to become a big book, even if it's a category book. The big hitters in courtroom thrillers are John Grisham and Scott Turow. In horror, you have V.C. Andrews, Stephen King and Dean Koontz. When a celebrity writes a novel, especially a stand-up comic turned television star, it's usually a big book, no matter how badly it's written.

That's what makes it so tough to put a finger on elements common to big books, but I'll try anyhow.

The Elements of Big Book Style

I don't have to tell you that all big books require strong writing—the more magical, the better—and strong stories. The same holds true for almost any piece of fiction that gets published. Publishing professionals, those editors and agents who guide books and authors into print, are perfectly able to recognize good writing and good stories. What they're looking for are qualities that distinguish great stories from good ones.

THE BIG BOOK NEEDS A CATEGORY-LIKE HANDLE

Courtroom thriller. Coming-of-age story. Political murder mystery. Romantic thriller. Medieval saga. Improbable love story. Women's adventure. Psycho thriller. Offbeat spy novel. A story for Oprah.

Notice that some of these short descriptions show up routinely in the brief passages of best-seller lists. Publishing people understand them because the terms are often identified with big books with exceptional track records. But there's a downside. A courtroom thriller, for instance, means to an editor or agent—and you, for that matter—that you will have to go up against the likes of John Grisham. There's no room on most publishers' lists for courtroom thrillers that are not as good as or better than one of his stories.

Notice, too, that several categories borrow on the word *thriller*. Everybody loves a thriller. I think you could invent a unique big-book idea for a novel just by connecting any word to thriller: western thriller, computer thriller, classroom thriller, medical thriller, legislative thriller, thriller thriller, publishing thriller.

The downside to using *thriller* is that unless you can write adrenaline-pumping action and suspense from the very first pages of your novel, your attempt will soon be discredited by its failure to live up to your thriller billing.

You must follow up that handle with a phrase that tells the publishing pro that something different has just come across her desk. It must be enough to tempt her to ask to see writing samples and to inspire you to write something fresh and exceptional enough to live up to your own expectations.

GIVE YOUR PACKAGE A SHOWBIZ TWEAK

By this, I mean a phrase that jogs the imagination. Even if it's a bit hokey, it's something that performs two important functions:

One, it connects your idea to the world of Hollywood. Broadway, high-profile celebrity, sport, politics, pop culture or even the classics.

Two, it tells what your story's about. Suppose the first line of your query letter is:

> *Congratulations on your success as editor of the Gulf War epic novel* Saving General Principle. *From the feel of that wonderful book I suspect you'd like to take a look at my battlefield thriller,* Genetic Attack.

You've given the novel's title and a handle that places the book in a general area of interest. And because you've done some research, you know the editor handles books of that type.

Your next line will be a single stroke of your finest creativity in startling a jaded editor, who's inundated by queries because he's been so successful with *Saving General Principle*, into paying attention to your pitch. So you tweak his interest by writing:

> *In my near-future war novel,* Jurassic Park *meets World War III as genetic weapons threaten to wipe out humankind.*

Some other examples of startling tweaks:

> *"Les Miserables" comes to roost in Little Rock, Arkansas, in the aftermath of an earthquake twice as devastating as that in Turkey.*

Or:

> *Lewinsky-gate in reverse. A cabal of presidential hopefuls expose the youthful foibles of members of the media.*

Or:

> Gone With the Wind *plays out in East LA in the year 2000.*

Like that.

I'm thinking that's a bit hokey.
No, make that very hokey.

Yes, it is. And you wouldn't dare make such a statement unless your story packed all the punch you've promised and then some. And you really wouldn't want to say another word of hyperbole throughout your entire query. All you're doing with this eye candy is getting attention in a shorthand way.

You see, editors and agents talk to each other in such telegraphic language all the time. If you were to overhear the "let's do lunch chatter," you'd likely hear editors and agents using terms like:

"Dracula meets Hannibal Lecter."

"*Megatrends* implodes when the Y2K bug hits."

"*The Blair Witch Project* takes place in a Sisters of the Unhappy Souls convent."

"Cosmo Kramer runs for the Senate from Texas."

All the statement does is place the topic of a new work of fiction into a context. It arouses interest. It evokes this important response: "Oh, yeah? How does it go?"

From this point on, you must stop trying to sell sizzle and begin to deliver substance.

THE BIG BOOK CAPTIVATES WITH ITS MAJOR CHARACTERS

I can't think of any classic novel or film whose blockbuster success could not be attributed in great part to dazzling characters, great and small. Characters rich and realistic. Characters quirky and complex. Characters demonic, or at least dark. Characters that the audience feels honored to have met in fiction or too frightened to ever meet in reality. Or both.

No matter how good or evil, these characters must connect with readers of your fiction. People must wish that they themselves could be as heroic as your heroic characters. They must see in those characters things they fear finding in themselves, even in the good guys. They must applaud when the characters overcome those awful flaws within themselves in order to achieve whatever plot quest you have established for them. On the other hand, readers sometimes find moments of compassion for your most villainous characters as well. Think of the two tag-team villains in *The Silence of the Lambs*, for instance. Jame Gumb, the serial killer, is tormented by his ambiguous sexuality. And Hannibal Lecter has that soft-spoken, sensitive side. You find yourself sympathizing with them momentarily. Think about it. Sympathizing with a serial killer and a cannibal. That can't be healthy for you, even for a moment. But it is a remarkable quality when you can evoke it in your own fiction.

THE BIG BOOK ALWAYS DELIVERS DISTINCTIVE MINOR CHARACTERS

Nobody is ordinary in big-book fiction or blockbuster film. Remember *Shakespeare in Love*? Remember the realism that was created because everybody in the film was somebody? The minor characters came to life. But they did even more than live. We saw them as people with goals and interests and opinions. They each had an effect, however minor, on the story. And Queen Elizabeth, whose character spent only eight minutes on film, could have stolen the film. As it was, actress Judi Dench did steal that Oscar as best supporting actress. You can say the same thing about a Tom Wolfe novel. An Anne Tyler story. Stephen King. A Quentin Tarantino film. The movie *Fargo*. The really big stories always have big little people.

THE BIG BOOK ALWAYS DEALS WITH A DOMINANT ISSUE WITH A TWIST

The dominant issue dictates the overall personal stories of individual characters. The example that first swims to the surface in my mind is *Schindler's List*. The Holocaust and all its horrors occupied center stage on-screen, overshadowing yet another huge theme, World War II. Nothing happened in the film unless it was caused by the Holocaust or its perpetrators and victims. That's a big issue to end all prominent issues. The twist in this story is a German industrialist con man who suppresses his own mercenary interests to save Jews from the gas chamber.

Let's look at some others:

Shakespeare in Love—Dominant theme: love. Special twist: The preeminent literary figure of the western world, whom we know almost nothing about in terms of his personal life, falls in love while writing the ultimate love story, *Romeo and Juliet*.

Jaws—Dominant theme: fear, especially the universal fear of sharks in the ocean. Special twist: An immense great white shark develops a vendetta against a resort community whose lifeblood depends on tourism during the summer season.

Saving Private Ryan—Dominant theme: war, treated as hell in a way only veterans have seen until this film. Special twist: Saving Private Ryan, a worthy goal that came with one hell of a cost.

THE BIG BOOK HAS THE POWER TO STUN

Shortly after filmmaker Stanley Kubrick's death, I read a piece by Janet Maslin in the *New York Times* titled: "A Visionary, a Mindblower, Kubrick Never Failed to Stun." Here are two excerpts from that piece:

> *Kubrick's small (only eight films after 1960) but amazingly varied body of work was unified not only by bizarre brilliance but also by its rare ability to disturb. He anticipated, even prophesied, all manner of assaults on the soul of mankind, and he gave voice to its most insidious fears. . . .*

> *. . . He preferred an eerie formal elegance, a detached and chill-inducing fascination with detail, to more familiar means of capturing an audience's attention. . . . The Kubrick style was defiantly, mesmerizingly feel-strange.*

What struck me about this evaluation more than anything else was its similarity to an evaluation by another great talent from an entirely different world, that of literary criticism. In *The Western Canon*, Harold Bloom writes:

One mark of. . . originality. . . for a literary work is a strangeness that we either never altogether assimilate, or that becomes such a given that we are blinded to its idiosyncrasies. Dante is the largest instance of the first possibility, and Shakespeare, the overwhelming example of the second. Walt Whitman, always contradictory, partakes of both sides of the paradox.

This notion of strangeness fascinates me for two reasons. One, because I recognize that the most memorable stories I've experienced, either in books, film or television, had some quality of weirdness: *The Catcher in the Rye, M*A*S*H, A Clockwork Orange, Lonesome Dove, Fargo, Ulysses, One Flew Over the Cuckoo's Nest, Angle of Repose, August 1914, Andersonville, Seinfeld, All in the Family, The Monk, The Detective, The Treasure of the Sierra Madre, Apocalypse Now, Avalon, Pulp Fiction, Homicide, American Beauty,* almost anything Elmore Leonard—you get the idea and have your own list.

Two, because the line between strange and over-the-top is so tricky that only the very best sense of balance permits a writer to walk it.

The weirdness in *Fargo* sets its hooks in you and never lets go, while the weirdness in *Twin Peaks* wears out halfway through the first episode.

The fourth viewing of any *Seinfeld* rerun tops next season's highly hyped finale of *Just Shoot Me.*

Pulp Fiction works. *Natural Born Killers,* every bit as strange, repels (in my opinion).

 What is that single quality of strangeness in a work that attracts but does not repel?

I'll give you a list. I can't tell you whether your own stories will fascinate powerfully enough to attract without becoming repellent. You'll have to work this brainstorming problem out all on your own.

Think of your favorite works of fiction as I list these qualities. See if I'm on point with my observations. Not all great stories have all of the qualities, but every great story has one or more:

The Brainstormer's Catalog of Acceptable Strangeness
- Characters so odd but likable, you want to meet them.

- Dangers so weird but so familiar, you're afraid they might happen in your own life.
- Techno-possibilities so fascinating you're not sure whether they're fact or fiction.
- Language so inventive, so graceful, so slightly off-key that it could only have been written by a complex genius, yet simple and elegant enough that you understand it.
- Ideas so powerful you wish you'd thought of them first, yet you're grateful that the writer introduced them to you, because they might make a difference in your life.
- Tragedy so avoidable that nobody but a human being like you would allow them to occur.
- Humor so fresh and original that all the popular sitcoms will steal it in the coming season.
- Stories so personal that you grieve or rejoice as if they happened to you.

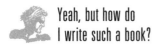 Yeah, but how do
I write such a book?

Here's a brainstormer tool for a big book of your own.

The Brainstormer's Big Book Tool

FILL IN THE BLANKS FOR YOURSELF.

1. Category _____
2. Title with stopping power _____
3. Shorthand identification _____
4. Striking character traits _____
5. Dominant issue _____
6. Twist on the issue _____
7. Stunning quality _____

I'll do it for one of my own yet-to-be-published novels as an example:

Category—Romantic thriller.

Title with stopping power—*Love Busters, Inc.*

Shorthand identification—*Seinfeld* meets *Sleepless in Seattle*. The heroic character becomes a con man who ruins other peoples' relationships and nearly gets himself killed in the bargain.

Striking character traits—Con artist as heroic character whose own fear of relationships leads him into breaking up others.

Dominant issue—Love and relationships.

Twist on the issue—A young con man breaks up a marriage only hours after the wedding, and a grateful father-in-law pays him in gratitude. Armed with this dangerous precedent, the con man starts up a business dedicated to destroying relationships for hire.

Stunning quality—Who's to say? A lot of publishing professionals have looked at my one-page synopsis, which, of course, incorporates all of the above. But heck, I haven't sold it as of this writing.

So let's get busy writing and rewriting, shall we? Until we can both break the big-book barrier.

 Tomorrow. I can't find the motivation. Maybe I've got writer's block. What do you think?

Writer's block. *Bah!*

"Writer's block is a hoax."

—RICHARD WALTER

CHAPTER 12

The Fourth Habit of Highly Effective Writers

Ignoring writer's block

P eople have written entire books on dealing with the ailment called writer's block. I have a better idea for you.

Imagine yourself dressed in a gown, mask and surgical gloves, and standing in the center of an operating theater. By eavesdropping on the conversations of the nurses and surgeons, you discover that you are the principal surgeon scheduled to transplant a brain from the picnic cooler beside you into the head of a dying patient. Your assistants have already peeled back the man's scalp and removed the half-dome of his skull. Everybody in the room has begun staring at you expectantly.

"What are you people looking at?" you say.

Your chief assistant says, "It's time for you to transplant the brain."

You reply, "Maybe tomorrow. I can't find the motivation. Maybe I've got surgeon's block. What do you think?"

I think you have overindulged yourself on a steady diet of baloney for far too long. There's no such thing as surgeon's block. If the doctor doesn't do the operation, it's because she's lost her nerve, lost her enthusiasm or doesn't know what she's doing. Why do writers think they have the privilege of a special dispensation for not working? What is this mysterious white lie known as writer's block? Face it—if you're not writing, it can only be because you're too lazy or you don't know what you are doing.

I've learned two things about creative writing. The first is that creativity doesn't strike sparks in you like a bolt from the ionosphere. You can't expect much from wandering around idyllic settings waiting for an inspiration. The most effective aids to creativity continue to be a simple pen and blank pad. You create sparks by striking one against the other. Write an idea down. Develop that idea. Resort to some of the brainstormer strategies from chapter 1, turning that idea inside out. That's where creativity comes from. The second thing I've learned is that writing does not occur by thinking about it. Writing only happens when you do it, so plant your butt in a chair and get busy. Keep busy. After you create a million or so words, you will have established yourself as a serviceable writer simply from the experience. If you've worked hard at learning from your experiences along the way, you'll probably be a creative writer. That's how it works.

And by the time you've written those million words, you will have forgotten that the condition of writer's block even exists, except in the minds of dilettantes.

> "Fiction is not a dream. Nor is it guesswork."
>
> —MARGARET CULKIN BANNING

CHAPTER 13

The Fifth Habit of Highly Effective Writers

Texturizing with transitions and tie-backs

T ransitions and tie-backs give a story continuity and flow. The highly effective writer never permits her fiction to develop that feeling of this happened, then that happened, then this happened, yadda, yadda.

No, the effective writer somehow creates the impression that words, sentences and paragraphs flow inevitably from one to the next. Each new chapter seems a logical progression from the previous chapter. These units of construction don't stand alone as separate entities that somebody dropped into place like building blocks. When you reach a moment of truth in such a story, you realize that that literary instant results from a confluence of a hundred facts and circumstances you've read earlier in the story. Every iota is a related, orderly part of a whole that cannot be taken out without damaging the overall structure. When you read a work that gives you this feeling, you know it was written by a master of transition.

Advanced Transitional Techniques

If you need a review of common transitions, take a peek back at chapter 7. The devices you find there will help the effective writer create serviceable transitions. Now we want to transcend the ordinary.

The really brilliant effective writer always keeps two notions at the top of his awareness. The first is simple cause and effect. The second is motivation.

CAUSE AND EFFECT

Something that happens in the present scene will result in something happening in a later scene. Perhaps nobody can say for sure what that effect will be. A good writer will have a number of possible consequences to create and sustain a feeling of suspense. She might achieve surprise by inventing a possibility that even the sharpest reader could not anticipate. But by keeping to the fictional rule that actions cause reactions, the writer keeps the reader hooked. This feeling of suspense acts as an emotional form of transition. You feed a reader cause and effect often enough and she will come to expect it. She will keep track of unsolved issues, waiting for you to spring your solution.

In the film *The Truman Show*, you might remember an early scene where Truman is outdoors and a rain shower is soaking him and the space within an arm's reach around him. That scene hits you between the eyes because it's an image right out of the comics and cartoons. Yet, I didn't get the point of it for a time. When it did strike me later, it was a truly *oh, wow!* moment. Of course, being a man-made world, the huge soundstage of *The Truman Show* was subject to the occasional glitch. Later, such glitches tipped off Truman as to what was happening to him. But at the moment of that shower, neither he nor I understood what was going on.

MOTIVATION

We already discussed this when we talked about characters. Motivation is a second abstract transitional device. As you develop a character, the reader begins to see what causes that character to tick. As the reader begins to know and understand the character, he realizes that the events now happening in this fiction will, sooner or later, rub up against the individual motivation, which has a certain predictability to it. When that happens, and a character begins reacting, the reader expects to see certain semipredictable responses.

It's an adage among playwrights that anytime a gun is introduced in the first act, then somebody had better be shot with it before the curtain in the third act. The same can be said about cause and effect and motivation and response. You simply cannot put a madman's dynamite temper into play in the opening pages of your novel, light the fuse in the middle pages (carrying the reader ahead in the form of an abstract transition) and fail to provide an explosion in the climax.

As you write, you probably don't have to worry too far ahead about the simple transitions from word to word, sentence to sentence, paragraph to paragraph, scene to scene and chapter to chapter. For any writer of modest talent, those things take care of themselves like the automatic bodily responses of heartbeat, digestion and breathing. If you fall short in these areas, they are also easy to fix during the editing process.

Tie-Backs

I think of tie-backs as transitions in reverse. They add a professional texture to every story.

As you will recall, I suggest writing the central story line first in your fiction, using the ten-scene technique. This helps minimize detours on secondary plots, inadvertent word padding on secondary action and wasted development on lesser characters. But that technique also creates ellipses in the action, gaps that you have to account for during the revision and editing of your manuscript. It's a simple process to read the story, find those gaps and look backward into the work to find a spot where a logical transition can be placed. Then you can tweak both locations, connecting the logic so you can keep the reader onboard.

It's a fairly routine process of keeping your eyes open for instances where the jump from one scene to the next is too abrupt. Simply use one of the transition techniques we've already discussed to fix the problem.

TIE-BACK TECHNIQUES

The flashback. Everybody knows about the flashback. Moviegoers see them all the time, usually brief scenes of a past event that help explain the motivation for a current event in the film. Novelists write them all the time, often in a distinctive typeface or format such as italics. Most often a character will tip off the flashback by remembering the previous event, and then the event is played out. Sometimes without explanation or preamble, a scene appears, plays out and the story resumes where it left off. Even these rough cuts or transitionless jumps usually don't bother readers or viewers.

If there's any problem with flashbacks, it is that they have become something of a cliché. Writers use them because they easily explain things. The trouble is, any form of explanation stops the story, whether exposition, narration or pseudo-action played out in the trappings of the dreaded dream sequence.

Finally, remember this: All writers great and small use flashbacks, but the really talented writers use them as only one tool in an entire tool kit of transitional and texturizing devices. Lazy writers drop a flashback into the story because they don't have the energy or imagination to find some more creative method.

Refer to this brief list any time you're considering writing a flashback:

1. **Don't.** Find another, more artful technique. Examine some of the possibilities that follow.

2. **If you must resort to flashbacks, ration them.** Use them sparingly, and never in the climax.

3. **Be brief.** Illustrate your point, and get back to the story in the present.

FORESHADOWING THE BIG SCENE

You see this technique most often in film because Hollywood tends to be so obvious about it. In the movie *Braveheart,* an early scene of betrayal set up the possibility of a pivotal betrayal at the climax of the story. (And just to be sure that we didn't fail to get it, Mel Gibson's heroic character turns fatally stupid, allowing himself to be duped so often that by the film's end, he deserves to die of terminal stupidity.)

The trouble with this device is its familiarity and tendency to give away the outcome of a critical scene. Once you sense that the climactic scene has developed the feel of an earlier scene, you know how the story is going to turn out. At least in flashbacks you see new information revealed, facts from the past that explain the present. When you see a scene being played out as you have already seen it, all you're getting is repetition. And a repetition that spoils the ending besides.

Once again, all writers use this technique, and I wouldn't dream of eliminating it from your own tool kit. Instead, I have these tips.

Foreshadowing Tips

1. **If you must foreshadow** a big scene, do it no more than once. Don't assume that readers are too stupid to get the point. Too much foreshadowing of the same issue diminishes the effect of later scenes.

2. **Foreshadow in such scenes by using different characters.** Playing the same trick on one character will only make her look like an idiot.

3. **Introduce a surprise effect.** You can add a delicious taste to your art by creating seemingly predictable situations, then springing unexpected results on your characters and readers.

I find the most stunning example of such a surprise in Larry McMurtry's Pulitzer Prize–winning *Lonesome Dove*. McMurtry develops his characters thoroughly and distinctively. You can see he is as fascinated by them as we are. However, unlike most authors, he allows some of the best characters, both minor and major, to die horrible deaths. Yes, the bad guys often do get their just desserts. But all too often, to my tastes, the good guys also get their unjust desserts. It's all part of McMurtry's portrayal of the West as an unforgiving environment. And it sets up the violent death of one of modern fiction's most endearing characters. By the time that heroic character dies, so many others—good and bad—have gone before him, you can't guess how things will turn out. You can only hope. And, I think, the ability of that novel to cause me to invest such emotion in it is the reason I list it as one of my favorites.

TEXTURIZING WITH TIE-BACKS

Here you employ the finest craft that you can summon to your writing. You make connections, both subtle and obvious, between separate events in your novel, engaging the reader in the kind of interactive participation that makes an audience rave about your fiction.

Here's a checklist of such techniques and some examples of how they might be employed. Using this brainstormer tool, you ought to be able to enrich any tale you tell.

Texturize using a seemingly trivial detail. Writers often drop a small object or event into the narrative, especially early in the story. Left in plain sight, characters and readers overlook it until it comes into play at some critical moment late in the story. This technique works wonderfully when the detail isn't *too* obvious. Remember in vintage films how the director would subject such a detail to an extreme close-up? And just in case we didn't get the possibility that it would later play an important part in the story, the soundtrack hit you in the eardrums with a crescendo of ominous music. Nowadays you need to hire a crew of investigators to watch the film with you to pick up such minor details.

But the best trivial details work when they have been planted so well that when they crop up, you instantly recognize them and even give yourself a slap on the forehead for overlooking them earlier.

In writing a first draft, you usually don't have a handle on all the details, trivial or otherwise. That's what makes it so convenient to texturize with tie-backs. How do you do it? Simply go straight to the climactic or other important scenes of your story, usually toward the end of the book. Find a detail that's critical. Then see if you can locate an earlier spot to plant that detail in plain sight.

Texturize with seemingly small words and ideas. I like this technique the best of all the texturizing devices because you can enrich the manuscript by using them in a number of variations. Here are two:

1. **Repeat a distinctive thought or phrase of dialogue in the story.** This connects an earlier part of the story to a later one without having to rely on an overt transitional device. Television shows frequently overuse this technique, giving one character a pet phrase that he repeats ad nauseum. One way to vary the device is to give it a different meaning each time it's used. On *Seinfeld*, all the principal characters would use the same phrase, often with different meaning, all in the same scene, creating a device all of its own.

2. **Plant the story's ending in the first thousand words.** Simply review your ending. Transplant a telling word or thought directly into the beginning of the story. Massage the context so it doesn't become a crude giveaway, but rather a well-crafted throwaway line that turns out to be not so throwaway after all. Between the beginning and the end, don't fall victim to the temptation to continue hammering away on that singular thought or phrase. Let it lie. Clever readers will pick up on it.

Texturize using consistency of character. Both motivation and cause and effect come into play during texturizing. Review each character's goals and motivations. Then take a look at every situation where the character comes into play. Satisfy yourself and your readership that the character's behavior is consistent with her motivation. And that consistently motivated behavior causes predictable effects. Look at small situations as closely as you examine the big events. Look for opportunities to reaffirm character consistency in the smallest ways.

Finally, look for changes as characters develop, either as they grow or deteriorate. Characters often do change. Your job as the writer demands that any change is consistent with sufficient motivation and not just a whim of the author. Then, once that change is established, decide whether the character remains consistent to the end of the story or whether she backslides. Both are elements of effective texturizing.

Texturize using conflicting points of view. This is another favorite device because it lends itself to creating art in your writing. When you tie back characters who are in conflict to an event that involved both of them, look for opportunities to show how they differ in their recollections. When a significant event occurs within a novel, it should not be forgotten by the characters. And characters in conflict should remain in conflict even during the memory of that earlier scene.

Texturize using that element of surprise. Nothing texturizes like surprise. As you revise your fiction, take a close look at scenes that might be too methodical, too predictable. It's one thing for you to remain true to plausible motivation and believable cause and effect. It's quite another for your story to plod forward, technically correct but boring.

I'm not talking about trick endings where you unmask the narrator as the heroic character's pet kitten. That's too stupid for words. And I don't mean you should pull the rug out from under your readers at the climactic scene or other major moments.

Rather, I suggest you use one of the strategies we discussed in chapter 1 to find an unexpected ending to a scene, an unpredictable sentence to finish off a paragraph or an unusual word choice to color a sentence. Surprise your readers. Better yet, surprise your characters. Best of all, when you can, surprise even yourself.

If you use this checklist faithfully as a way of looking at your writing, you will find ways to improve it, moving down the path toward the big book. Even if you don't sell the piece in a big book, in the end, you'll have improved the quality of your work.

> "Effective description occurs only when the naked eye merges with the imaginative eye."
>
> —REBECCA McCLANAHAN

The Sixth Habit of Highly Effective Writers

Inventing advanced images

I groan every time I read this writing advice or any of its clones: "Employ accurate description to enrich your writing." You might as well tell a sculptor to use sharp chisels.

Just in case you think my advice is just as useless, namely, *create lively images in place of static description*, I have a few exercises that will help you sharpen your skills.

The Brainstormer's Advanced Imagery Video Exercise

1. **Find a video of a film that closely parallels** the kind of work you want to write in your fiction. Use *Fargo* if you want to publish quirky drama. Rent *One True Thing* if you're interested in writing about dramatic family relationships. And so on. You might find it useful to experiment with a video in which the story has been adapted from a published novel. If you can find it in video, its original novel and a published screenplay—all in your area of interest—you've hit a home run.

2. **Review the video,** looking for one important scene in each of the following categories:
   - **A silent scene.** A powerful scene or portion of a major scene without

dialogue. Make sure it involves at least one major character. If you have chosen a movie adapted from a novel, see if you can find that scene within the novel for later comparison. Don't read the scene; just find it.

- **A scene of dialogue.** A powerful scene or portion of a major scene in which two characters, at least one of them a master character, talk to each other. If it's a memorable film, almost any conversation will involve conflict. That's fine. But try to find a scene that doesn't rely on intense physical action. Once again, it's best when you can find how the author originally wrote that scene in the novel from which the film is adapted.

- **An action scene involving major characters and dramatic physical play.** If you find intense dialogue, no problem. No need for car chases or gun battles. But even if the actors merely storm around the room pointing fingers and scowling, that is action enough. Once again, find it in the novel if that's possible.

3. **Novelize the silent scene.** That's right, just watch the pictures on film and re-create those images in writing. You might want to review the standards we discussed in the ACIDS test. Try to be brief, accurate and active, even when talking about static pictures. Stretch your abilities to find fresh ways of looking at familiar scenery. The wonderful thing about this brainstormer exercise is you don't have to invent images out of whole cloth. What's more, you won't be searching your memory banks to recall an experience of your own. You don't even have to rely on a static photograph or picture of the setting. Once your imagination is freed from having to invent or recall events, you can concentrate on simply creating the image in words as it appears to you on-screen. When an artist uses a sketchbook to capture elements of a setting some distance from her studio, she's doing much the same thing. She's literally capturing aspects of an image. If she doesn't return to the setting with a canvas, easel and paints, at least she'll be able to refer to the sketchbook, plug into her memories and produce images. That's what you'll be doing.

When you're finished novelizing, make the following comparisons:

- **If possible, see how the screenwriter handled this scene.** Of your novelization, the original author's published version and the screenplay, the film script is likely to be the briefest. And it will address only the most significant aspects of that setting. The screenplay uses shorthand terms to describe the elements that the writer believes he must convey to the director and cinematographer as being most important. That gives you the chance to see if you identified the same important aspects as you created your own image. How did you do?

- **Compare yours to the original author's published version.** Did the screenwriter and author agree? And did your descriptions fall into line with the author's intent? You needn't be too hard on yourself in making these comparisons. After all, you're probably putting your writing up against polished professionals who already had the benefit of editing and best-seller status.

4. **Novelize the scene of dialogue in the video.** Don't get ahead of me here. Follow these steps:

- **Capture only the spoken lines, word for word,** from the film, not the novel or the screenplay. Enclose the spoken remarks in quotation marks, but use only a minimum of attribution or not at all. That is, identify the speaker only as much as necessary. For instance, if a man and woman are speaking, use "he said" or "she said," but only occasionally. If three or more people are talking, or if both people are of the same gender, use a modified script techniques such as,

> Sam: "I don't understand you, Diane."
> Norm: "Why not?"
> Sam: "This is insane."
> Diane: "No, you're insane."

To get the most out of this exercise, transcribe at least two or three pages of dialogue exchanges.

- **Rewind the video to the beginning of the scene.** Mute the volume.
- **Play the scene without sound.** Watch for action that accompanies the language in the dialogue you have captured. Notice the emotions and other images supplied by the actors. Examine telling images going on in the background of the primary action. Pay attention to elements on film that the director and cinematographer highlighted by lighting, camera angle, focus, cuts, close-up and other techniques.

- **Rewind and play back the scene as many times as necessary as you write the essential narration.** Don't merely confine yourself to telling what happens next. Don't only supply mechanical transitions. Observe images. Capture those images in words and supply the lines an author might write between sections of dialogue. You needn't write half a novel to get the benefit of this exercise. In fact, it's better if you stick to a minimalistic approach. Don't interfere with the continuity of the dialogue, which you ought to be quite familiar with after transcribing.

- **Compare your final product** to both the screenwriter's and the original author's. Once again the screenwriter is most likely to have the briefest of passages. He will have mentioned only the images and emotions that are critical to the success of the scene. In fact, most actors and directors will reject any attempt by the screenwriter to tell them how to do their jobs. So when you see any directing instructions in the screenwriter's script, you know it's critical.

How did you do in comparison to the original author? Use the same standards that you applied for pats on the back in the silent scene.

5. **Finally, perform the same exercise on the action scene.** Begin with a transcription of pure dialogue as you did in the last exercise. Then create action and images from what you see on-screen with the volume on. Action scenes often require noisy sound effects. Dialogue might not be the most essential element within the scene, so the images you create often will be more violent and sensory.

   When you have finished, make the same comparisons as before. The screenwriter might well have written half a page or more describing the action that will take place in high-intensity moments of his film. And the original author might devote many pages to suspenseful scenes. The exercise, even if it requires you to write several thousand words you can never publish as your own, will be a valuable experience in your personal writing development.

Let's discuss a handful of techniques you can apply to your own writing. Let's revise a low-intensity scene in a way that gets the point across using an economy of words but creating a powerful effect.

The Brainstormer's Guide to Advanced Imagery Techniques

1. Replace labored descriptions with a single image.

The ice fog distracted him with its sparkle, its glitter, its dazzle. It was like a shower of shimmering, weightless particles of glass.

Becomes:

The ice fog glittered like a dust storm of glass.

We used nouns and verbs instead of adjectives. *Glittered* includes all the notions of *sparkle*, *shimmer* and *dazzle*. One sentence replaces two.

2. Replace strings of microscopic details with one small but telling image. Note how *a dust storm of glass* doesn't need to be clarified as a shower of shimmering and weightless particles anymore. And notice how a dust storm suggests an element of danger, which comes into play later.

3. Set static situations into motion as dynamic sensory images.

He felt like a kid again.

Becomes:

He opened his mouth to collect the particles. He couldn't feel them, but he could taste them. And surprise, they tasted like dirt.

Precise verbs and concrete nouns in the active voice. And a peculiar jolt of finding that an ice-palace scene tastes like dirt. Now instead of the ice fog distracting him as it would a child, he's doing things that affect his senses, just as a kid would (and without saying so).

4. Emphasize character awareness over author awareness.

He should have known better than to dally in the cold while he was still a mile away from camp.

This might be the narrator speaking, but as it stands now, without context, the voice sounds like the author chiding the character—treating him like a kid, in fact. It's an easy fix:

He knew better than to dally while he was still a mile away from camp.

What does this change have to do with imagery? Written this way, the passage confirms character awareness. It emphasizes the sensory effects of preceding images. And it sets up the punch line to have more punch because you'll read *how the character experienced the action and imagery* rather than *how the author reported the experience.*

5. Tie the images to the overall ACIDS package.

But he fooled around until the sun came out and brought him to his senses. He shielded his eyes and set off toward camp, but before he'd gone even half a mile, he was snow-blind.

If you read the original versions of this exercise in order, you get a feeling of: *So this looked like that. Then the other happened. Then another thing happened. Until finally the guy was blind.* The scene feels like a hasty ad-lib, an unpolished first draft.

6. Above all, don't overwrite imagery. Avoid images that stand in the way of action, conflict and dialogue.

Nothing distracts a reader more than stopping a story's momentum to describe. In the next example, I'll exaggerate an even more egregious sin: interrupting dialogue.

She found him kneeling on the trail.

"Ross?" she called to him, breaking into an awkward hippety-hop run through the knee-deep snow. "Are you all right?"

He straightened up and tried to get to his feet, but he was trapped, waist-deep in a snowdrift, a low wall that had begun drift to his shoulders. "Sara? Is that you?"

Becomes:

She found him kneeling on the trail in a waist-deep drift, his fists pressed into his eyes.

"Ross?" she called. "Are you all right?"

"Sara? Is that you?"

Two things. One, let your people talk. Two, don't belabor a point by endlessly recasting an image. There's no need to trip up both characters in snowdrifts.

7. Try cutting imagery altogether. Have you ever considered eliminating passages altogether in your writing? Using the hidden text feature of your word processor, eliminate a selection. Do you find anything missing between the previous scene and the successive scene? If you can revise either with a few transitional words, consider leaving the intervening passage out. Ask yourself whether you'd like to keep it, but only because there's a personal gem of writing in it that you cannot live without. I suggest having it both ways. Delete the passage from your text and save it in a separate file for later. Maybe you can use it in your current piece of fiction. Or maybe in your next novel.

My agent once made a deep impression on me in a discussion about *The Bonfire of the Vanities*. She said, "Sometimes I wish Tom Wolfe wouldn't describe so much and in such excruciating detail. Sometimes I wish he'd just leave a little bit to my own imagination."

Best advice about imagery I've ever gotten.

8. **Bring your imagery to life with the effective use of dialogue.** Which leads us to the next chapter.

> "In fiction, the characters must always get right to the point when they talk."
> —DEAN KOONTZ

CHAPTER 15

The Seventh Habit of Highly Effective Writers

Writing stunning dialogue

I f you want to learn how to write superb dialogue, study the best plays and films of our literature. If possible, study them both in performance (live or video) and in print. Read plays and screenplays to get the feel of the writing on the page, and, in the best scripts, what type of writing it is—pure dialogue unadulterated by music, actor expression, pictures or narrative transition supplied by an author. Read it aloud to yourself to get a flavor of the emotion contained within the word choices made by the writer. Playwrights and screenwriters who succeed at their craft are probably the best writers of dialogue you can study. By looking at such refined gold, you can learn from them more than from any ten books that tell you how to write dialogue.

Let's dig into dialogue.

The Brainstormer's Dialogue Exercise

If you want to advance your study to the graduate level, follow these steps.

- ☐ Rent a video of a play or film that's best noted for its writing rather than its pretty actors and pictures. Any nominees in the Tony Awards or the screenwriting award in the Oscars will do.
- ☐ Buy a copy of the screenplay of the film or play.
- ☐ Decide which scenes of dialogue make the strongest impression on you. If you can't come by a copy of the screenplay, take notes as you watch the film.

☐ Return to those scenes and transcribe them if you don't have the screenplay. Print out the transcriptions so you have hard copy in hand for the next step.

☐ Watch your chosen scene again with the sound muted. Read all the parts of the dialogue to yourself as the video plays silently. Don't get ahead of or fall behind the pace of the film. Try to lip-sync each actor's part.

You'll be impressed by this exercise for several reasons. Not only will you reap the benefit of the screenwriter's words, but also a director's influence on how those words are accompanied by pictures and action. Not to mention the effect of the language spoken by professional actors and all the decisions that are made about word choice, diction, timing, emphasis, pace and pauses—in essence, how everything comes together and flows in the performance. All without narrator intrusion. Especially in plays, dialogue rather than special effects carries the story. Learn from them.

Let's take a time-out for a couple of quick puzzlers. See if you can identify the actors or characters and the films, plays or televisions shows in which these lines were delivered. (You'll find the answers on page 278.)

You can't handle the truth.

Kill Claudio.

I'm your number one fan.

I can eat fifty hard-boiled eggs.

Is that your final answer?

You could probably quote a dozen lines from current movies, lines that have become catch phrases that fall into use, then overuse in the popular culture. I think even more remarkable are those simple, plain expressions that strike sparks in your recollection because the wording is distinctive, and you instantly connect them with images from a film, play or superb piece of fiction. That's the kind of dialogue you should be striving to write. Memorable dialogue.

Rather than study dialogue that other, more brilliant writers than us have created let's storm our brains and create some distinctive dialogue of our own, shall we?

Eliminating the Basic Bugaboos of Bad Dialogue

Try this exercise to sharpen your dialogue-writing skills by measuring techniques you probably have already learned through experience and from other writing handbooks and seminars. After we get through this drill, we'll tackle more advanced techniques.

The exchange takes place among three characters. You won't find anything overtly exciting in the passage, although it does have the potential for tension and action. But don't try to rewrite it. Simply identify one problem in each segment of dialogue, preferably the most serious problem. Then, again without rewriting, correct the problem and go onto the next segment. If a succeeding segment contains two errors, including one of a type you've already corrected, fix both. We'll meet again at the bottom of this exercise and proceed. And, oh yes—add necessary quotation marks in the proper places.

DIALOGUE EXERCISE

> *I'm leaving now, Wilma stated.*
>
> *I wonder if you should go at all, her mother countered.*
>
> *You're not going! And that's all there is to it, her father said angrily.*
>
> *Wilma snorted, I've made up my mind, and you can't stop me.*
>
> *Oh, dear, said her mother. She began rocking ever quicker and quicker in her rocking chair, unable to decide whether anything she might say could change her daughter's mind without sending her husband over the edge.*
>
> *Her father moved to the doorway and declared, Over my dead body. He folded his arms. He stood looking squarely at Wilma, taking a deep breath, standing up on his toes to make himself look bigger, daring her to try anything physical.*
>
> *Wilma walked across the room and stood before him. Good-bye, Father.*
>
> *Good-bye, Wilma. He stood aside.*
>
> *I love you both, she said. Then she was gone.*

Correcting the Common Bugaboos

> *I'm leaving now, Wilma stated.*

Change to:

> *"I'm leaving now," Wilma said.*

Simple as that. Any reputable writing handbook will tell you *said* is an invisible word that doesn't require dozens of synonyms in writing lines of dialogue. Almost any word besides *said* breaks the rhythm of a dialogue exchange. If you want to break that rhythm intentionally, fine. Do so. Otherwise use *said*.

I wonder if you should go at all, her mother countered.

Change to:

"I wonder if you should go at all," her mother said.

Same solution, different problem. The words inside the quotes contain the notion of contradiction, weak as it is. No reason to use *countered* as a tacked-on concept in the attribution. Again, don't break the rhythm of a potentially smooth exchange.

You're not going! And that's all there is to it, her father said angrily.

Change to:

"You're not going. And that's all there is to it," her father said.

I made two fixes to a single problem. I removed the exclamation point because writers should never use punctuation to indicate high emotion in a statement. The exclamation point used in that example is an attempt to prop up weak language inside the quotes. Same with the adverb *angrily.* If the line of dialogue doesn't carry the emotional freight, not even a dozen adjectives and adverbs can move the train.

Wilma snorted, I've made up my mind, and you can't stop me.

Change to:

"I've made up my mind, and you can't stop me."

Here, one fix corrects two problems. You can't grin, sneer, chuckle or snort words. All you can do is look like an amateur trying. If you don't believe me, snort the problem sentence into your handkerchief. Convinced? As to the second problem, the context inside the quotes tells us who's speaking. No need to repeat it with an attribution.

"Oh, dear," said her mother. She began rocking ever quicker and quicker in her rocking chair, unable to decide whether anything she

might say could change her daughter's mind without sending her hus-band over the edge.

Change to:

"Oh, dear," said her mother.

I confess, I planted an entire army of sins in the second sentence to distract you. If you engaged in fixing the redundancy between *rocking* and *rocking chair* and the repetition of *quicker* and *quicker* and the internal monologue of the mother, who's clearly a minor character in this scene, you missed the point. As would any reader. The problem includes all of those things because the writer went off on a tangent. As we discussed in the previous chapter, don't break up the continuity of dialogue exchanges by extraneous action, excessive imagery, distracting narration or letting the characters muse. Sustain the momentum of the scene by eliminating everything useless.

Her father moved to the doorway and declared, "Over my dead body." He folded his arms. He stood looking squarely at Wilma, taking a deep breath, standing up on his toes to make himself look bigger, daring her to try anything physical.

Change to:

Her father blocked the doorway. "Over my dead body."

Assuming that Wilma is the most important character in this exchange because she initiates the confrontation, I deleted all the narrative devices that stand in her way. I simply allowed the father to stand in her way instead. That allowed me to use the line inside the quotes without attribution.

DIALOGUE RULE OF THUMB: When one character acts or thinks in a scene and that scene also contains a segment of dialogue, there's no need to attribute the dialogue. Your readers will assume that the character speaks the line.

After all, once her father blocked the doorway, who else inside the room would say those words? If you determined that the father's words are a cliché, congratulations. I agree. I could argue that it's not the writer resorting to the cliché but the character. But I won't.

Wilma walked across the room and stood before him. "Good-bye, Father."

Change to:

Wilma walked across the room and stood before him, chin thrust at his chest.

We have reached the moment of truth in this scene, the confrontation between father and daughter. Words inside quotes aren't necessary when body language will do better.

"Good-bye, Wilma." He stood aside.

Change to:

He folded his arms and stood looking squarely at Wilma, taking a deep breath, standing up on his toes to make himself look bigger.
She raised her head and stared into the eyes that dared her to take him on. She did, but not in the way he could have withstood her, not physically. She simply enveloped his eyes in hers and touched his soul. He surrendered in stages, first blinking, then dropping his head to break her grip on him. He swallowed hard, wavered and stood aside.

Perhaps I've overdone this revision, but I did so to make a point. In the original problem line, the change in attitude was all too sudden and apparently unmotivated. The original situation had all those lines of narration interfering with the continuity of the exchange. Yet at the decision point, with no explanation, the father changed his mind and spoke too quickly, making himself and the writer look like morons.

The revision gives you an image of silent confrontation—again, no dialogue. Finally, believably, he gives in to Wilma. The correction allows a reader to take a pause as the action plays out subliminally—during a logical pause in the dialogue exchange.

Leave the final line unchanged.

"I love you both," she said. Then she was gone.

Let's move on to write some advanced dialogue. I'm going to give you a check-list of the most important elements to consider in writing your dialogue. As with the basic considerations we just discussed, I'll give you a moderate to good line of dialogue. You try to revise it to a better line. We'll discuss and look at a possible revision that I suggest. Then you make a second revision. At the end of this segment, I'll reduce all this wisdom to a single checklist that you can copy and use anytime you decide to revise a section of dialogue in your own fiction.

Conflict

Conflict ought to be the decisive consideration in whether to use dialogue at all. As Dean Koontz says, in fiction, people should always get to the point. And, as Richard Walter (*Screenwriting*, Plume) argues, they should always argue.

Check your own work. If you have used dialogue exchanges simply to give information, you're probably making a mistake. The one thing that makes the ears perk in overhearing somebody else's conversation is conflict.

So use it in your dialogue. If you prefer to give information inside quotes, find a way to incorporate conflict. Otherwise, do the job using some other narrative device. Here are some possibilities for you to consider in using conflict to spice up dialogue by incorporating conflict into every exchange.

16 BRAINSTORMER TECHNIQUES FOR PUMPING UP THE DIALOGUE
The following are overall approaches to conflict. You might have minute word changes or additions—small fixes—that accomplish each.

- ☐ **Overt aggressiveness.** I doubt you need my advice on how to write action or language that inflicts or threatens some form of abuse.

  She pulled a stun gun and pointed it. "One more step, and you're a break-dancer."

- ☐ **Passive aggressiveness.** A far more interesting form of hostility, in which a seemingly submissive character can wreak havoc on a dominant one.

  She set the casserole on the table. Gray chunks floated up in steaming chartreuse sauce. "Tuna and beet goulash, Mother Parker."
  "I hate beets."
  "Oh, really? Randall says it's your favorite."

- ☐ **Provocation.** When one party in the scene taunts or dares another, you can achieve two levels of conflict: one directly in the challenge, and another in the event the challenge refers to.

"Ron," he said. "You have to confront her now. If you don't, she won't stop calling you."

☐ **Undercurrents.** Using this device, conflict occurs but remains beneath the surface.

He raised his glass. "A toast to our undying love." He said it without so much as a smile.

Here the conflict is not directly in the words as in the contrast to the inappropriate expression.

☐ **Ambiguity.** The reader and characters might not be able to decide whether conflict might actually be taking place beneath the surface. Only the writer knows for sure, and since conflict is going to take place in every written dialogue exchange, conflict it is.

He poured. "Taste this Zin. It's to die for."

If a later scene reveals the truth of that declaration, the ambiguity is revealed and resolved.

☐ **Subliminal conflict.** The characters engage in what they think it's innocent banter. Readers know that disaster looms right around the bend in the river. You know what I'm talking about. Every horror movie in existence uses this technique.

☐ **Word choice.** Clipped Anglo-Saxon words can suggest conflict. All the best curse words in English derive their power from the Anglo-Saxon sounds.

Contrast:

"Would you appreciate having your gluteous maximus impacted by my podiatric appendage?"

With:

"Want me to kick your butt?"

☐ **Sentence length.** Abrupt sentences elevate conflict. Same with strings of abrupt sentences

For example, this:

"I don't like your attitude and if you don't apologize—and promptly— I'm afraid we'll have to stop seeing each other."

As opposed to this:

"I don't like your attitude. Apologize. Now. Or else we're through."

☐ **Paragraphing.** Short paragraphing suggests higher emotions, if for no other reason than readers read them faster. Higher emotions hint at conflict. Combining short paragraphs and short sentences can increase the effect. Read the previous paragraph, then this revision:

"I don't like your attitude."
He looked down.
"Apologize."
He studied his nails.
"Now."
He found something to gnaw at on one finger.
"Or else we're through."
He sighed and held out the finger to her. "I need an emergency manicure, don't you think?"

☐ **Rhythm.** Rearranging words can suggest conflict, especially if you create snap at the ends of sentences and paragraphs.

Compare:

"Listen when I'm talking to you."

To:

"When I talk, you listen."

☐ **Repetition.** Key phrases add emphasis when repeated. However, be aware if you're doing this one to death.

"When I talk, you listen and listen good."

☐ **Put it in the affirmative.** I mentioned this in chapter 8 on editing. Which of the following suggests a higher level of conflict?

"I'm not kidding."

Or:

"I'm serious."

☐ **Imperative forms** add emphasis to the most neutral statements. They pump up any term with potential for conflict, especially when you use several techniques at once.
Notice the difference between:

"I don't think you should tell her the truth."

And:

"Don't tell her the truth. Lie. Lie your tail off."

☐ **Typographical emphasis.** Do **NOT** rely on this "AMATEURISH" technique!!!!

☐ **Body language.** Overt actions and passive behaviors indicate conflict.

"I don't exactly hate you," she said, blinking with only one eye.

☐ **Character recognition.** Neither the author nor the narrator gives away the hostility, but one character sees conflict in an otherwise innocent situation. By saying so, he tips off everybody else.

"You say you've forgiven me but I can see the muscle cramps in your temples."

Anytime I present a seminar, this is the point at which somebody raises a hand. Before word passes from her mouth to my ears, I know that she has been sitting there all along mentally arguing with my first bold statement: Conflict must be present either overtly or potentially in every exchange of dialogue—people in fiction must always argue. The question always comes out:

I'm writing a (women's, children's, senior's—you fill in the blank) novel about (romance, family values, virtues, spirituality, kittens, puppies—

again, fill in the blank) because there's already too much violence in the popular culture. I want to write about good things. Happy things. So there's no room for conflict in my dialogue.

Good luck. I suppose you could tie up a woman, child or senior and make them to stay put as you force-read your story to them. Short of that, nobody in the reading or listening world, let alone the publishing industry, is going to pay any attention to your work, let alone pay money for it. And, if you have to use bondage to acquire an audience, that in itself is a form of conflict, isn't it?

That's what I want to say, although I never do.

I do say this, though. Conflict sells. More so than sex, which in all its forms and treatments usually can be condensed into conflict anyhow.

I doubt you can name any title or category in commercial fiction in any medium that is not bound up, so to speak, with conflict. Conflict occurs in:

- The most wholesome family shows—*Father Knows Best*
- Animated features—*Cinderella, Tarzan, The Lion King*, you name it
- Obscenity-free fiction—anything by Jan Karon or Danielle Steel
- Prize-winning children's stories—*Shiloh* by Phyllis Reynolds Naylor
- The Bible—everywhere from Genesis to Revelation

In a word, everywhere.

You see, hostility, violence and strife aren't by themselves objectionable in fiction. True, some forms of writing glorify such things and even worse things. But that's not what I'm saying in this chapter. I'm saying two things:

Thing one—Good characters can't be interesting unless they triumph over something, normally evil things. This involves conflict. The stronger the conflict, the more precious the victory. It's one of the more fundamental facts of life. You can look at up. The Bible is a good place to start.

Thing two—One of the best places to exploit conflict is in dialogue exchanges.

Discussion over. Let's move on to the other elements we can use to improve our writing of dialogue.

Miscellaneous Brainstormer Tips to Writing Dialogue

Always keep these principles in mind:

Economy of words. I have alluded to this characteristic in the earlier discussions, but let me address some specifics of the point.

- Characters shouldn't "speechify." Be wary of writing any text inside quotation marks the moment the speech reaches the third line. If it's a personality trait of the character to be long-winded, fine. Even at that, don't overdo it. Break up long speeches with action, images or conflict-laden responses from another character.
- Don't let characters talk as we do in real life. All writing manuals agree. No *wells*, *okays*, or other forms of chitchat, such as:

> *"How are you?"*
> *"I'm fine, how are you?"*
> *"Fine, I guess."*
> *"You guess?"*
> *"Yeah."*
> *"You gonna get to the point?"*

That's what I want to know.

- Avoid clutter. I'm talking about the space between lines of your speakers. Let the dialogue flow. Read the following example, first as it is, then only the first line in each paragraph. Get the point?

> *"Spit it out," she said, fiddling with his necktie. She seemed unable to make eye contact with him. That confirmed it for him. He thought he'd be on safe ground telling her why he'd been so cool toward her lately.*
> *He yanked the tie from her hands. "I don't trust you." He adjusted the knot and made sure the point of the tie touched the middle of his belt buckle.*

Precision in word choice. Study every line of dialogue to ensure it says exactly what you intended to say.

A good exercise would be to return to a technique we used when transcribing video. Create a backup file of the scene that includes dialogue exchanges. Remove or put into hidden text everything that is not inside the quotation marks. Then try to carry the conversation only by the language inside the quotes, with no helping phrases outside the quotes.

Imagery, both inside and outside the quotation marks. Paint images. Once you condition your readers to love the dialogue exchanges, your story will move faster.

Rhythm, pace and snap that mirrors the master story model. To create memorable dialogue exchanges, tell miniature stories in every scene, especially those with dialogue.

Start out strong, never boring. Consider competing points of view (conflict) as reversals. End the scene with snap, a high emotional content. For an example of how this works in the most innocuous exchanges, go back to the illustration we used earlier, the girl leaving the house (see pages 252-255).

Irony. From the overt to the subtle, irony acts like an injection of adrenaline, pumping life into dialogue.

Overt:

> *"I'm such an idiot," she said.*
> *"Yes," he said. "You are."*

Middling (with thanks to Ring Lardner):

> *"Are we lost, daddy?" I asked.*
> *"Shut up," he explained.*

Subtle (I think):

> *"I'm such an idiot," she said.*
> *He didn't answer.*

Distinctiveness of Voice

We've traveled a long way in this discussion about dialogue. Even at that, I doubt we've scratched the surface of the possibilities for improving your fiction by writing powerful, effective exchanges. I do know one quality above all others separates the best-sellers from the also-rans, and if you can master this skill, you can overcome any deficiency in anything we've already talked about.

Any writing genius you care to name, from Shakespeare to Toni Morrison, derives much of their reputation from the ability to create a unique voice for every character. As you read their material, you realize who is speaking by the attitude, word choice, pacing, phrasing, power of vocabulary and so on.

You know when you are reading an amateur's work when every character thinks and sounds alike, deriving their lack of individuality by adopting the same points of view and voice as the author.

To help you avoid this, it pleases me to introduce a new brainstormer tool.

THE BRAINSTORMER'S DISTINCTIVE VOICE TOOL

To help you remember this tool of voice, I've identified five qualities, all beginning with the same letter as *voice*.

Vocabulary. The word choices made by the character, pet phrases they use and their general vocabulary level. Give your characters distinctive words.

Verbosity. On a scale of brevity to the opposite extreme. You can create a distinctive voice just by controlling the length of a character's thoughts and speeches.

Velocity. The pace and rhythm of a character's speech and thoughts. This is reflected in how you arrange words, sentences and ideas.

Viewpoint. First, this is the overall attitude toward elements and characters in the story. Second, it's the literal point of view and omniscience allowed that character by the author.

Venom. You might consider this a quality within the overall category of viewpoint. I included it so we might isolate the attitude of a character, her emotional intensity and the capacity for mood swings. When you're talking about emotion, you hit upon a central issue in the character's makeup. I don't want that quality mixed up with other, more academic or mechanical considerations.

Using this tool to identify qualities you can jot down on your character cards, you can establish distinctive voices for every character in your novel. Then, when a character comes into a scene after having been absent for fifty pages or so, you can refresh your memory about what makes him unique.

> "Never try to walk across a river just because it has an average depth of four feet."
> —MARTIN FRIEDMAN

CHAPTER 16

Bonus! The Eighth Habit of Highly Effective Writers

Sketching action into the white space

I f you have studied any art like painting, sculpting, or photography, you already understand the concept of including white space or negative space into the composition of an image.

The technique I admire most in the true artists among our writers is the ability to communicate a point seemingly without writing about it. Or, as I call it, writing in the white space.

Take the quote at the top of this chapter. The irony in that sentence comes from what's not written. And the charm comes from the reader's participation in supplying the necessary information in the white space of the statement.

A more familiar example of writing in the white space is the description written as a reflection. Consider the obvious, outright narrative description, as in:

He was tall, six-feet-two, with a nose to match—tall, thin and straight.

That's the author talking.

The Mirror-Imaging Technique

The writer bounces an image literally off a mirror:

He caught sight of his six-feet-two reflection in the window of a bagel shop, paused and studied his thin, straight nose both in profile and straight on. Straight on, he decided, always show his nose to her straight on. Never from the side.

Same information, different approach—one that gives the facts without stopping the story as if to say, *I'm going to describe somebody now.* At the small cost of a word increase, we see the reflection through the character's eyes, not the author's keyboard. We see action, both actual and implied—turning his head to study his profile is suggested. Plus we learn something about the character's personality: He's vain about his nose.

That's writing in the white space.

Let's move on to some other common and uncommon techniques of writing in the white space.

The Smash Cut

The term *smash cut* comes from film writers. It implies a jarring, abrupt scene change. For instance, the closing shot in one scene might be a beautiful woman sipping her Folgers as the red sun rises over the mountains. Smash cut to the red fireball of an earsplitting terrorist explosion over the mountainous landscape of a city skyline. Get it?

The fiction writer's smash cut can save a lot of miles in writing transition and explanation of how a character got from one place to the other. The best way to illustrate this is by example.

Here's a chapter's ending sentence:

He was so proud of himself and couldn't wait to hear what Mama would say when he told her what he had done.

Followed by a page break and the opening of a new chapter with:

"You imbecile," Mama said. "You scant-wit, slack-jawed, mouth-breathing, knuckle-dragging idiot."

Nothing but the turn of a page stands between the character's wondering what Mama will say and what Mama actually says. No taxi ride. No bus transfer. No subway graffiti. Not even a description of how a proud son broke the news to his incredulous mother. The writer assumed *you* could assume anything you wanted between his wondering and her reacting. The result's better, too.

DIALOGUE THAT ELIMINATES THE NEED FOR NARRATION

As much as we've discussed dialogue already, I do want to point out its capability of helping you write in the white space. As an example, take a look at Mama's line of dialogue above. The word choice indicates enough emotion. There's no need to say *Mama said in disbelief* or *Mama said angrily.*

LETTING THE CHARACTER TELL

The conventional wisdom holds that you should always show, not tell. But not always. Here's an example where telling works well:

> *"What?"*
>
> *"What do you mean, what?"*
>
> *"I mean, why are you wearing that stupid smile?"*

There's no author to tell you character two is smiling, no narrator to comment narratively that it's a stupid smile. Both drop out of sight to allow character one to tell you that the smile exists and that he considers it stupid.

SHOWING BY CONSEQUENCE RATHER THAN ACTION

Sometimes you can achieve a powerful effect by skipping over the action and showing the result.

> *"I told you not to talk to me like that, Randy," she said. "I told you what I was going to do if you talked to me like that again."*
>
> *He blew a stream of air between his lower lip and upper teeth. The sound reminded him. "Get me a brew."*
>
> *"What did you say?"*
>
> *"You deaf? I said get off your butt and get me—"*
>
> *He cradled his nose in his hands, huffing blood through his fingers and down his elbows.*
>
> *"See?" she said, standing over him, her fist still balled. "See what you made me do?"*

No wind up, no punch, just the punch's effect.

THE NARRATOR TALKS TO THE CHARACTER, NOT THE READER

Did you notice this in the previous characters' dialogue exchange? The narrator resisted the temptation to say, "The sound reminded him of a beer can snapping open." That would be telling the reader. Instead, the character said, "Get me a brew." Most readers would be able to supply the notion that the sound of blowing between upper teeth and lower lips can sound like a beer opening. If some didn't, they didn't miss anything important. If they did, they can feel a bit superior to everybody else.

DO, DON'T TELL

Once in a while, if you keep your eyes open, you'll find an opportunity to exploit an interactive narrative device.

> One-thousand-one, one-thousand-two, one-thousand-three.
> *He clenched his eyes and plugged his ears. Any second now. She should see the snake.*
> One-thousand-four.
> *She should be screaming by now.*

Rather than tell that the character counted to three, the narrator does the counting. Thus, the reader counts along with the character.

LET THE READER SETTLE DISPUTES ON HIS OWN

Occasionally, keep your narrator above the fray. Allow one character's point of view. Let another character hold a contrary opinion. Don't settle the argument for the reader. Leave the outcome ambiguous. The negative space you create let's the reader participate in your fiction by supplying her own result. An example from film might be found inside that briefcase that glowed every time it was opened in *Pulp Fiction*. What *was* that thing?

101 MISCELLANEOUS TECHNIQUES FOR WRITING IN THE WHITE SPACE

I have toyed with this concept of writing in the white space for so long that sometimes I think I'm risking style over substance. After all, hundreds of writers have proven that straightforward description and plain narration can succeed in publishing fiction. You need not rely on sleight of hand and tricks of prose to create an appealing work.

With that in mind, here are a few more tricks I have resorted to but have not named, all taken from that yet unpublished novel *Love Busters, Inc.*, the one about a con artist who starts the business breaking up relationships for hire.

Miscellaneous Technique No. 1

> *The old man says, "I'd like a word with you, Tugster."*
> "Yes, sir." Wit. He says he'd like a word wit me. I'm dead. Surely. Didn't I see a movie where bricklayer was a euphemism for hit man?

I used the word *wit* to illustrate that the bricklayer had an accent, without actually giving him one between the quote marks.

Miscellaneous Technique No. 2

> *"I'm Andrea Barron. And your last name is—?" Her hands windmill between us.*
> *"Grey. With an e. Tug. Grey."*
> *"Why are you speaking so slowly, Mr. Tug Grey?" A lift of both her flute and one full eyebrow, a living, loving toast to our insanity. "Do you have a speech impediment or something?"*
> *"Yes."*

An excess of ordinary punctuation—four periods in the second, six-word paragraph—creates pauses on the page rather than ellipses, dashes or narration to indicate the character's deliberate hesitations. When you read those words, you "hear" Tug speak in halts.

Miscellaneous Technique No. 3

> *All because she loves me. Not even knowing my name. She runs at the sensuous mouth for a full minute before she even asks.*
> My name is damnation, woman. *But I don't say that. I tell her an alternate truth.*
> *"Tug?" she says. "As in tug-boat?"*
> *"Yes. Tug."*

Since the first-person narrator talked about her not asking his name, I didn't go through the formality of putting her question in quotes. Writing in the white space, I simply went to the answer.

Miscellaneous Technique No. 4

> *. . . the guy staring up at the center of my face makes me wonder if my fine, straight nose is going to leave the party in the condition it crashed the party. He's a full foot shorter than me, five feet and change, thighs like fireplugs, a chest like a beer keg, a pony keg stacked on top for a head—no neck.*

I describe Tug by creating the image of somebody else and showing the contrast. You learn that Tug is six feet tall, plus change. Tug also wonders whether his fine, straight nose will be broken, showing us the image of it without actually letting on that we're describing it, a technique better than the mirror thing.

Miscellaneous Technique No. 5

> *She loves me. Not the first eleven words of our relationship have lapsed, and Andrea lusts for me like Lucifer for a second chance. Not married an hour and already she's destined for scarlet lettering, the A-train to D-court, T-man at the throttle.*

These are the opening lines of the novel *Love Busters, Inc.* I referred to adultery without saying the word by echoing Nathaniel Hawthorne's *The Scarlet Letter*, using the *A*, which stands for adultery. *D* suggests divorce court. *T*-man will later prove to be a reference to the narrator's name.

Miscellaneous Technique No. 6

Did you notice the first two sentences? Especially the first four words?

> *She loves me. Not. . . .*

Those four words foreshadow the contradiction in the first sentence. Tug says she loves him and he loves all women. The scene will show that neither loves the other, after all. The word arrangement tells all.

Miscellaneous Technique No. 7

> *"Mar-*tee*!" Sturgis groans through his grin, "what's happening?"*
> *"He's talking to Andrea—no, he's looking this way again—uh-oh."*
> *"What?"*
> *"He's coming over and he's got his army with him."*
> *"Oh God, Tug, you've gone and done it now," says Sturgis.*
> *"Son, I wonder if I might have a word with you?"*
> *"Me, Mr. Barron?"*
> *"No, Marty, I wanna talk to a guy name Tug Grey."*

An elaboration of an earlier technique, I let three characters describe the action to one another, almost entirely between quotation marks. The narrator stays out of the picture.

Miscellaneous Technique No. 8

> *It's as if the bricklayer is reading my mind. "Nah, you're going to do it because you want to. I seen something there when I named the price."*
> *Greed, maybe? I have to hand it to the bricklayer. He is a man of vision, a blue-collar Clark Kent, able to look quite through me. I'm going to have to work on dummying up my face—like Marty's.*

Thanks to the television show, *Lois and Clark,* I was hoping this expression would trigger the image of the alias for Superman and refer to his X-ray vision. You can enlist other familiar types, titles and situations as a starting point for images of your own. Elsewhere in this manuscript I referred to champagne as Love Potion No. 1, playing off the song "Love Potion No. 9."

Miscellaneous Technique No. 9

> *"Could we go out a few times?"* Daddy will pick up the tab.
> *"That I couldn't do."*
> Oh.
> *"Stop pouting. I'm doing it for your own good."*
> How is this for my own good?
> *"Jason. He's got a dark side. He carries a razor."*

"I knew *it."*

"How?"

Did I say that aloud?

In this exchange, Tug speaks part of the time to hold up his end of the conversation, and the remainder of the time he is silent as Andrea reads his body language and supplies the unspoken declarations in it.

Miscellaneous Technique No. 10

"Why didn't you just pay Jason to leave your daughter alone. He doesn't look like a guy who would—well, you know—refuse an offer too good to—you know."

"I did try to pay him off, kid. I offered him five large. He got greedy. The little turd tried to shake me down for ten. Can you believe the audacity?"

Soon after the Godfather movies, the expression *he couldn't refuse* entered the popular culture to stay. I didn't want to use it because it has become a cliché. So I began the thought and left it hanging. I let the reader and characters complete the thought without ever fully using the cliché. Hey, maybe it is a bit hokey, but you did finish the thought, didn't you?

Miscellaneous Technique No. 11

Marty launches into his Einstein speech again—once he's had an idea to gnaw on, he doesn't let it go too readily. I tune him out. Sprouting there among the weeds of my mind is my own idea, one the bricklayer planted. Back and forth I go. Maybe I could start up a business doing what I did today. No, that was a lucky accident. I can't go around getting brides to kiss me. How would I get up momentum? Where would I find disgruntled in-laws like Mr. Barron? Naw, face it. It couldn't be done. There just wouldn't be enough goofy clients for a service like that—would there? Besides, what do I know about running a business?

Something causes me to tune in on Marty for a second and ask, "What'd you say?"

"I said two things. I said you made four hundred eighty thousand

bucks an hour—almost half a million. That's four million a day, you
know, minus some chump change."
 The march of the moron's mind is slow but certain.
 "And I also said I want to freakin hire you."

While Tug was thinking over the possibilities of starting a company to break up relationships, the action in the novel remained in motion offstage. Namely, his companion had kept on talking. When Tug became aware of it, so did we.

Miscellaneous Technique No. 12

Night Runner had backtracked almost to ground-zero when he saw
them. Six—no, seven—men coming over the ridge.

This is from my second Force Recon novel. It's night. It's difficult to see exactly how many are coming over that ridge. I didn't say so, though. I simply allowed the character to amend his count, which told us the difficulty he was having in seeing.

Miscellaneous Technique No. 13
Remember the grizzly attack and this line?

"Bill? Bill? Bill? Bill? Bill?"

Another way to put it would be an escalation of stress like:

"Bill? Bill? Bill? Bill? BILL?"

In that way, the author creates the rising tension typographically. In the first version you, the reader, are left to supply your own emphasis to the white space.

Miscellaneous Techniques No. 14 through No. 101
Sometimes you simply have to know when to stop writing and leave enough white space for a reader to fill in.
Like now.
One final puzzler: Find eighty-eight techniques of your own for writing in the

white space. You're a certified brainstormer. And I know you have the tools to get it done.

Or if you'd rather, put your mind and my tools to work on a fiction project of your own instead of solving riddles.

Good luck with all your fiction writing.

APPENDIX 1

PUZZLER SOLUTIONS

Page

2—uryy4me? Or miee e uuuu?—Are you too wise for me?—Or am I too easy for you?

4—THEBEGIN—Begin at the end.

5—Solutions to the maze:

Solution 1 is below. This is a likely solution if you start at the beginning and adopt the conventional rules of solving mazes by entering the maze where you are told to start.

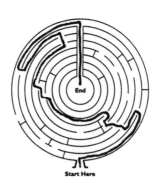

Solution 2. This is a likely solution if you begin at the end, although it is certainly a possibility for anybody willing to suspend their disbelief at the beginning and to follow a route too direct to be true. Beginning at the end often eliminates several wrong turns immediately.

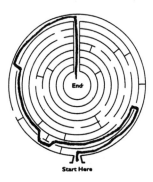

Finally, Solution 3. This is the best, most creative solution in getting from start to finish—or finish to start. It's most likely you'd choose this one by studying the puzzle at arm's length, disregarding conventional maze rules altogether *and* beginning at the end. If ever a drawing illustrated the expression, "Cut to the chase," this is it.

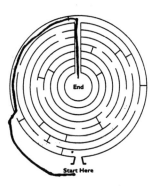

8—A cocklebur inspired Velcro, a failed shock absorber gave us the Slinky toy, a twisted loop allowed audio cassette tapes to be played without turning them over, a pie plate led to the Frisbee and failed synthetic rubber resulted in Silly Putty.

24—The letter *f* occurs eight times in the sentence. If you try to read the passage and pick out the letters, you'll very likely miss the two that do not have the hard *f* sound. Go back and check. To tally the letters, take the passage a letter at a time. Simple?

27—"liar of the worst magnitude" is derived from "liar of the first magnitude," William Congreve, *Love for Love*; "stiff-necked people" comes from *The Holy Bible*, Exodus 32:9; "they are better strangers than friends" is from "we may be better strangers," Shakespeare, *As You Like It*; "there is safety in stupidity" comes from Thoreau, *Walden*.

32—Solution to Brainstormer Strategy 8 puzzler:

Rather than beating your brains out literally trying to find five vowels to eliminate, cross out, in order, all of the letters in the words, *five vowels*.

O̶F̶P̶I̶E̶V̶N̶E̶V̶Y̶O̶O̶W̶U̶R̶E̶E̶L̶Y̶E̶S̶S̶

The message to prospective brainstormers:

OPEN YOUR EYES

33—He can eat only one egg on an empty stomach. After he eats the first one, his stomach is no longer empty. And my father's name is James V. Smith. I'm a Junior and my name is all over this book for you to see.

48—Puzzler Final Quiz

theIN	**B**egin at the end (Big *in* at *the* end)
ject ject alwisconventdom	**R**eject conventional wisdom
act crazy	**A**ct a little crazy
impimagossible standard standard . . .	**I**magine impossible standards
never _____	**N**ever settle
fy	**S**implify (simply fy)
geniustapgenius	**T**ap into genius
uropiiii	**O**pen your eyes
ytiralop	**R**everse polarity
stemakewordwordad of excuse excuse	**M**ake words instead of excuses

The first letters of which spell BRAINSTORM.

51—Chapter 2 puzzlers:

    pppod—Two peas in a pod

    cumorrowmorrow—See you tomorrow

    bprepre—Be prepared

    8brutebrute—Et tu Brute

    ci ii—See eye to eye

81—First lines: *Moby Dick*; *Out of Africa*; *Forrest Gump*; *Bright Lights, Big City*; *Blue Highways.*

82—Last lines: *Angela's Ashes*; *M*A*S*H*; *Forrest Gump*; *Ulysses*; *The Catcher in the Rye.*

100—"Romeo and Ethel" was the spoof title within the movie *Shakespeare in Love*, referring to Romeo and Juliet, of course. *War, What Is It Good for?* is the original title for *War and Peace*, or so Jerry told Elaine on a "Seinfeld" episode, embarrassing her in front of a Russian author. *Lost Moon* is the title of the book on which the film *Apollo 13* was based on. The novel *Horseman, Pass By* became the film *Hud*. *American Hero* was the novel that led to the movie *Wag the Dog*.

113—Punctuation Quiz:

    He said, "No, I won't go," digging in his heels and screaming, "Never."

Or, if you like: . . .screaming, "never." Lose the exclamation points.

    "Who wants to know?" she asked.

    "Who said, 'I won't go'?" she asked.

    He ran away from home. His dad didn't even know he was gone.

115—Chapter 4 puzzlers:

    big MAN—*Little Big Man*

    foslter—*Ellen Foster*

    kacitizne—*Citizen Kane*

    conGverosadtions—*Conversations With God*

    NOTICE—*Black Notice,* of course

134—Chapter 5 puzzlers:

    oleander—*White Oleander*

    kill kill bimockrd—*To Kill a Mockingbird*

    enutrof—if you turn it around, *Reversal of Fortune*

    get ᴛ—*Get Shorty*, of course

    cles cles—Pericles

158—Chapter 6 puzzlers:

Wrong is almost always pronounced wrong.

Write, right, rite and Wright are usually pronounced right.

Fiction always begins with an *f*, and end always begins with an *e*.

The alphabet.

A quick brown fox jumps over the lazy dog.

181—Chapter 7 puzzlers:

1. i an an an I—An eye for an eye.

2. = old fool—There's no fool like an old fool.

3. $\frac{\text{statement}}{\text{credwhatanible}}$—what an incredible understatement

habirdnd = butwosh—A bird in hand is worth two in the bush.

i l w8 u u u u ever ever ever ever—I'll wait for you forever.

189—Exercise No. 1:

The estate nestled like a caress between the meandering rivers. Lord Smith-Piper had ruled that peasants could not hunt there, but Avery and his band had never abided by such lordly rules.

190—Exercise No. 2:

Deena decided to catch his eye. With style. Any woman could attract a man by dropping her dress. Not Deena. She would use finesse, let him believe it was his idea. That's how you got a man, by making him think the seduction was his idea.

251—Catch phrases:

You can't handle the truth.—Jack Nicholson in *A Few Good Men*

Kill Claudio.—Beatrice in Shakespeare's *Much Ado About Nothing*

I'm your number one fan.—Kathy Bates as Annie Wilkes in *Misery*

I can eat fifty hard-boiled eggs.—Paul Newman in *Cool Hand Luke*

Is that your final answer?—Regis Philbin in *Who Wants to Be a Millionaire?*

APPENDIX II
BLANK FORMS

WRITE Task List

Date_____

Goal:
Writing-related
Radical
Inspirational
Timed
Explicit

PRIORITY	TASK	NOTES

The WRITE Task List for setting brainstormer goals and objectives.

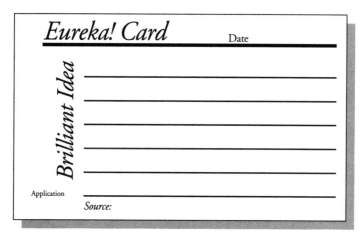

The Brainstormer's Eureka! Card.

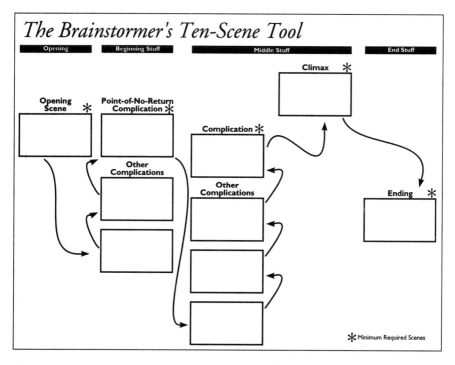

The Brainstormer's Ten-Scene Tool.

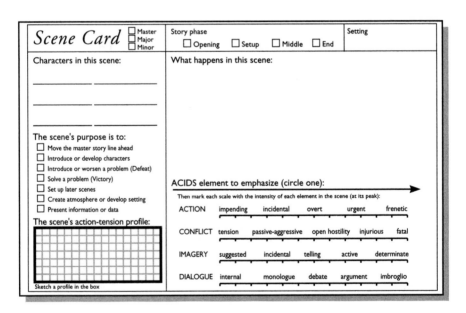

Character ☐ Master ☐ Major ☐ Minor Role/Title:

Pertinent Bio	Physical	Distinctive Language
	Ht./Wt. _____	
	Hair _____	
	Eyes _____	
	Nose _____	
	Mouth _____	
	Hands _____	
	Striking Feature	

Goal/Motivation	– Fatal flaw	
1. Mission-Duty		
2. Career-Selfish	+ Saving grace	
3. Romance-Sex		
4. Quirk		

Name: _____ " _____ " Age: (_____)

The annotated Character Card.

Scene Card ☐ Master ☐ Major ☐ Minor

Story phase ☐ Opening ☐ Setup ☐ Middle ☐ End   Setting

Characters in this scene:

_____ _____

_____ _____

_____ _____

What happens in this scene:

The scene's purpose is to:
☐ Move the master story line ahead
☐ Introduce or develop characters
☐ Introduce or worsen a problem (Defeat)
☐ Solve a problem (Victory)
☐ Set up later scenes
☐ Create atmosphere or develop setting
☐ Present information or data

The scene's action-tension profile:

Sketch a profile in the box

ACIDS element to emphasize (circle one):

Then mark each scale with the intensity of each element in the scene (at its peak):

ACTION	impending	incidental	overt	urgent	frenetic
CONFLICT	tension	passive-aggressive	open hostility	injurious	fatal
IMAGERY	suggested	incidental	telling	active	determinate
DIALOGUE	internal	monologue	debate	argument	imbroglio

The Brainstormer's Scene Card.

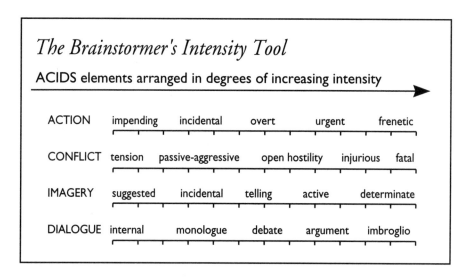

The Brainstormer's Intensity Tool.

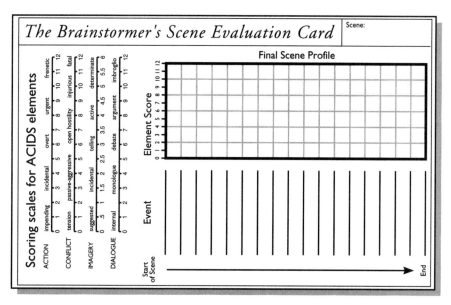

The Brainstormer's Scene Evaluation Card.

Brainstormer's Editing for Readability Log

Selection: _____

	Ideal	Original	Edit #1	Edit #2	Edit #3	Edit #4	Edit #5	Edit #6	Edit #7	Edit #8
Word Count										
Sentence Count										
Graf Count										
Avg.# Sent/Graf										
Avg.# Words/Sent										
Avg.# Char/Word	4.25									
% Passive Voice	0-5%									
% Readability	80⁺%									
Grade Level	4-6									

Brainstormer's Readability Log.

INDEX

qualities of, 101-102
series, 221-222
working, 64
writing in journal, 47
Tone, setting, 85
Topic sentence, 191
Touched With Fire, 41
Transitions, 191-192, 236-238
 vs. smash cuts, 265-266
The Truman Show, 63, 237
Tyler, Anne, 229

Verbosity, 263
Verbs, action-bearing, 152
Video exercise, advanced imagery,
 243-246
Visualizing, 37
Vocabulary, and voice, 263
Voice
 distinctive, 262-263
 passive, 196, 202-203

The Western Canon, 43, 230-231
White space, writing in, 265-273
Wilson, Jerry, 37
Wolfe, Tom, 229
Word(s)
 economy of, 260-261
 first hundred, 84-88
 first ten thousand, 92-93
 first thousand, 88-91
  story's ending planted in, 241
 intrinsic power of, 172-173
 last hundred, 97-98
 last ten thousand, 93-96

last thousand, 96-97
length of, 197-200
 applying test, 211-212
 omitting needless, 202-203
 placement, 173-174
 short, 203
 striking, 86-87
Word attitude, 171-180
Word choice, 159
 concrete, 162-164
 dialogue, 257
 exploring, 210
 inventive, 162-165
 precise, 261
 repetition, 176-177
 specific, 162-164
Word count, 184-185, 188
 managing, 210
Word-of-Mouth Marketing, 37
WRITE system of setting goals, 16-18
 task list, 280
Writer's block, ignoring, 234-235
Writing
 awkward, 176
 grade level of, 199
 ideal standard, 200-202
 mechanics, 111-114
 and mood, 41-42
 standing up, 44-45
 See also Paragraph structure, Sentence structure, Word choice
Writing sample
 to editor or agent, 225
 mission, 92

Yeats, W.B., 27-28